INDIAN HISTORY CONGRESS MONOGRAPH SERIES

ESSAYS IN ANCIENT INDIAN ECONOMIC HISTORY

IN THIS SERIES

RECORDING THE PROGRESS OF INDIAN HISTORY:
SYMPOSIA PAPERS OF THE INDIAN HISTORY CONGRESS
1992–2010
Edited by S.Z.H. Jafri

ESSAYS IN MEDIEVAL INDIAN ECONOMIC HISTORY
(2nd edition)
Edited by Professor Satish Chandra

ESSAYS IN MODERN INDIAN ECONOMIC HISTORY
(2nd edition)
Edited by Sabyasachi Bhattacharya

HISTORY, IDEAS AND SOCIETY:
S.C. MISHRA MEMORIAL LECTURES IN HISTORY
Edited by S.Z.H. Jafri

INDIAN HISTORY CONGRESS MONOGRAPH SERIES

ESSAYS IN ANCIENT INDIAN ECONOMIC HISTORY

Second Edition

Edited with an Introduction by
BRAJADULAL CHATTOPADHYAYA

INDIAN HISTORY CONGRESS
in association with

PRIMUS BOOKS
An imprint of Ratna Sagar P. Ltd.
Virat Bhavan
Mukherjee Nagar Commercial Complex
Delhi 110 009

Offices at
CHENNAI LUCKNOW
AGRA AHMEDABAD BANGALORE COIMBATORE DEHRADUN GUWAHATI HYDERABAD
JAIPUR KANPUR KOCHI KOLKATA MADURAI MUMBAI PATNA RANCHI VARANASI

First published 1987
Second edition 2014

ISBN: 978-93-80607-55-9

Published by Primus Books

Laser typeset by Digigrafics
Gulmohar Park, New Delhi 110 049

Printed and bound in India by Replika Press Pvt. Ltd.

Contents

PART 3
Land, Agriculture, Surplus Appropriation and Distribution of Labour

PART 4
Crafts Production and Craftsmen

PART 5
Aspects of Exchange in Early Indian Economy: Trade, Organisation of Traders, Interest, Coinage

PART 6
Patterns of Setbacks and Tensions in Early Indian Economy

Preface to the Second Edition

THE INDIAN History Congress has emerged as a representative organization for a large section of historians in India, providing its members with a forum to present their unpublished research work, using data from across the country. The annual sessions of the Indian History Congress are invariably attended by senior historians, who provide guidance to young researchers in their endeavours. In its multi-pronged activities, the Congress is perhaps one of the few organizations in India to provide a research and publication forum. To this end, it brings out an edited volume containing a selection of the research articles presented at various sessions. In fact, it is the meticulous selection of essays and rigorous editing of the volumes that has given cause for the University Grants Commission to recognize these proceedings to the level of a referred journal for the purposes of granting promotion to college and university teachers under the Career Advancement Scheme.

During its Golden Jubilee Celebrations in 1987, the Indian History Congress decided to publish three thematic volumes focusing on the Economic History of India. This three-volume set, entitled *Indian History Congress Golden Jubilee Year Publication Series* together contained over a hundred essays, with an introduction by eminent historians. The series met with much success, as it provided a panoramic view of 50 years of changing focuses and emphases of scholars on art, religion, and society and issues related to the historical roots of economic backwardness and the resultant economic under-development in India's colonial past.

These volumes on economic history were also important from another perspective. While inaugurating the first session of the Indian History Congress in 1935, Sir Shafa'at Ahmad Khan remarked that, 'economic history is almost a virgin field'. In the years following 1935, research in this area gathered depth and pace. In the subsequent decade and, in particular after Independence, considerable literature too was produced on the various aspects of the economic history of India. A nationalistic critique of colonialism during the process of decolonization was a major factor in developing interest in this topic. Meanwhile, since the mid-1950s the Marxist approach too gathered acceptance in the academic world of historians as an important factor in the explication of historical development. Together, the twin discourses of nationalist critique and Marxist approach became important contributory factors for a heightened interest in the economic aspects of India's historical past.

In challenging the imperialist historiography, Indian historians evolved considerable interest in studying society, religion, and art. They posited that

Indian cultural past was essentially composite in nature and different communities lived side by side in a spirit of syncretism. In doing so, historians also examined the nature of religious identities and their role in shaping the contours of societal developments in our past.

Prints of the 1987 three-volume set were soon exhausted. Keeping in view their usefulness and steady demand among scholars as well as students, the Executive Committee of the 71st Session of the Indian History Congress, at University of Gour Banga, Malda, West Bengal, decided to reprint the three volumes, possibly with a new introduction by their respective editors.

To this end, I am grateful to Professor Satish Chandra, Professor Sabyasachi Bhattacharya, and Professor B.D. Chattopadhyaya for contributing substantial pieces for the new editions. And, it is indeed a pleasure to have these volumes released as a part of the preparations for the celebrations of the Platinum Jubilee Session of the Congress.

5 December 2013

SAIYID ZAHEER HUSAIN JAFRI
Secretary
Indian History Congress
Department of History
University of Delhi

Preface to the First Edition

THE EXECUTIVE Committee of the Indian History Congress at its meeting in Srinagar in 1986 had constituted the Golden Jubilee Celebrations Committee, which decided, amongst other things, to bring out a few thematic volumes containing articles published in the Proceedings of the Congress since its inception. Four volumes that are being brought out as part of the Golden Jubilee Celebrations deal with Indian art, religion, society and economy through the ages.

It may not be out of place to recall here the expectations of the founding fathers of Congress, Sir Shafa'at Ahmad Khan, the President of the first session in 1935, said: 'I have no doubt whatsoever that this body . . . is destined to play a momentous part in the building up of a vigorous school of Indian historians. . . . It knows no politics, it will not serve the interest either of our national life and thought propagandists who paint the glories of their country's past in a flamboyant language . . . nor will it support writers who are obsessed with prejudice and racial pride, have completely ignored those features which have maintained and preserved the continuity of our cultural life . . . I dread the prospect of long line of histories of India written by Muslims, Mahrattas, Sikhs, Bengalis and Pathans, each from their own point of view. . . . Should history be tied to the chariot wheels of perverted sectionalism which is now acting as a most serious obstacle to the growing nationalism of India on a whole?'

To what extent has the Congress, which has truly grown into an All-India body and is the largest organization of professional historians in the country, lived up to these expectations? The readers could perhaps look for an answer in the collections being presented here.

Each of these four volumes is preceded by short introduction from the editor, who has already provided the rationale of the concerned anthology. It is hoped that the series will reflect the commitment of the Indian History Congress to scientific and secular history and prove useful to all students of history.

I take this opportunity to thank Professor B.D. Chattopadhyaya of the Centre of Historical Studies, Jawaharlal Nehru University for taking up the responsibility of editing the present volume at a very short notice. On behalf of the editor as well as on my personal behalf, profusely thank Shri Kishore Kumar Singh for very significant help rendered by him. Dr Bhairabi Prasad Sahu's unflinching help in proofreading is also gratefully acknowledged.

We are grateful to the Indian Council of Historical Research for making a handsome grant which has enabled us to meet partially the cost of publishing these volumes.

New Delhi
15 October 1987

D.N. Jha
Secretary
Indian History Congress

Introduction to the Second Edition

The essays in this collection on different aspects of the economic history of ancient India were, originally presented at the annual sessions of the Indian History Congress and have been published in the Proceedings of the Congress. The volume was put together by scrutinizing carefully the Proceedings of the Congress during the first fifty years of its existence. The publication of this four-volume series in 1987 of which Essays in Ancient Indian Economic History was the first, was intended to mark the Golden Jubilee Anniversary of the Congress, in 1987.

It is little more than two and a half decades since. By now, this collection and its companion volumes have all gone out of print, but it seems there is still a demand for them. Ideally, this new edition should have been updated by including new essays published in the Proceedings of the Congress in the last twenty-five years, and by locating them within the global trend of economic history writing during this period. It would indeed have been interesting to have considered the general state of economic history after its heyday in the sixties and seventies of the last century and the nature of historiographical drifts towards social formation oriented studies, and further, to examine how these drifts are reflected in the contributions at the Congress. That task, one hopes, will be taken up soon, at least in the centenary year or Platinum Jubilee of the Congress. All that needs to be stated here is that all the issues which are represented in this collection continue to be of relevance to serious historical studies.

I thank the secretary of the Indian History Congress for asking me for a new Introduction to the re-issue of the collection, and I shall look forward to its post publication reception.

30 September 2013 Brajadulal Chattopadhyaya

Introduction to the First Edition

JOURNEYING THROUGH the interesting assortment of contributions in the *Proceedings of the Indian History Congress* with the objective of preparing an anthology on a theme can be a meaningful exercise in many ways. It has been so to me. I started with certain ideas derived from broad familiarity with the historiography of the field I was investigating but soon came to realize that this was a somewhat inadequate perspective with which to approach the *Proceedings*, for the *Proceedings* do not seem to offer an easy correspondence with historiographic trends that one, perhaps a little too hastily, tends to reconstruct on the basis of pioneering research monographs and seminal articles in research journals. If my historiographical ideas did not get fully confirmed by going through the entire *Proceedings* series, it was because, I became aware, the contributions to the *Proceedings* represent a different academic context. The context is one in which the contributors are not addressing anonymous readers but are participating in a live forum. Since the Indian History Congress is a forum where participation is broad-based and where the participants are not necessarily all exclusive specialists but are drawn from various levels at which Indian history is taught and learnt, the contributions addressed to this forum annually reflect perhaps more authentically the state of the discipline in the wide arena of its dissemination than do monographs and seminal research papers by specialists alone. This is neither to say that the *Proceedings* constitute a parallel historiography nor that the state of the discipline has remained static in its pages. Almost fifty of the *Proceedings* offer a substantial volume of historical writings where shifts from one kind of concern to another—and shifts in the craft as well—are evident enough; what one cannot simply assume is that the contributions to the *Proceedings* would necessarily and neatly fit into a schema of rapid historiographical change. Perhaps in considering historiography as a serious theme of study one needs to go beyond the material selecting chosen and envisage exploring several levels and paces of change simultaneously. The *Proceedings* will then surely come in for far more serious analysis than it is possible to offer here.

The theme that I am required to prepare a collection on is economic History of Early India, and besides searching for contributions for the collection, my main curiosities have been (i) to examine the changing status of early Indian Economic history in the annual meet of Indian historians and (ii) to see if there has been any noticeable change in perceptions regarding early Indian economy in this forum. By the early forties some major monographs on early Indian economic history had been published; in the early *Proceeding;*

interest in economic history, on the other hand, seems to have remained peripheral. If, in a fashion uncharacteristic of an ancient Indian historian, I am to succumb to the lure of figures and cite them, it would appear significant that between 1938 and 1961 the number of papers on early Indian economic history presented at the Congress was a meagre twenty-five against a formidable three hundred on political and administrative history. Throughout the sixties economic history seems to have maintained almost an equally low profile, if in the Agra session in 1956 not a single paper on economic history was presented, in the Ranchi session eight years later, out of thirty-six papers on ancient India, only one on economic history figured in subsection V. In retrospect, it is the seventies and eighties that have seen the beginnings and crystallization of a noticeable change in the status of economic history in the Ancient India section of the Congress. I would not pretend to be able to offer an adequate explanation of this change; what is evident is that among many new practitioners of the craft, the major focus has shifted in a significant way, and it is not only that economic history is no longer peripheral to the interests of the participants at the Congress; the practitioners have also started taking to this craft differently.

The change of status and of orientations of early Indian economic history, which is perhaps the *raison de être* of this collection, is borne out further if one keeps in mind the ground that has been covered. Individual contributions in single volumes of the *Proceedings* may sometimes appear to be too specialized and isolated; taken together, contributions which have appeared over the years cover a wide range of economic aspects. However, if it were only for the fact that the contributions relate to a variety of themes, this collection would have conveyed hardly any historiographical sense. What is important is that new themes have come to be added to earlier ones, new source material has been used resulting in the broadening of the scope of early Indian economic history and more significantly economic history has gone beyond narrow frontiers by relating itself to areas which are of general historical relevance. From economic history as 'also an area of History' the movement has been such that it is usual to find in the pages of the *Proceedings* today explorations into relationship between technology and economy, patterns of regional economic transformation or into areas of socio-economic tension.

It would be incorrect either to assert that the changing historiographical trend at last encompasses all levels or to attribute it solely to the labours of the seventies and eighties. After all, historiography of the *Proceedings* cannot have been and is not really separated from the totality of historical research in India, and what happens outside the forum of the Indian History Congress is also what is present in it. As the first article in the present collection should sufficiently demonstrate, the concern to view economic history not an end in itself but meaningful only in the context of broader historical generalizations has been very much present in the Congress and is not a rootless contribution of today's history alone.

The following brief points are by way of clarifying how the present collection is organized. Selecting the articles for the collection has been a difficult task; despite the best of intentions one is torn between alternatives and perhaps cannot help surrendering to personal preferences in the end. There are, however, a few criteria I have tried to adhere to. I have tried to include as many contributions as possible from the old issues of the *Proceedings*; at the same time, I have had to resist the temptation of including more than one contribution by an author. It has also been my endeavour to provide a general view of early Indian economy—chronological as well as spatial—through the contributions in the *Proceedings*. There are, to be sure, wide gaps, but the gaps exist not because any period or any region has been deliberately excluded from this collection but mainly because the *Proceedings* still await meaningful contributions relating to such periods and regions as have gone unrepresented. Hopefully, a future anthology would be more comprehensive on both counts. The chronological span of the collection extends to the twelfth–thirteenth century. Without going into an argument as to whether subscribing to a conventional scheme of periodization is justifiable or not, it may simply be underlined that it is a choice of convenience. In the Congress itself the scheme of periodization of Indian history has changed from time to time, further, in some *Proceedings* volumes, contributions relating to the same period appear under different sections. Accepting the conventional periodization of ancient in relation to medieval was thought to be a way out to reduce these variations.

So far as the contributions themselves are concerned, the versions which appeared in the *Proceedings* have been reproduced. Certain changes however had to be carried out. Efforts have been made to add diacritical marks, to correct misprints and to follow a uniform system with regard to italicization and citation of references. In any case, the volume had to be prepared in great haste and it has been beyond my competence to ensure uniformity and accuracy.

Brajadulal Chattopadhyaya

PART 1

Early Indian Economy: General Themes

1

Role of Property, Family and Caste in the Origin of the State in Ancient India

Ram Sharan Sharma

IN THE study of the origin of the State reference has been generally made to the state of nature depicted in the Buddhist sources[1] but no attempt has been made to present its complete picture on the basis of all the sources including the Purāṇas, *Māhabhārata,* and the Jaina traditions.[2] A study of these sources not only furnishes an idea of the early state of nature but also of the circumstances which led to the origin of the State. Although the pictures differ in details from one another, four essential characteristics of the early state of nature stand out clearly.

First, the earliest means of subsistence was the fruits and roots of trees. The description of *kalpavṛkṣa* as the main source of the livelihood of the people is a very common affair in the Brahmanical and Jaina traditions.[3] The Buddhist traditions refer to *vanalatā* and some sort of roots (*bhūmiparpaṭaka*) as the earliest means of sustenance.[4] It is natural that in the earliest stage of his life which generally correspond to the *Kṛta* age of the Purāṇas and Epics, men should have lived as food gatherers and not as food producers. This is supported by anthropology and is true of the people of paleolithic age.[5] As Morgan points out, the first livelihood was 'natural subsistence upon fruits and roots on a restricted habitat.'[6] Nobody could then conceive that the fruits and trees belonged exclusively to him. It was a period of savagery when 'a passion for its (property's) possession had scarcely been formed in their (men's) minds, because the thing itself scarcely existed. It was left to the then distant period of civilization to develop into full vitality that greed of gain (*studium lucri*), which is now such a commanding force in the human mind.'[7]

Second, except in the *Mahābhārata,* the traditions about the state of nature give no clear indication of the origin of the monogamous family in which the father is supreme and all the domestic activities centre round the wife. As it is stated in the Śānti Parva: 'A householder's home, even if filled with sons, grandsons, daughters-in-law and servants, is regarded empty if destitute of the

*14th Session at Jaipur, 1951.

housewife. One's house is not one's home; one's wife is only one's home.'[8] But how did this home originate? It can be said on the basis of Epic and Puranic traditions that formerly there existed a state of promiscuity when children could be produced merely by *saṃkalpa* to co-habit. In the *kṛta* age there was neither like-marriage (*maithuna*) nor recognised monogamous marriage system (*dvandva*).[9] The *Mahābhārata* says that in the land of Uttarakurus the institution of marriage did not exist. This is also supported by Āṭānāṭya-sutta in *Dīgha Nikāya* which refers to the land of Kuru in these words: "There do men live calling no goods their own, nor as their chattels any womankind."[10]

Third, it is clearly stated in the Purāṇas that there were no *varṇas* in the *Kṛta* age. The Buddhist sources also do not mention the division of the people into classes in their account of the earliest life of mankind.[11]

Fourth, it can be said on the basis of the clear statements of the Śānti Parva that in the early stage of the state of nature, the institution of State did not exist.[12] According to Kauṭilya in certain lands called 'Vairājya' there was no kingly office and the people thereof had no sense of thine and mine.[13] This implied that the absence of the ruler coincided with the lack of private property.

A study of primitive societies existing in recent times establishes that the institutions of property, family and class (or caste) were conspicuous by their absence in the earliest stage of man's life. It is not just a mere coincidence that in ancient India in absence of these institutions, the State also did not exist. As it will be shown later there was a vital connection between the existence of these institutions and the rise of the State in ancient India. Although people living without these institutions cannot be called civilized, they enjoyed a sort of harmonious life free from cares, anxieties and greed.[14]

But this harmonious tenor of life was destroyed due to the discovery of the art of cultivation[15] which enabled the people to produce more than they could consume. There began the tendency to store rice[16] and the people appropriated to themselves by force and violence rivers, fields, hills, trees, shrubs and plants.[17] For the first time they established their separate houses which required the sanction of the law. Rice fields were divided and boundaries were set up round them saying—'This is thine, this is mine.'[18] But when people began to snatch away the rice of others without their consent, there arose the necessity of some authority which would protect their respective fields. And that led to the creation of the office of the 'Mahākhattiya' or protector of fields.[19]

The Buddhist sources not only emphasise the importance of the rise of private property in the origin of the State but they also vaguely refer to the role of the family in this connection. They inform us that when sexual congress began between man and woman, in order to conceal their sin they built houses (or huts).[20] Probably one house was meant for one family. According to the Tibetan Dulva (vol. V) this was the first appearance in the world of division by houses (or families?), and this division was made lawful or not lawful according to the king's decision.[21] At one place Śānti Parva refers to the rise of *dvandva* or monogamous family in the Kali age but does not connect it with the rise of the State.[22]

The importance of *varṇas* in the rise of the State is chiefly dealt with in the Purāṇas. According to them, when the means of subsistence had been provided, people were divided into four *varṇas*. Brāhmaṇas were meant for praying, Kṣatriyas for fighting, the Vaiśyas for producing and the Śūdras were addicted to manual tasks.[23] This division worked in favour of those who fought and prayed and therefore it might have been resented by the conscious producers. Therefore the Purāṇas say that the duties of the castes were settled but they did not fulfil their respective duties and came into mutual conflict. "Having become aware of this fact the Lord Brahmā prescribed (*daṇḍa*) criminal justice and war as the profession of the Kṣatriya."[24]

It is in the Śānti Parva that the *role* of all the three institutions of property, family and caste in the origin of the State can be seen at one place. The circumstances that led to the creation of the State are set forth clearly: 'The wealth of one is snatched away by two, that of those two is snatched away by many acting together. He who is not a slave is made slave. Women, again, are forcibly abducted. For these reasons the gods created kings for protecting the people.'[25] And when the people made compact to put an end to such a state of affairs, two main conditions were that they should throw out those who abduct other people's wives or rob other's wealth.[26] Besides, the compact was made to 'inspire confidence amongst, all *varṇas*.'[27] In order to place the compact, on a permanent footing they went out in search of a king. They were prepared to give him certain share of their own property and beautiful maidens in marriage.[28] The result would be that the king would have a vital and permanent interest not only in the preservation of his property and family but also those of his subjects. It was on such conditions that Manu finally accepted the kingship.

Besides Manu, the Epic and Puranic traditions make Pṛthu, the first traditional king.[29] The tradition says that one of the main grievances of the people was that dishonest men seized the property of their neighbours. When Pṛthu was consecrated, he removed the grievances of the people.[30] At the time of his coronation, the first king Pṛthu assured the people in these words: 'I shall establish the *svadharma, varṇadhcirma* and *āśramadharma,* and enforce them with the rod of punishment.'[31] It is further said that the first king was equally honoured by all the four *varṇas*.[32]

While the above direct references to the origin of the State throw sufficient light on the importance of property, family and caste in it, certain indirect evidences may also be examined. One line of approach may be: what would happen if the State does not exist? The one recurrent tone both in Śānti Parva and Ayodhyā Kāṇḍa which contain long description of *arājaka* states is that family and property would not be safe.[33] It is stated that if the king did not exercise the duty of protection, no body, then, with reference to any article in his possession would be able to say this is mine. Wives, sons, food and other kinds of property would not then exist.[34] It is further mentioned that the strong would forcibly appropriate the possession of the weak.[35] Bhandarkar has quoted five passages which suggest that the kingly office arose to protect the weak against the strong.[36] Possibly it may not be correct to interpret the 'weak' as poor and 'strong' as rich. But there are certain references which give the impression that the kingly office was meant to support the haves against the combined attacks of the have-nots. Thus it is said that in absence of the royal protection the wicked men would forcibly appropriate the vehicles, robes, ornaments and precious stones and other kinds of property belonging to others.[37] Obviously only the wealthy could own such items of property. It is also said that if the king does not protect, the wealthy would have to encounter death, confinement and persecution.[38] In such a case two persons combining together snatch the wealth of one, and many acting in concert rob the two.[39] The Ayodhyā Kāṇḍa informs us that in a kingless State the wealthy feel insecure and they cannot sleep keeping their door open.[40] Further, under such conditions, all restrictions about marriage and intercourse cease, and the institution of marriage ceases to exist.[41] It is said that in the absence of the king, the *varṇavyavasthā* would be destroyed and an intermixture of castes would take place.[42] Exactly the same consequences follow if *daṇḍa,* the symbol of the power of the State, disappeaears. It is pointed out that it was by means of *daṇ. da* that the misappropriation of other people's possession was stopped and that is why it was called *Vyavahāra*. But once, when it disappeared, the results were disastrous. 'There were no restraints in the matter of the union of the sexes. All idea of property ceased. All creature? began to rob....'[43] Thus it can be argued that since the absence of the rule or *daṇḍa* has been regarded in the classical traditions as a great menace to the institutions of property, family and caste, the State arose due to the necessity of protecting them.

The chief duties of the king also can throw light on the purpose for which his office was created. It is well-known that one of the main duties of the king was the protection of private property by punishing the thief, and that of family by punishing the adulterers. So great was the responsibility of protecting property that it was incumbent on the king to restore to a subject the stolen wealth at any cost.[44] At one place it is said that a king of strict rule was one who cherished the poor.[45] But there is also an evidence to the contrary. It is stated that the king should always honour those of his subjects that are rich because in every kingdom the wealthy constitute an estate. Further, there is no doubt that a wealthy person is the foremost of men.[46] Besides, the protection of the family and the prevention of adultery was another great responsibility of the king. Manu enumerates eighteen offences into which the king should look. Out of them ten offences are connected with the property and two are connected with the family.[47] Similarly Kātyāyana lists ten wrongs deserving attention by the king. Out of them five are connected with property and one with family.[48] Kātyāyana is specially particular that there should not be sudden accession of riches in the case of an indigent man.[49] Similarly, according to *Śukranītisāra* offences against the State included murder of women, inter-mixture of castes, adultery, thieving, pregnancy without husband.[50] Out of seven conditions which Buddha laid down for the success of the Vajji state: two can be said of be related to property and family. One condition was that the Vajjis should act in accordance with the Vajjidharma as established in the old days. If Vajjidharma is explained in the light of the extract from Aṭṭathā quoted in *Dīgha Nikāya* (Hindi translation), it means that the thief should be punished according to law.[51] As to the second condition it clearly said that they should not detain among them by force or abduction women or girls belonging to them.[52] Specially, according to the Buddhist sources punishment of thieves was one of the primary charges of the king and the thief could be summarily killed at the order of the king either by hanging or by the removal of his skin, flesh and bones, etc.[53]

The Buddhist sources, however, do not refer to the maintenance of the castes, which according to the Brahmanical sources[54] was one of the most important duties of the king. According to the *Rāmāyana* under the ideal rule of Daśaratha members of the different castes pursued their respective avocations.[55] The inscriptions also refer to the connection of the king with the four *varṇas*. One of them describes the king Rudradāman I as being approached by the *varṇas*[56] and the other represents Gautamīputra Sātakarṇi as the preventer of the confusion of the four castes.[57] Among the ancient Indian law-givers, Manu laid special emphasis on the preservation of the caste system by the king. In his view the kingdom would prosper only so long as the purity of castes is maintained, otherwise it will perish together with its inhabitants.[58] Presumably, taking it for granted that the Brāhmaṇas and Kṣatriyas would perform their duties, Manu ordained that the king should carefully compel the Vaiśyas and Śūdras to perform the work prescribed for them; if these two castes swerved from their duties, they would throw this whole world into confusion.[59] It appears that the existence of the State or the ruler was so completely identified with the maintenance of the institutions of property, family and the caste system that Śānti Parva provides the same punishment for a person guilty of arson, theft or such co-habitation with women as may lead to inter-mixture of castes as is prescribed for the person guilty of compassing the death of the king.[60]

It is commonly accepted that the king in ancient India was the upholder of *dharma*. The Buddhist sources also want him to become *dharmadhvaja*, *dharmaketu* and *dharmādhipati*.[61] What *dharma* meant in case of the Vajjis has been explained above.[62] But what were the concrete contents of the Brahmanical Dharma which the king was asked to uphold? This may be known from the *Dharmaśāstras*—the lawbooks to be followed by the kings. They contain elaborate chapters on property laws, marriage relations and caste system. The Śānti Parva which describes *dharma* as resting upon the king[63] refers to the consequences of its disappearance in these words: 'When sinfulness is not restrained, no one can, according to the rights of property as laid down in the scripture, say—this thing is mine and this is not mine. When sinfulness prevails in the world, men cannot own and enjoy their own wives, animals, fields and houses.'[64] It was also said that *dharma* was meant to aid the acquisition and preservation of wealth; and besides, if *dharma* increased it caused a confusion of castes.[65] In the address of the sages to the tyrannical king Vena, *dharma* is explained in similar terms. They warned him that *dharma* was the greatest friend of men of all castes. If the king renounced *dharma,* nobody's wife, wealth or house would be his own. According to Kauṭilya when all *dharmas* perish, the king becomes the promulgator of the *dharma* for the establishment of the four-fold caste system and the protection of morality.[66] Thus, it seems that in concrete terms the king's maintenance of *dharma* signified nothing but the defence of the social order based on the institutions of family, property and caste system.

Therefore, from whatever point of view we study the problems of the origin of the State—the circumstances in the state of nature leading to the rise of the State, the conditions obtaining in a kingless State, the chief duties of the king, the meaning of the upholding of *dharma* by the king—it is difficult to avoid the conclusion that property, family and caste played the primary and vital *role* in the rise of the State in ancient India.

Note–Editions of the Original Sources Consulted in the Article

Brahma Purāṇa	Ānandāśrama Series, 1895
Brahmāṇḍa Purāṇa	Venkateśwara Press
Kūrma Purāṇa	Calcutta, 1890
Mārkaṇḍeya Purāṇa	Bibliotheca Indica
Vāyu Purāṇa	Calcutta, 1880
Viṣṇu Purāṇa	Wilson's translation
Vṛhannāradīya Purāṇa	Calcutta, 1891
Padma Carita	Bombay, vs 1895
Śānti Parva	Chitraśālā Press, Poona, 1932
Ayodhyā Kāṇḍa	Bombay, 1913
Bāla Kāṇḍa	Bombay, 1912
Mānavadharmaśāstra	Edited by V.N. Mandalika, Bombay, 1886
Kauṭilya	Shamasastry's edition
Kāmandaka Nītisāra	Trivandrum Sanskrit Series
Śukranītisāra	Madras, 1882 and S.B.H., Allahabad

Bṛhaspati A.S.	Punjab Sanskrit Series
Kātyāyana Smṛti	Kane's edition
Dīgha Nikāya	Pāli Text Society, London, 189–1911
Mahāvastu, vol. I	Senart, Paris, 1882

Notes

1. Ghoshal, *Hindu Political Theories*, pp. 118-20; Bhandarkar, *Carmichael Lectures*, 1918, pp. 115–22; Bandhopadhyaya, *Development of Hindu Polity and Political Theories*, pp. 275–7; *Public Administration in Ancient India*, p. 34ff; Beni Prasad, *Theory of Govt, in Ancient India*, pp. 205–6; and Dikshitar, *Hindu Administrative Institutions*, pp. 17–18.
2. *Mārk. P.*, 49th ch.; *Vāyu P.*, ch. 8; *Kūrma P.*, ch. 29; *Brahma P.*, ch. 5; *Viṣṇu P.*, Bk. I, ch. VI; *Brahamāṇda P.*, chs. 29–31; *Padma Charita*, ch. 3; Tibetan Dulva quoted in Rockhill's *Life of Buddha*, pp. 2–9; *Mahāvastu*, vol. I, pp. 340–48: *Dīgha Nikāya*. Aggañña Sutta; *Mbh.*, XII, chs. 59, 67, 69 and 206.
3. *Vāyu P.*, VIII-84; *Padma Charita*, ch. III, 55.
4. *Mahāvastu*, vol. I, pp. 340–1.
5. Childe, *Man Makes Himself*, ch- IV.
6. Morgan, *Ancient Society*, p. 20.
7. Ibid., p. 27.
8. Sānti Parva, chs. 144, 546. *Mbh.*, I, 4–9, 12.
9. नचैषां मैथुनो धर्मोबभूव भरतर्षभ।
संकल्पादेव चैतेषामपत्यमुपपद्यते।।
द्वापरे मैथुनो धर्मस्तेषामपि जनाधिपे।
तया कलियुगे राजन् द्वन्द्वमापेदिरे जनाः।।
SP, ch. 207, 38 to 41:
तासां विशुद्धात् सङ्कल्पज्जायते मिथुनाः प्रजाः।

—*Vāyu P.*, VIII, 57
10. °Santi Parva, chs. 102–26, Bombay; Rhys Davids, *Dīgha Nīkāya*, pt. III, p. 192.
11. *Vāyu P.*, VIII, 60; Rockhill's *Life of Buddha*, pp. 2–6; *Mahāvastu*, vol, I, pp. 340–8; Rhys Davids, *Dīgha Nikāya*, pt. III, pp. 82–7.
12. न वैराज्यं न राजाऽसीन्न दण्डो न च दाण्डिकः

—SP., ch. 59, 14
13. वैराज्यं तु जीवतः परस्याच्छिद्य 'नैतन्मम' इति मन्यमानः.....*A.S.* VI.I, 2. The sense of this passage has been given above on the basis of Jayaswal's translation, *Hindu Polity*, pt. I. p. 94.
14. *Vāyu P.*, ch. VIII, 48, 52, 62 and 63; विशोकास्सत्वबहुला एकात्रबहुलस्तथा ..... ता वै निष्कामचारिण्यो नित्यं मुदितमनसाः, *Kūrma P.*, ch., 29.
15. *Vāyu P.*, VIII, 128, 142–45 and 154; *Mārk P.*, chs. 49–59, 60 & 74; . . . . तस्मिं वनलते अन्तर्हिते तं शालिं अकणं अतुषं सुरभिततण्डुलफलं आहारमाहरन्ता चिरं दीर्घमश्यानं तिष्ठेन्सु, *Mahāvastu*, vol. 1, p. 342.

16. Rockhill, *Life of Buddha*, p. 5; *Dīgha Nīkāya*, op. cit., p. 86; *Mahāvastu*, vol. I, p. 343.
17. पर्य्यघृहणन्त नदी क्षेत्राणि पर्वतानि, *Vāyu P.*, VIII, 31; *Mārk P.*, chs. 49–62; *Kūrma P.*, ch. 29.
18. *Life of Buddha*, op. cit., pp. 5–6; *Dīgha Nikāya*, op. cit., p. 87.
19. *Life of Buddha*, op. cit., pp. 6–7; *Dīgha Nikāya*, op. cit., p. 88; *Mahāvastu*, vol. IX, pp. 347–48.
20. *Mahāvastu*, vol. I, p. 343; *Dīgha Nikāya*, op. cit., p. 85; *Life of Buddha*. op. cit, p. 4.
21. *Life of Buddha*, op. cit., p. 5.
22. SP, ch. 207, 40.
23. वर्णधर्मेजीवन्त्यो व्यरूध्यन्त परस्परं *Vāyu P.*, VIII, 155–59, cf. *Padma Carita*, III, 240.
24. ब्रह्मा तमर्थ बुद्धत्वा यु याथातथ्येन वै प्रभुः
    क्षत्रियाणां बलं दण्डं युद्धजीवमादिशत्।। —*Vāyu P.*, ch. VIII, 161
25. Śānti Parva (SP), ch. 67, 14 and 15.
26. SP, ch. 67, 17 and 18.
27. SP, ch. 67, 19.
28. SP, ch. 67–23 and 24.
29. SP, ch. 59, 125.
30. *Viṣṇu P.*, Bk. I, ch. VIII.
31. *Samarāṅgaṇa-Sūtrādhāra*, ch. VII.
32. *Brahma, P.*, ch. V, 116–21.
33. SP., ch. 68; Ayodhyā Kāṇḍa, ch. 67.
34. SP, ch. 68, 15, 33 and ch. 57, 46; of Ayodhya Kāṇḍa (AK), ch. 67, 10, 11 and 31.
35. SP, ch. 68, 14.
36. Bhandarkar, op. cit., pp. 115–18.
37. SP, ch. 68, 16.
38. SP, ch. 68, 19.
39. SP, ch. 90, 39 and 40.
40. AK, ch. 67,18.
41. SP, ch. 68, 21 and 22.
42. SP, ch. 68, 29.
43. SP, ch. 191, 13, cf. *Manu*, VII, 20, 24.
44. SP, ch. 75, 10; *Āpastamba Sūtra*, II, 10, 27.4.
45. SP, ch. 139, 97.
46. धनिनः पूजपेत्रित्यं पानाच्छादनभेजनैः
    अङ्गमेतन्महद्राज्ये धनिनो नाम भारत।
    ककुदं सर्व भूतातां धनस्थो नात्र संशयः।।

    —SP, ch. 88, 29 to 30.
47. *Manu.*, VIII, 4–7.
48. *Kātyāyana.*, 947 and 8, Kane's edn.
49. Ibid., p. 949–50.
50. *SNS*, ch. IV, sec. V, 161–2.
51. *Dīgha Nikāya* by Rāhula Sāṇkṛtyāyana and Jagadiś Kaśyapa, pp. 118–19.
52. Ibid., p. 118.

53. Ibid , pp. 201, 204, cf. p. 236.
54. *Arthaśāstra,* Bk. III, ch. I; *Kāmandaka Nītisāra,* sec. XIII, 41 and 58; *Brhaspati A.S* , III, 18; *Manu.,* VII, 17 and 35; *Kātyāyana.,* 949–40; Śānti Parva, ch. 15, ch. 63, 27, ch. 65, 12 and ch, 77, 11–17; *Brahma P.,* ch. 222, 103; *Viṣṇu P* , 57, Bk. III, ch, VIII.
55. Bāla Kāṇḍa, VI, 17 and 19.
56. Junāgarh Rock Insc., in *Select Inscriptions* by Sircar, vol. I, p. 171.
57. Ibid., p 199.
58. *Manu.,*. X, cf. *Śukranītisāra,* IV, see. I, 215–16.
59. *Manu.,* VII, 418, cf. IX, 253; *Vṛhannāradīya P.,* ch. 140–62.
60. SP., ch. 85, 22.
61. *Dīgha Nikāya,* (Hindi), p. 234.
62. See fns. 50–52.
63. SP., ch. 90–95.
64. SP., ch. 90, 9 and 10.
65. Ibid., ch. 90, 17 and 35.
66. *Kauṭilya,* Bk. III, ch. I.

2

Economic Condition of Western India During 200 BC–AD 500

A.S. Altekar

TRADE, INDUSTRY, agriculture and the connected arts and crafts were the mainstray of the economic life of the society in Western India during our period. Rayatwari system seems to have been prevailing in the Deccan during our period, as it does now. We usually come across small pieces of lands being owned by ordinary individuals. Thus one donor at Junnar makes a gift of a field of 15 *nivartanas*[1] at the village of Puvanada, and another of 12, 8 and 4 *nivartanas* at Vatākaka. Obviously land was divided into small units and owned by individual proprietors. It is, however, likely that the Mahāraṭhis, Mahābhojas and Mahāsenapatis, who were feudal chiefs or high officers, may have owned fairly extensive pieces of lands. For instance, Uṣavadāta is seen in the enjoyment of a field of 200 *nivartanas* at the village of Kakhaḍī.[2] Revenues of villages and houses may have also been assigned to civil and military officers, as is recommended in the Smṛtis. We get some instances of monasteries being assigned the revenues of entire villages; the same could as well have been the case with the Amātyas and Mahāmātras.

The state owned some pieces of arable land, in different towns and villages, which it used to get by escheat or purchase. These are described as royal lands *(rājakaṁ khettaṁ)*, in one Nasik record.[3] When the king possessed no personal land of his own and desired to make a land grant, he had to purchase the land required. We find Uṣavadāta purchasing a field for 4000 *kārṣāpaṇas* (= Rs. 1,500) in order to gift it to the monks at Nasik.[4] Waste and fallow land belonged to the state, but under the Gupta administration the village councils had to be consulted at the time of their disposal. Such formalities are not mentioned in connection with land transfers described in western Indian records. We, however, find that land transfers were regularly recorded in the registers kept for the purpose in the city and village councils.

Some Nasik records refer to the donations of entire villages. Thus Nasik inscription no. 19 refers to the donation of the village of Samalipada in

*14th Session at Jaipur, 1951.

exchange for the village of Sudisaṇa. This exchange obviously suggests that the gift of the village meant the gift of its royal revenues; it did not interfere with the private ownership of land. When ownership in private land was transferred, it was usually of small fields which kings purchased or which belonged to the state.

Our records supply no data to determine the incidence of land taxation; nor do we know anything about the share which the lessee received from the lessor. Probably his share varied from 40 to 50% of the gross produce.[5] There is no datum to determine the price of land in western India during our period; Nasik inscription no. 10 refers to the sale of apiece of land for 4000 silver *kārṣā-paṇas* (= Rs. 1,500) but we do not know the dimensions of the field purchased. In the Gupta empire the arable land was usually sold at about three *dīnāras* (= two and a quarter tolas of gold) per *kulyavāpa*. But the precise dimension of the *kulyavāpa* is not known and so we do not get any definite idea of the land prices, *Nivartana* is the land measure frequently occurring in our records, but its precise measure is not known. It appears that it was about four acres in extent.

Crops grown in our period were probably the same that are grown at present in western India, *viz*., jwar, bajra, wheat, sugarcane, rice, gram, cotton, oilseeds and betel leaves. Timber and fire wood were important forest products and they figure among the exports to foreign countries. Lead mines were worked in the Deccan and supplied the metal for the Sātavāhana currency. It is likely that the gold mines near Maski may have been worked in our period, as also the diamond mines near Golkunda.

Cotton industry seems to have been the most thriving industry of the Deccan during our period. Rough, fine and coloured cotton cloth figures prominently among the exports from Bharoch, as described by the *Periplus*. Tagara, most probably Ter in Hyderabad state, and Pratiṣṭhāna, the capital of the Sātavāhana empire, were great centres of the cotton industry. The Andhra province also had a large number of the centres of this industry.

During the first century of the Christian era, there was considerable trade carried on with the outside world through the ports of western India. Bharoch was the most prominent among them. Among the imports of this port, the *Periplus* mentions Arabian and Italian wines, copper, tin, lead, coral, topaz, fine and rough cloth bright coloured girdles, storax, flint glass, antimony and gold and silver coins. For the use of kings costly silver vessels, singing boys, beautiful maidens and choice ointments were imported. The exports of this port included spikenard costus, bdellium, ivory, agate, carnelian, onyx, stones, lycium, cotton cloth of all kinds, silk, long pepper and such other things as are brought from various market towns.

Bharoch was the main centre of foreign trade, but there were other ports on the western coast which had their own share of both foreign and coastal trade. Among these may be mentioned Sūrpāraka or Sopara in Thana district, which figures as a harbour in the Jātakas also. Kalyan in Thana district was a flourishing port. For a time, it was the rival of Bharoch as most of the Sātavāhana exports and imports took place through it. During the Śaka Sātavāhana struggle, the Śakas tried to block it several times. Kalyan had several flourishing merchants, some of whom figure as donors at Kanheri and Junnar during the second century AD.[6] As late as the sixth century AD, Cosmos Indieopleustes enumerates Kalyan among the five chief marts of western India with trade in brass, cloth and timber and fire wood.

Seumulla or Chawlse near Bombay, Mandagora (probably situated on the Rajapuri creek), Palaipamai (either Pal near Mahad or Dabol), Buzantion (Vaijayanti or Vijayagada) are other ports mentioned by the *Periplus*. Some of the above ports like Sopara and Kalyan have now become land-locked. Dvārkā, Prabhāsa and Valabhi were the principal ports of Kathiawar and Khambayat of northern Gujarat.

From the *Periplus*, we get a clear idea of the routes of the overseas trade. Ships from the western countries started from Arabia Felix (Aden) and followed the Arabian coast as far as Kane, from where the route to India diverted; some ships sailing to the Indus and on to Bharoch, and others direct to Arabia in July, as they could thereby utilise the monsoon to accelerate their speed.

Ujjayini in Malwa, Paithan in Maharashtra and Tagara, probably Ter in Hyderabad state, were the chief inland centres of trade. There were brought down to Bharoch from these market towns various articles, through bullock carts or on pack animals. Among the minor trade centres, we may mention Junnar, Karahāṭaka (Karhad in Satara district), Nasik, Govardhana and Vaijayantī. Roads were bad or non-existent according to the author of the *Periplus*, but he is probably over-drawing the picture. They appear to be sufficiently good and workable. We find residents of Vaijayantī in Karnataka making donations at Karli, residents of Karhad and Nasik in Maharashtra making gifts at Bharhut in Bagelkhand and citizens of Dattamitri in Sindh donating caves at Nasik. Sea communications were also well developed; Buddhist monasteries at creek Kanheri show that priests also travelled by the sea in the company of merchants, who built or excavated monasteries for their use. River traffic was not much in vogue; rivers in western India usually flowed through hilly country and petty streams, along the Tapi and the Narmada, however, there was some traffic in Gujarat.

Thanks to the numerous donative records, we get a fairly good glimpse into the different cross-sections of the trading community. Trades in corn, (*dhāñikas*), drugs (*gandhikas*) and jewels (*maṇikāras*) are frequently referred. Garland makers (*mālākāras*), ironsmiths (*lohavāṇijakos*) or (*kammāras*), goldsmiths (*suvarṇakāras*), braziers (*kāsakāras*), stone-cutters (*salavanijakas*), artisans (*āvesanis*), carpenters (*vadhikas*), weavers (*kolikas*), potters (*kulārikas*), hydraulic workers (*odayantrikcis*) and oilmongers (*tilāpiṣakas*) are seen vying with one another in making donations for religious objects connected with Buddhism and Hinduism. Caravans were the arteries of trade and are referred to as donors in several places. Farmers did not lag behind the traders and caravans in their religious zeal; they are referred to as *kuṭubikas*, *kālayikas* and *gahapatis*. The general impression produced by the votive records is that society was rich and prosperous and that the artisans, traders, caravans and farmers contributed a good deal to its well being.

Guild organisation was a special feature of trade and industry during our period. Guilds were known as *śrenis* and their aldermen were known as *śresṭhins*. Our records refer to the guilds of weavers, potters, braziers, oilmongers, hydraulic workers, bamboo workers, etc.[7] Sometimes, as at Govardhana, there were two guilds in the same town of one and the same industry, *viz*., weaving. Guilds had executive committees of their own, consisting of four or five members, whose president (*śresṭhin*) carried on the executive work with their help. The guild must have been primarily intended to safeguard the interest of the particular trade or industry. It, however also conducted banks, whose services were availed of not only by its members but also by the general public. Guilds and their banks were regarded as stable institutions, more enduring than kingdoms and empires. When Uṣabadāta, the son-in-law of the great king Nahapāna, who was most probably the governor of northern Maharashtra, desired to make permanent arrangements for the annual supply of a fixed income to certain monasteries near Nasik, he did not issue orders to the local treasury officers to make an annual remittance. His endowment took the form of a permanent deposit in local guild banks, with instructions to hand over the annual interest to the beneficiaries. Obviously he regarded the guild banks as more enduring than the government of which he was a distinguished member. Empires were established and destroyed in the course of a few years or decades, but guilds and their banks lived from age to age. A Gupta record shows that guilds would carry out their liability even if they changed their headquarters. Precaution, however, was often taken to get the permanent endowment at a guild bank registered in the office of the town municipality or *nigama sabhā*, which was expected to see to it that the guild banks carried out their obligations from generation to generation.

It is a great pity that we should not have so far found the seals or sealings of even a single guild of the Deccan and western India. The numerous guild sealings found at Vaiśālī gives us quite a vivid picture of the working of the organisation during the Gupta period, showing how there were joint guilds of bankers, traders and caravans with their membership spread over a large number of towns. It is likely that similar organisations may have existed in the Deccan also during our period, as they certainly did five hundred years later.

Let use now consider the currency problems. The larger part of the ordinary daily transactions were probably done by barter.[8] But silver, lead and copper currency was also in existence to supplement them. We have not so far found any specimens of gold currency current in western India. The gold coins or *suvarṇas*, one of which is equated to 35 silver *kārṣāpaṇas* in a Nasik record, were probably the gold pieces weighing about 120 grains which were issued by the Kuṣāṇas in northern India, some of which occasionally travelled down to the south with trade. Neither the Sātavāhanas nor the Śakas, neither the Ābhīras nor the Traikūṭākas issused any gold currency.

Kārṣāpaṇa is a term applicable both to the silver and copper coins, but in our records it usually refers to silver ones. The Nanaghat inscription of Nayaṅikā refers to her husband giving a *dakṣiṇā* of 24,400 *Kārṣāpaṇas* on one occasion and of 11,000 on another. At that time the Sātavāhanas were issuing no silver coins. Probably the *Kārṣāpaṇas* or punch-marked coins of northern India were current in the kingdom or were minted in it by some private moneyers. At Kondapur several moulds of punch-marked coins were discovered which were in vogue in the Sātavāhana period. Only a few later Sātavāhana kings sporadically issued silver currency in the second century AD.

The Western Kṣatrapa currency was on the other hand predominantly in silver. Each piece weighed about 30 grains. These coins were known in contemporary times as *Rudradamakas,* after the most powerful king of the dynasty, but this name does not occur in our records. A Nasik record tells us that 2,000 *suvarṇas* were equal to 70,000 silver *kārṣāpaṇas.* If we ignore the alloy in both the coins, this equation shows that 1050 (35 × 30) grains of silver were equal to 120 grains of gold. This gives the ratio between the prices of gold and silver at about 9:1. Silver being not indigenous to the country was dearer in India in the terms of gold; this was also one of the reasons as to why so much of Roman gold flowed into the country.[9]

We possess no data at present to give either the nomenclature or the relative value of the copper and lead currency that was profusely issued by the Sātavāhanas.[10]

Our records give us a good idea of the money market. Nahapāṇa's son-in-law Uṣavadāta invested 2,000 *kārṣāpaṇas* in one bank of the weavers' guild at Nasik as a permanent deposit on which an interest at 12% per annum was guaranteed. Another weavers' guild at the same place however agreed to pay only 9% interest to the same person. It is difficult to understand the causes for this difference in the rate of interest. When permanent deposits were fetching interest at so high a rate as 9 or 12% per annum, we may well conclude that short term loans must have been possible even for solvent parties at about the rate of 20 or 24%. The *Manusmṛti* mentions 24%[11] as the normal rate of fair interest and its statement is thus confirmed by the epigraphical evidence in our age.

There is no sufficient evidence to reconstruct the price level of the period. One Nasik inscription gives 4,000 *kārṣāpaṇas* as the price of a piece of land, but since no information is given either about its size or yield, the statement is not of much value As regards the price of cloth we are on surer grounds. We find that usually 12 *kārṣāpaṇas*[12] were sufficient for the three robes of the monks. A *kārṣāpaṇa*, weighed about 50 grains and was thus somewhat heavier than the four anna silver piece. So about three rupees and a half were sufficient for the underwear, the upper garment and the robe of a monk. These clothes required about 12 yards of cloth and so the price of one yard was about 4 annas.

We have no sufficient data to determine the cost of living during our period. Unfortunately no votive records give us any data about the money necessary to feed one monk every day. Northern Indian records of the Gupta period, however, show that one *dīnāra* or ¾ tola of gold was usually sufficient to feed a monk throughout the year. The monthly cost of one sumptuous meal was thus about Rs. 2 in the pre-war value of that coin.

Notes

1. See Junnar nos. 9, 14, and 18. The dimension of a *nivartana* is not definitely known, but it was probably equal to four or five acres.
2. *EI*, VIII, p. 71.
3. Nasik inscription no. 3.
4. Nasik no. 10.
5. *Yājñavalkyasmṛti*, undoubtedly composed during this age, permits the lesser 50% share. I.166.
6. Among the donors from Kalyan, some are merchants, some goldsmiths and some blacksmiths.
7. See Nasik inscriptions nos. 12, 15; Junnar inscriptions nos. 16 and 31.
8. This is the reason why some of the governments of the day like the Ikṣvāku and the Vākāṭaka administrations did not issue any coins at all.
9. In one Nasik record no. 12, the term *prati* is also used as a synonym for *kārṣāpa. na*.
10. Dr D.R. Bhandarkar's view that the silver coins introduced by Nahapāṇa were known as Kuṣāṇas *(IA*, 1919, p. 81) is untenable. *Kuṣaṇamūla* like *Chīvaramūla* was a sum given to the monks for the expense of purchasing *Kuṣaṇas*. What they were we do not know.
11. Ch. VIII, 140–1.
12. One record at Kanheri however provides for 16 *kārṣāpaṇas* for the robing of each monk. This was rather an unusual and liberal provision.

3

Family and Inheritance in Early South India

R.N. Nandi

SOCIOLOGICAL STUDIES of ethnic survivals indicate that the earliest family in south India was both matrilocal and matrilineal. Traces of matrilocal family can be found along the Malabar coast while matriliny is practised by a large number of castes and tribes in different parts of the peninsula.

In the beginning of the Christian era, however, the nature of family had changed considerably under the influence of Brāhmaṇa patriliny and sanskritization.[1] The elite groups which submitted to the northern patriarchal tradition adopted the patrilineal and patrilocal family as the normal feature of social organization. The Sātavāhana family, which was at once patrilineal and patrilocal, paid no more than customary respect to matriliny when they publicised their mother's ancestry in inscriptions. The Sālaṅkāyanas, the Ikṣvākus, the Viṣṇukuṇḍins, who were all Brāhmaṇa dynasties, mentioned only the ancestry of their father. But the early Kadambas, the Cālukyas of Badami and the eastern Cālukyas of Veṅgi, who seem to be of non-Brāhmaṇa origin, describe themselves as belonging to the paternal Mānavya *gotra* and as the sons of Hārīti, their ancestress. Some of the later Pallavas also occasionally mentioned their mother's decent, though the paternal clan-name Bhāradvāja figures uniformally in all their records. The Valayur and Velurpalaiyam grants[2] refer to the Pallava ruler as Cuṭu-Pallava, which means that the king was born of the marriage of a Cuṭu girl with a Pallava prince. Similarly, the Gaṅga king Anantvarman, who described himself as a Codagaṅga, did not hesitate to publicise that he was born of the union of the Gaṅga Devendravarman and the Coḍa princess Rājasundar.[3]

*15th Session at Gwalior, 1952. The paper has special reference to the inscriptions of early medieval Karnataka and Andhra.

The vast majority of non-elite families which were less affected by the patriarchal formulations of the Brāhmaṇa law-givers, however, continued with the matrilineal tradition, some temporarily reverting to matriliny until a male heir was obtained and others practising it as an accepted norm of social conduct. Temporary reversion to the descent through daughter (*marumakkathayam*) is evident from inscriptional references to dedication of daughters as *bāsavīs*, among whom descent is always in the female line.[4] In 800, one Aridari Poleyamma of the village Mayile dedicated a virgin to local temple along with 8 *mattras* of land, 1,000 cows and a swing for the use of the deity.[5] In 974 the blacksmith Bidi dedicated two young girls to another temple of the Shimoga district.[6] While the donations of property emphasize the donor's desire to obtain religious merit and social publicity, the dedication of daughters illustrate the tendency of certain families, which had not yet broken away from the matriarchal tradition, to temporarily revert to the system of descent through daughter in the absence of a male heir in the family. The practice is further illustrated by a record of 889. The inscription mentions the prostitute (*sule*) Kadacchi and her husband Mayadamarasa,[7] who had a daugher but no son. The couple dedicated their daughter to a local temple, the purpose being to convert her into a *bāsavī* who would be entitled to inherit the mother's property under the *marumakkhathayam* law. Kadadde, the dedicated girl, in her turn, took a mate of her choice and tried to procure a male issue for the family of her father. Unfortunately she, too, had a daughter named Ayacabbe. Ayacabbe, in her turn, renewed the attempt but gave birth to a daughter, Kaliṅgabbe. Kaliṅgabbe's marriage with one Pallaraki again resulted in the birth of a daughter, also named Kaliṅgabbe. The second Kaliṅgabbe ultimately gave birth to a son whose name was Parakayya. The inscription which stops with Parakayya is meaningful inasmuch as it suggests that Mayadamarasa's lineage was continued by temporarily reverting to the *marumakkhatthayam* system. The inscription does not name any of the husbands or mates of the several women who are named. This is in keeping with the present insignificance of a male partner in the *bāsavī* system. Kaliṅgabbe I's husband is mentioned as matter of gratitude, because it was his daughter who succeeded in procuring a son and thereby helped the family to revert back to the descent through son (*makkathayyam*). The record, which describes Parakayya as one belonging to lawful descent (*dharmasantati*) also anticipates the present position of children of a *bāsavī*, who do not suffer from any social stigma.

The practice of dedicating a girl to some deity in absence of male heir is very much prevalent among certain castes in the peninsula. Hutton observes that in Bellary and its neighbourhood, in the absence of a male heir, a daughter is offered to the temple.[8] After her dedication she becomes by established custom the heir of her parents' property and can perform their funeral rites as if she were a son. She takes to herself a man of her own selection, of any equal or higher caste, but continues to live in her father's house and her children take her father's name and belong to his family and not be their father's.[9] If she has a son, he inherits the property and the question of dedicating a daugher as *bāsavī* does not arise. But, if she has a daughter then again she beomes a *bāsavī* and renews the attempt to procure a son for the family.[10] The women of the Madiga caste are often made *bāsavīs* or dedicated as *devadāsīs*. In the case of the left hand Kaikkolan caste, which observes temporary reversion to the *marumakkhathayam*, the women often belong to the right hand faction.[11]

But, while the lack of a male heir led some families to temporarily revert to the descent through daughter system, other families practised it although male issues were not wanting. A record of about the eighth century refers to a donor, probably a lady, who after saluting her preceptor, her elder brother and blessing her son, announced that 'if the inheritor be without a husband, or having a husband, has all daughters, if they obtain husband and marry, it is not a violation of this agreement.'[12] Evidently, the inheritor was a lady, a daughter of the benefactress who was, probably, the wife of Timmapa Odeya. The statement in the inscription implies that the daughter was to inherit, in preference to the son, the property of her mother.

The practice of the *aliya santana* or descent through the sister's son, which is reminiscent of the maternal uncle's influence in a matriarchal family, is also illustrated by the inscriptions of the early medieval period. Earlier, the prevalence of the custom is confirmed by the southern lawgiver Baudhāyana who mentions cross-cousin marriages.[13] Marriage with the *mātula-kanyā* is also mentioned in the early Tamil classic, the *Maṇimekhalā*.[14] Inscriptions show that the *aliya santana* rule was popular with the Brāmaṇa families of Karnataka and Andhra. Gaṇḍanārāyaṇa, who was a feudatory of the eastern Cālukya king Badapa and who received a village from the king, regranted it to Candana, the son of his own sister. Two Brāhmaṇa brothers Svāmiyaśas and Viṣṇu-yaśas, who received a village from Jayasiṁhavallabha, also of the eastern Cālukya house, donated a ninth portion to their own sister's son Viṣnuśarman; Viṣnuśarman belonged to the Gavisni *gotra*, and was a student of Bahvṛca *śākhā* and his maternal uncles belonged to the Vatsa *gotra* and were students of the Chāndoga *caraṇa*.[15] The law of *aliya santana* which indicates the survival of matrilineal influence in patrilineal society, became more popular among certain castes in later medieval times.

Though the Brāhmaṇa elite society rejected matriarchy in preference to patriarchy, it could not altogether destroy the legal position to which the women had become entitled over centuries. This would explain the contrast between the northern women who remained over subdued to their men folk and almost confined to the four walls of the house and the southern women who inherited, administered and bequeathed property and public officers alike notwithstanding the denial of such rights to women by lawgivers.[16]

Women of the princely families owned and managed property in their own right. The Sātvāhana queen Nāganikā, who spent royal resources on the performance of Vedic rituals,[17] evidently had a right to do so. Similarly, the queen Vijayamahādevī of the eastern Cālukya dynasty, who ruled as a sovereign during the minority of her son, donated plots of land to Brāhmaṇas.[18] The fields formed part of the crown land which the queen inherited from her deceased husband. Gifts of villages as freehold estates to priests and temples also indicate the right of princely women to property.[19] Examples of priestly women receiving landed property in donation either jointly or singly, also point in the same direction. In 688 the village Navatula in the Ganjam district of Orissa was granted jointly to a Brāhmaṇa woman Pillikasvāminī and her brother Pilasarmā as a freehold estate.[20] Similarly, the 12 *nivartanas* of land granted to a Brāhmaṇa woman for the performance of the *prājāpatya* rite was as much the property of the priestess as the 25 *nivartana* of land donated to the priest Āditya of the Kauśika *gotra* for the same purpose.[21]

Cases are also on record to show that public offices and personal estates could be inherited and administered by the wife and the daughters is succession. An inscription of the Shikarpur taluk of Karnataka refer to the wife of a district headman (*nāḍgāvuṇda*) who succeeded to the office of her deceased husband, and enjoyed privileges and emoluments which the office carried with it.[22] The lady-officer also inherited the estate of her late husband. Later, the daughter of the widow succeeded both the office and the estate which her mother had inherited earlier. Another woman who had lost both her husband and son and was living with the four sons of her widowed younger sister, appears to have inherited the entire property of her deceased husband, a man of some influence in the government, so as to be able to spend profusely on the works of public welfare and religious merit.[23]

However, with the progressive alienation of landed property, administrative authority and trade rights by the state to the Brahmanical families, the roots of Brāhmaṇa patriliny struck ever deeper resulting in corresponding weakening of the matriarchal institutions. At present, the matrilocal and matrilineal family survives among certain tribes and lowly Śūdras who live on the periphery of the Brahmanical society but are seldom recognised as parts of it. In matters relating to property rights, the women of Brahmanical castes in south India need as much the protection of modern legislation[24] as do their counterparts in other regions of India. The present tension between the Brāhmaṇa and Śūdra communities of Tamil Nadu, where status-displacement following the introduction of patriarchal institutions was greater than in other parts of peninsula, can be related to the conflict of two mutually incompatible social systems one of which gave social and economic power to the patriarchal Brāhmaṇa elite and the other gave such authority to the numerically superior matriarchal families of unbrahmanical origin.

Notes

1. The inscription of the early medieval period bear out the eagerness of tribal families and petty bureaucrats, who lived in intimate contact of the Brāhmaṇa elite, to adopt Brāhmaṇa *gotras* and practise Brāhmaṇical rites in an attempt to find a place in the status system of the Brahmanical society, See R.N. Nandi, 'Gotra and Social Mobility in the Deccan', *Proceedings of the Indian History Congress*, 32nd session, Jaipur, Delhi, 1972, pp. 118–23 and 'Clan-name and Social Mobility in the Deccan', *Proceedings of the Indian History Congress*, 33rd session, Muzaffarpur, Delhi, 1973, pp. 111–18.
2. *JRASB*, 8, p. 3.
3. *JAHRS*, 12, p. 118.
4. J.H. Hutton, *Caste in India*, p. 162.
5. *EC*, 8, *Sb*. 9.
6. *EC*, 7, *HL*, 64.
7. *EC*, 11, *Dg*. 17, p. 29.
8. Hutton, op. cit.
9. Ibid.
10. Ibid.
11. Ibid.
12. *EC*, 11, *Dg*. 17.
13. *Baudhāyana Dharmasūtra*. I, 1926, cited in P.V. Kane, *Dharmasastra Ka Itihasa*, vol. I, p. 280.
14. *EI*, 19, no. 24, p. 137ff.
15. *EI*, 31, no. 20 B, p. 133ff.
16. Earliest law-givers including Baudhāyana described women as dependent on father in childhood, on husband in youth and on son in age, see *Manusmṛti*, 9, 185; 9. 217. *Nāṛadasmṛti*, 24–26, cited in Kane, op. cit., pp. 906–7. Medhātithi states that whatever a wife acquires belongs to her husband and that ordinarily the wife is not to inherit the prorerty of her dead husband, *B.C. Law Volume*, I, p. 160. But a widow of sonless husband may inhert property if she is virtuous.
17. *B.C. Law Volume*, I, p. 159.
18. *IA*, 7, no. 53.
19. *EI*, 4, no. 50.
20. *IHQ*, 20, p. 232, AD 688.
21. *IA*, 6, p. 88.
22. *EC*, 7 *Sk* 219.
23. *EC*, 8, *Nr*. 35.
24. The Hindu Succession Law of 1956 which gives equal rights to male and female successors seems to compromise the positions taken by patrilineal and matrilineal communities.

PART 2

The Early Pattern of Socio-Economic Transformation

4

Agricultural Production During the Early Iron Age in Northern India

M.D.N. Sahi

During the recent years there has been an increasing awareness amongst scholars of the need to discuss in specific terms the impact of the use of iron-technology as an instrument of socioeconomic change in India. Ghosh[1] held the view that the effect of iron was not significant, that the metal did not produce any spurt in the material prosperity of the society and that the introduction of iron did not immediately involve a march towards urbanism. Sharma[2] ascribes the rise of Magadhan power to the availability of iron in south Bihar in 600 BC. In his later work Sharma[3] states that the total picture of the Painted Grey Ware (PGW) settlement does not warrant their characterisation as urban as has been done by Wheeler. However, he concedes that towards the end of the PGW period they can be called protourban at best. He further observes that, all told, the PGW people practised field agriculture but iron does not seem to have played any role in it. Chakrabarti[4] is of the opinion that iron did make the already existing village structure economically more productive but he is not prepared to ascribe any revolutionary role to it in social change preceding 600 BC. Niharranjan Ray[5] argues that at the present state of our archaeological knowledge, there is yet no absolute case for iron-technology effecting in the clearance of forests even at the earlier NBP Ware level of the culture. The same seems to have been the case in regard to the assumption of extensive plough cultivation; the sort of agricultural operations which could provide sufficient surplus for bringing about a new social phenomenon, namely, urbanisation. Following Ray and Sharma, Thakur[6] holds that the much discussed iron-aided extensive agriculture is a myth in the context of the economy of the sixth–fifth centuries BC and apparently there is hardly a direct and perceptible connection between iron and the origin of towns on this count.

*43rd Session at Kurukshetra, 1982.

In the present paper we seek to study the position of agricultural production during the early Iron Age (Painted Grey Ware) and thereby the role of iron in it; and to examine the validity of the views mentioned above.

Archaeological evidence as it stands today indicates that iron was introduced into the Indo-Gangetic plain by the unpainted Black-and-Red Ware people at Noh. But very soon the technology was mastered and popularised by the PGW people who colonised northern India between 1100–800 BC.[7]

Iron objects used by the PGW people may be classified as under:

(a) Weapons used for warfare or hunting and fishing, viz. arrowheads, spearheads, daggers, lances and fish-hooks; (b) House-hold objects like nails, pins, needles, knives, clamps, rings, bangles and tongs: (c) Craft tools—*viz.*, adze, axe, chisels and borers: (d) Objects used in agricultural operations including spade, sickle, hoe, axes, (socketed and plain) and plough-share.

The hard alluvial soil and the deeply forested areas of the Gangetic plain posed themselves as the two ecological handicaps before the copper Age (OCP) people. Probably the broken pieces of socketed axes from Hastinapur and simple type axes from Atrañjikhera. Jakhera and Noh, were used by the PGW people for cutting the stumps of the burnt down trees of the dense forests, facilitating reclamation of land for agricultural purposes. The ploughshares from Alamgirpur[8] and those from Jakhera[9] must have been very helpful in breaking the hard alluvial soil of the Gangetic plain and making the fields fit for cultivation. A complete sickle (without handle) from the proto PGW levels at Jakhera (Period II A) and a smaller one from Atrañjikhera (period III) must have facilitated, the agricultural operations of the PGW people. Thus in all likelihood the newly acquired iron-technology was harnessed by the PGW people for overcoming the ecological handicaps and ushering in an era of large scale settlements and agricultural production.

The impact of the use of iron tools is also reflected in the multiplicity of cereals and grains and beginning of cultivation of an important cereal (wheat) evidenced at Atranjikhera and hitherto unknown in the Gangetic Valley during the Copper–Bronze Age. The excavations at Hastinapur and Noh brought to light the remains of rice (*oryza sp.*) from the PGW levels. It may be noted that barley and rice were the staple food of the Gangetic plain during the Copper-Bronze Age. The two cereals are reported from Hulas (Harappan), Lai Quila, Atranjikhera, Noh and Sringaverapur in the OCP context. Evidence from Atranjikhera[10] clearly establishes that besides rice and barley the PGW people started cultivating wheat (*Jriticum compactum*). In the same context, referring to rice from Atranjikhera, Chowdhury mentions that it was found in heaps and was mostly without husk. They further hold that from these facts one would be led to presume that production of cereal was then not only enough to meet the requirements of the entire community but there was also some surplus.

About the cultivation of wheat Watt[11] observes that during the rains in June and July the land is ploughed two or three times and smoothed. If rain has been plentiful and the ground remains moist, seed is shown broadcast in October, November and December. The ground is then again ploughed and promoted and the beds formed. If there is subsequent rain the fields are irrigated from wells six or seven times; if there is no rain, nine or ten times. It means that cultivation of wheat requires the field to be ploughed least four or five times. Moreover, for this winter crop artificial means of irrigation are also a necessity inspite of the rains. It implies that iron tools were not only useful in breaking the hard alluvium of the Gangetic plain but also for procuring water for irrigation by tapping artificial sources of water such as digging of wells, tanks and canals. This was more easly to be achieved with the help of iron tools. Kachcha wells are attested at Jakhera and Atranjikhera associated with the PGW levels. At Jakhera a moatlike water-channel has also been noticed,[12] which may have been used for irrigating the fields as well.

In this context it is also interesting to note that Vedic texts also refer to the practice of providing artificial source of water for irrigation by digging channels. *Khanitra*, a shovel or spade for digging, is mentioned in the *Ṛgveda* and the later texts. *Khanitrima*, meaning produced by digging, is epithet of *apaḥ* (water). It clearly refers to artificial water channels used for irrigation as practised in the times of the *Ṛgveda* and the *Atharvaveda*.[13] This reminds us of the spade found in the core of the rampart with a moat at Ujjain in a PGW-associated level.

Though most of the PGW settlements are situated close to and along the major river banks, yet we have evidence of some settlement located away from the perennial source of water. Subsistence of such settlements would not be possible unless artificial sources of water are tapped not only for the daily needs of the people but also for agriculture. Dhansari, a PGW site in Aligarh, is situated about 5 km away from the nearest river bed of the Nim, a tributary of the Kalinadi. Out of 23 PGW sites explored in Kanpur district,[14] two single culture sites were found located away from the rivers. Around these there were big ponds and low lying swampy areas.

In order to have a better picture of agricultural production achieved by the PGW people it is desirable to recall the agricultural crops cultivated by the pre-PGW people.[15] In the pre-PGW context the grains reported from the Gangetic plain are rice and barley from Lal Qila, Atranjikhera, Sringaverapur and Chirand. Only rice has been reported from Hulas, Noh, Mahagara, Koldihwa, Chirand, Baidipur, Pandurajar Dhibi and Mahisdal; field pea (*Pisum arvense*) from Chirand, garden pea (*Pisum sativum*) from Atranjikhera, horse gram (*Dolicos biflorus*), Urd (*Phascolus Mungo*) and *sarson* (*Br ssica compestris*) from Noh; *moong* (*Phaseolus radiatus*) and *masoor* (*lensesculenta*) from Chirand, *kesari* (*Lathyrus sativus*) from Atranjikhera and Chirand, gram (*Cicar arietinum*) from Lal Qila and Sringaverapur and *til* (*Sesame*) from Sringaverapur.

Though there are no definite archaeological evidences to demonstrate it, it may be presumed that most of the above mentioned grains (as we find in the case of rice and barley) may have continued to be produced and cultivated by the early Iron-Age PGW people. This presumption gets further corroboration from the corresponding literary evidence, *viz.* Late Ṛigvedic later Vedic and early Brāhmaṇic texts. Lal[16] and Sharma[17] have correlated the later Vedic and early Brāhmaṇic texts with the mature phase of PGW culture.

If seen in this light there is complete consonance between the archaeological and literary data. PGW culture definitely reveals a very stable agricultural base with agricultural tools like sickle obtained from the proto-PGW phase (Period IIA) at Jakhera and Atranjikhera (Pd. III). *Datra* and *Srīni* are two distinct terms which appear in the *Ṛgveda* for sickle. Words like *da, dau* and *daranti* may be taken as the derivatives of the former.[18] Another term, *lavitra* meaning reaping hook or reaping crop is found in the Brāhmanas. *Phāla*[19]and *Stega*[20] meaning plough-share occurs in the *Ṛgveda* and later Vedic texts. *Pavira* occurs in the *Ṛgveda,* applied to man, in the sense of having a goad or having a spear. Its derivatives *Pavirvant* or *Pavirva* which is found in the *Atharvaveda* and *Yajurveda saṁhitā* is used as plough apparently in the sense of having a metal share[21] like that of a lance. It may be interesting to note that the ploughshare of Alamgirpur (though not reported as such by the excavator) actually appears like a lance. *Lāṅgala* and *sira* are the regular words for plough in the *Ṛgveda* and later Vedic texts. In later texts it is described in a series of passages as 'lance pointed' and having well smoothed handle. In later Vedic texts[22] *sīra* was large and heavy as is shown by the fact that six oxen, or eight or twelve or even twenty-four were used to drag it.

Coming to the agricultural production of grains it may be noted that in the *Ṛgveda* and later Vedic texts, barley (*yava*) and probably rice too (*dāna/ dhānya*) occur. In the later Vedic texts the grains attested are rice (*vrīhi*), *plasuka* (fast-growing rice), *sāli* (rice); *upavaka* (barley); *godhwna* (wheat); *syam aka* (millet), *masura* (lentil); *khalakula* (kulattha—a kind of pulse); *mudga* and *kumāṣa* (beans), *til* (sesame); *khalva* (moong); *urvarn* and *urvaruka* (cucumbers), *garamut* (wild beans), *karakandhu, kuvala* and *badara* (jujube) and other unidentifiable grains such as *anu, amba, gavidhuka* or *gavadhuka, namba, priyaṅgu, masusya* and *śaṣya.*

Thus on the basis of combined, testimony of archaeological and literary sources it may be concluded that before the introduction of iron in the Gangetic Valley agriculture was extensive without proper ploughing and that irrigational facilities made it more and more intensive after the introduction of the iron tools leading to multifarious agricultural activities, producing some new crops, wheat being one of the most important.

Whether these agricultural activities of the PGW people were responsible for the surplus production as is claimed by Chowdhury (*supra*) can be judged properly if we recapitulate the vast area in which this culture flourished: the nature of its settlements and the density of population, which was related/ interlinked with agricultural production, not only for food but also for bartering it for the procurement of most of the raw material which was required for different industries but were not locally available. Food was also to be provided to a large section of smiths, potters, bead makers, bone-workers and so on who were probably not in a position to produce food for themselves.

To bring into sharper focus the extent of distribution of this culture it may be pointed out that from Lakiyopir in Sind to Kauśāmbī in UP it is about more than 1500 km and from Gharinda in Punjab to Ujjain in Madhya Pradesh about 800–900 kms. Within this area about 650 sites have been discovered so far.

This PGW sites are located generally along the river banks, the average distance from one site to another being about 10 to 12 kms. However, in favourable ecological environment it could be much less, even 5 kms.[23] In north Haryana where an intensive survey has been done, these have been found to cover as small an area as 1673 sq ms and as large as 96193 sq. ms.[24] Another very interesting feature emerges from Mughal's survey in Bahawalpur. Of the fourteen PGW sites discovered by him, as many as seven range between 1.1 and 2.1 hectares, which should be regarded as the normal run of the sites. Further, while three are less than a hectare each three others fall between 3 and 4 hectares. However, the most noteworthy point is that one of these fourteen sites is unusually large, *viz.* 13.7 hectares. This clearly shows on the one hand the emergence of a chief town amidst smaller villages—a pattern which in due course gave rise to local 'capitals' having been transformed into urban centres and on the other the fallacy of the views of the scholars quoted at the outse.

Notes

1. A. Ghosh, *The City in Early Historical India,* p. 10.
2. R.S. Sharma,'Iron and Urbanization in the Ganga Basin', *IHR,* vol. I, no. 1, p. 100.
3. R.S. Sharma, 'Later Vedic Phase and the Painted Grey Ware', *Purātattva,* no. 8, p. 64.
4. D.K. Chakrabarti,'Beginning of Iron and Social Change in India', *Indian Studies Past and Present,* vol. XIV, no. 4, p. 329.
5. Niharranjan Ray,'Technology and Social Change in Early Indian History—A Note Posing a *Theoretical* Question,' *Purātattva,* no. 8, pp. 132–8.
6. V.K. Thakur, *Urbanijation in Ancient India,* 1981.
7. B.B. Lal, 'Excavations at Hastinapur', *Ancient India,* no. 10–11 and 'Painted Grey Ware Culture', *A History of the Civilization of Central Asia,* 1981, ch. XVIII.
8. N.R. Banerjee, *The Iron Age in India,* pt. I.
9. M.D.N. Sahi, 'New Light or Painted Grey Ware People as Revealed from the Excavation at Jakhera', *Man and Environment,* vol. II, pp. 104–5.

10. K.A. Chowdhury, *et al*, *Ancient Agriculture and Forestry in North India*, pp. 63–6.
11. G. Watt, *Dictionary of Economic Product of India*, vol. VI, pt. IV, p. 125.
12. M.D.N Sahi, op. cit., p. 104.
13. A.A. Macdonell and A.B. Keith, *Vedic Index*, vol. II, p. 214.
14. Makkhan Lal, 'Settlement Pattern of the Painted Grey Ware Culruie in the Ganga Valley', paper presented at Indo-Pacific Prehistory Conference held at Pune, 19–22 December 1978 (mimeographed).
15. M.D.N Sahi, 'Early History of Agriculture in Pre-and Protohistoric India', *PIHC*, 1981, pp. 42–53.
16. Op. cit.
17. Op. cit.
18. Sharma, op. cit., p. 65.
19. Macdonell and Keith, op. cit., p. 58.
20. Ibid., p. 484.
21. Ibid., p. 509.
22. Ibid., p. 451.
23. B.B. Lal, 1981, op. cit., and Makkhan Lal, op. cit.
24. Suraj Bhan and Jim Shaffer, 'New Discoveries in Northern Haryana', *Man and Environment*, vol. II, p. 59.

5

Some Aspects of Early Orissan Economy and Society

Bhairabi Prasad Sahu

IN DEALING with the history of Orissa there has been a general tendency to concentrate on the littoral districts, although the rest of the state does not lack sources for historical study. This provides a distorted view of the actual historical and cultural developments in Orissa from *c.* 300 BC. It is well known that literary sources for this phase (*c.* 300 BC–C. AD 500) are meagre.[1] On account of this, archaeological data constitute our major source for the reconstruction of the early phase of Orissan history. Archaeological remains suggest that the process of cultural development was simultaneous, both in the littoral districts and the western rolling uplands, possibly with some forms of interaction existing between the two areas.

Two major systematic excavations unveiling the cultural sequence have been carried out in the coastal plains of Orissa–Sisupalgarh in Puri district, and Jaugada in Ganjam. The ruins of Sisupalgarh[2] are located about 3 kms to the east-south-east of Bhubaneswar. Excavation showed that the site was occupied from the beginning of the third century BC to the middle of the fourth century AD. There have been gradual changes in some industries, pottery being the most conspicuous, within the same integral culture. In the early period the pottery is essentially plain and devoid of decorations. It varied from dull grey to terracotta red. In the second phase the pottery was well fired, nicely finished and the bright red polished ware dominated. Incised and applied decorations appeared at this stage. Black-and-red ware of megalithic fabric appeared for the first time at the beginning of the period. In the late stages of the period the earliest specimens of the rouletted ware were found. In the succeeding period the bright red polished ware got increasingly weaker. In variety and execution the decorative patterns deteriorated. The most distinctive type of vessel, typical of Sisupalgarh culture, is a knobbed vessel, possibly a bowl-cum-lid, usually grey or greyish-black in appearance. From various, levels terracotta ear-ornaments, terracotta-bullaes, iron implements of war and peace (nails, spikes,

*41st Session at Bombay, 1980.

knives, sickles, borers, staples, arrowheads, caltrops, etc.) and beads of agate, carnelian, chalcedony, quartz and glass were found. Other finds included two fragmentary terracotta coin moulds, 9 finger-rings, 28 bangles of terracotta, copper, ivory, bone and glass, and numerous coins—a unique Murunda gold coin,[3] a silver Punch-marked coin, Kusana and Puri-Kusana coins and copper coins with the Ujjain and Eran symbols. The defences are square on, plain with each side being pierced by two gateways. Period II marked the beginning of the construction of the defences. Sisupalgarh revealed the use of baked bricks in good quantity.[4]

The fortified site of Jaugada, well known for a set of the Fourteen Rock-edicts of Asoka, is situated on the bank of Rishikulya in southern Orissa. Exacavations conducted by D. Mitra[5] revealed a full-fledged iron-using culture here. In period I, the pottery, being utilitarian in character, was essentially plain and devoid of paintings. The ceramic industry consisted of an ordinary dull red ware with or without slip, a black-and-red ware of well burnt fabric, generally with a polished surface, the dish-and-bowl being the common shapes, and a red polished ware. In period II the decorated pottery consisted of incised and applied patterns. The knobbed vessel which made its appearance in period I continued into this period, but the fabric degenerated considerably. Other cultural equipment included brick and stone structures, scantily represented in the small area under excavation, beads of shell, bone, carnelian, agate, crystal, quartz, terracotta and copper; and iron objects of peace and war. One Punch-marked and 2 Puri-Kuṣāṇa coins were collected from the site. The fortification is roughly square on plan, with two gateways on each side. It consists of an earthen rampart surviving to a height of 25 ft. at places. The defences began in the second phase of occupation.

With this brief description of the two sites in the coastal plains we move on to an early historic site in western Orissa. Excavations at Asurgarh[6] in Kalahandi district were directed by N.K. Sahu. In the upper phase of the third layer, assignable to the *c.* third century BC black-and-red pottery was found in abundance, together with black-polished ware. A piece of chunar sandstone showing the characteristic Mauryan polish was also found from this layer. The uppermost layer and the second layer contained pottery, iron objects like axes, hooks and door hinges and beads of semi-precious stones ascribable to the period from first to fourth century AD. Punch-marked coins and a copper coin of Kaniṣka were also collected from the site. The top layer contained floors of houses paved with brickbats. A circular structure of c. fifth century AD was exposed between the two trenches.

A comparative study of all these three stratigraphically excavated sites brings in certain interesting information. The earliest levels at Sisupalgarh have been dated to *c.* 300 BC and the latest to mid fourth century AD. The Asurgarh excavations unveil a similar trend. This site has also been dated to *c.* third century BC–*c.* fifth century AD. The report on the excavations at Jaugada, being provisional in nature, has not assigned any date to the different layers. But the ceramic evidence indicates its pre-Christian origin and the Puri-Kuṣāṇa coins in levels of period II sets the upper limit of the site.[7] Further, the identity of the material remains with those of Sisupalgarh and Asurgarh and the set of Aśokan inscriptions (which almost fixes the lower limit of site) proves beyond doubt that this site too is datable to the same time-bracket. Thus in all the three sites we encounter material remains dated back to *c*. 300 BC and the uppermost limits generally converge. The black-and-red ware and polishéd black-ware are evidenced in all of them. Punch-marked coins and Puri-Kuṣāṇa coins have been recovered from all the three sites. While at Sisupalgarh one encounters baked bricks in good quantity, brick and stone structures are scantily represented in the other two sites. This can be explained by the limited area and nature of the excavations. Remnants of floors of houses and brick-bats are noticed at Jaugada and Asurgarh, Iron implements of war and peace gathered from the three sites resemble each other to a considerable extent. The knobbed vessel first found in Sisupalgarh is also unearthed from Jaugada. Again in both the sites the fortification did not start with the first occupation. They were constructed in the succeeding period. The walls in both the cases were initially made of mud and later strengthened with Iaterite-gravel. At Sisupalgarh the fortification was 25 ft. high in the first phase of its construction. Similarly, at Jaugada the walls rise to a height of 25 ft. at places. Both the forts are square on plan and each of their walls is pierced by two gateways. There is a great deal of similarity in the archaeological data from these three different sites. These sites are located in three different parts of Orissa. They roughly form a triangle and are wide-spread in their distribution. The remarkable identity of material remains pre-supposes a certain degree of interaction between them.

Kharliagarh, the fortified site in Bolangir district at the confluence of the Tel and the Raul, is datable to the early historic period. It yielded sherds of coarse red ware which R.N. Das thinks resembles the Sisupalgarh type.[8]

Iron implements belonging to this early period have been unearthed from at least seven sites. Besides the three major sites discussed above, iron, agricultural and hunting implements are collected from Gangahar minor irrigation project area and Biratgarh in Mayurbhanj, Kharliagarh and Gudbhela in Bolangir. These artifacts from different sites though belonging to different periods are broadly dated in between *c*. 300 BC and AD 350.[9] Those from Kharliagarh resemble the Sisupalgarh tools.[10] The Gudbhela finds too resemble the implements from Sisupalgarh.[11] They are either contemporary or a little later in date than the Sisupalgarh finds.[12] The iron implements include agricultural and hunting tools. Sickles, pointed spearheads, arrowheads, nails, knives, hammer with hilt, chisel, swords and axes are the various artifacts that have been unearthed from the above sites.

As in northern India, the history of coinage in Orissa also begins with the Punch-marked coins. Barring the hilly tracts and the plateau regions the remaining eight districts have yielded these coins. B.B. Nath believes that they came into circulation in Orissa in the fourth century BC.[13] The upper limit of these coins is fixed by the Sisupalgarh finds—*c.* AD 100. The second major series of coins are the Puri-Kuṣāṇa coins. They are dated between *c.* second century AD and the fourth century AD. These in their distribution embrace the districts of Keonjhar, Mayurbhanj and all the four coastal districts.

The similarity of the material remains from the excavated sites, the early historic iron implements spread over different widely scattered districts and the wide distribution of the Punch-marked and Puri-Kuṣāṇa coins amply suggest that the growth of material culture in Orissa was just not confined to the coastal districts, as is often projected by the kind of historical writings we have. Keeping in view the above facts it will be naive to argue that the history of Orissa is the history of the coastal districts.[14]

Certain differences in the development of the material culture in the coastal plains and the rolling uplands has been highlighted by the available archaeological data. As a case in point one may refer to the relative paucity of Kuṣāṇa and Puri-Kuṣāṇa coins belonging to the early Christian centuries, in western Orissa. While from this one is tempted to believe that coastal Orissa in the early Christian centuries was a region of more hectic commercial and mercantile activity, yet no such conclusion can be reached till more evidences pour in. Despite the few minor differences, which could be due to insufficient exploration and survey, on the whole the similarities in the process of cultural evolution and development in both the regions are more striking.

To what period can one ascribe the beginnings of the early historic phase in Orissa? The earliest archaeological finds for this early period in Orissa, the Punch-marked coins are dated around the fourth century BC. In the three main excavated sites the earliest occupation levels have been fixed around 300 BC. The Kaliṅga war was fought in 261 BC. Rock-edict 13 of Aśoka records that one lakh persons were slain, one lakh and fifty thousand were carried away captive and many times that number perished from famine, pestilence and other calamities which followed in the wake of war. This information makes it amply clear that Kaliṅga of the third century BC was a well populated geographical entity. Its material culture was sufficiently developed to meet the needs of its people. All this presupposes a gradual and continuous evolution of the material culture in the preceding centuries. Piecing together these scattered facts one is inclined to trace the beginning of the early historic period in Orissa at least 100–150 years before the 3rd century BC.

Economy

Epigraphic records belonging to our period do not shed much light on contemporary economy and society. The two copies of the Aśokan inscription at Dhauli and Jaugada, the Hathigumpha inscription of Khāravela and the other few inscriptions assigned to our period of study help very little for any reconstruction of the economic history of ancient Orissa. However, certain epigraphs of our period, and some immediately succeeding it, thankfully, name a few types of land[15]—uncultivable (*Khila*), cultivable (*Khila-Śūnya)* and habitable (*Vāstu*). The term *kṣetra* probably meant land in general. The sources are conspicuously silent about the types of agricultural implements, the kinds of crops and cereals and methods of cultivation. From the Hathigumpha inscription it might be inferred that canals were dug out to insure against drought and to facilitate cultivation. From the hoards of iron implements unearthed from different sites, some, like the sickle and the axe, are agricultural tools and may help in forming some idea, however meagre, about the ways of agriculture. Surprisingly either ploughshares, hoes or spades have not so far been reported from any site. Their discovery would have helped in forming specific ideas about the agrarian economy of the period. The most important economic activity, as today, seems to have been a peasant agriculture based on irrigated rice cultivation.[16] There has been little climatic change during the last 2000 years in this part of the country, as is evidenced from the analysis of the wood-remains from Sisupalgarh.[17] All the six specimens from Sisupalgarh are found now in the forests of Orissa. Therefore, it may reasonably be suggested that crops and cereals may not have been very different in ancient Kaliṅga from what they are today in Orissa. One ventures to suggest that the people of Kaliṅga might have been familiar with wet paddy cultivation, atleast since the Kaliṅga war, if not earlier. Magadha must have influenced Kaliṅga in the production of this cereal. With the Aryans, rice formed an important part of the commonly observed religious rituals, either in the form of offerings or distribution, which constituted an act of merit. In Orissa, with the beginning of the northern Sanskritic culture (we do not use the word 'Aryanization' because it has a racial ethos) since the *c.* third century BC,[18] the cereal, if it did not exist earlier, must have been imported into the land from the north.

The Punch-marked, Kuṣāṇa and Puri-Kuṣāṇa, the Andhra and the few Gupta coins unearthed from different pockets throw a flood of light on the vigorous economic and brisk commercial activity in ancient Kaliṅga. The sheer volume of these finds (the punch-marked and Puri-Kuṣāṇa coins) rejects any explanation of their being imported, either by way of trade or through pilgrims They seem to have been locally manufactured for home consumption, The coin moulds from Sisupalgarh[19] and the twin coins from near Khiching[20] further reinforce our argument.

The agrarian pattern, as already discussed is not very clear, owing to the paucity of source material. Whatever meagre information we have access to is because of the land grant charters. The first recorded land-grant comes from Bhadrak and is dated to the second half of the third century AD.[21] It records the grant of eighty measures of land to a temple or religious establishment. The period intervening between the Bhadrak grant and the next series of grants is approximately a hundred years. The Matharas who rose to power in south-eastern Orissa in *c.* AD 350 issued a series of land grants In the land grants the villagers are instructed to do all the customary services and to pay all the dues to the donee. The cultivators are asked to attend to the donees as per custom and to offer them *Meya* and *Hiraṇya.*[22] The Baranga plates, the Sripuram plates, the Paralakhimundi plates, the Bobbili plates, the Tekkali plates, etc., which are all dated between the fourth and sixth century AD refer to grants of land. Quite interestingly, as in north India in the same period, so also here, the donors request the future rulers not to disturb the grants. All these are religious grants and only financial rights were delegated to the donee. Such grants were made not only to Brāhmaṇas but also to the religious and monastic institution[23] A careful analysis of these early grants may throw favourable light on the agrarian condition of early Orissa, and may reveal the genesis of a new socio-economic trend.

Society

The sources for our period do not provide much information about social life. They neither provide us a glimpse of the caste system. Some idea about the people's dresses, ornaments, pastimes and amusements may be fromed from the sculptural relics of the period. Invariably, all the records, beginning with the Hathigumpha inscription, refer to the Brāhmaṇas.[24] There is a dearth of information as regards the other castes whose existence however, cannot be denied. D. Das, relying on certain terms used in the inscriptions infers the existence of a section of people who, in their occupation, correspond to the Kāyasthas.[25] A. Sah, however, tells us that the inscriptions of Orissa do not indicate the existence, of a separate caste, such as the Kāyastha, prior to the tenth century AD.[26] About the Vaiśyas the records are once more strangely silent. Incidentally, the Jayarampur copperplate makes an isolated reference to *Gṛhaswāmī* and *Gṛhādhyakṣa,* which to D. Das seem to be synonymous with the *Gahapatis* referred to in the Jātakas.[27] Equally arduous it is to locate a dominant Kṣatriya section in the then society. Castes like the Khandayats, who constitute the regional Kṣatriyas, are invariably associated with professions more akin to the Vaiśya. Again, they as a separate section emerged only in later times. As regards the position of women, evidences are similarly meagre. One thirg that is clear is that there was no *satī* at this early stage. Not before the eleventh–twelfth century do we come across evidences of *satīi.*[28] Thus, the picture of society that emerges is a very ambiguous one. Clearly there is a deviation from the prescribed Brahmanical norms and this deviation can only be explained by investigating the actual caste stratification at various historical times.

In Orissa, in our period of study, social stratification based on the four-fold *varṇa* division presents its own problems. The Sanskritic culture coming from the north was yet (*c.* AD 500) to make its force felt fully. What we find in Orissa during this period is a process of interaction and assimilation between the bearers of the orthodox Sanskritic culture and the local tribal populace.

Together with the sculptural relics of Buddhism, Jainism, Śaivism and the Māṭhara grants which proclaim them as Śaivites and Vaiṣṇavites, we have evidence of Yakṣa, Nāga, Mother Goddess and other forms of tribal worship. As a specific point of reference one has the case of the Gaṅgas acknowledging the tribal goddess Saora as the 'Īṣṭa-Devatā' in the Mahendra mountains in the fifth century AD,[29] as a policy of appeasing the tribal sentiment. There are numerous other such instances. Therefore, what is discernible in this phase is a tremendous tribal influence on Orissan social life. To deduce from Māṭhara patronage of Śaivism and Vaiṣṇavism about the extent and intensity of Brahmanization would tantamount to an error of judgement. Quite possibly they patronised these religions with a view to acquire legitimacy in the eyes of people like the Sātavāhanas in the western Deccan, who resorted to Vedic sacrifices to achieve the same end. What seems highly probable is that the Brāhmaṇas, during this period, having been granted land in the peripherial areas initiated the process of acculturation and to expedite the process recognised the ruling chiefs as Kṣyatriyas and treated the rest as Śūdras. If this was so, then to an extent it could account for the absence of clear-cut orthodox four-fold *varṇa* society. This early phase was, thus, in a state of flux experiencing a transition. It thus becomes difficult to accept that the Aryan people came in large numbers and subjugated the local tribes and superimposed their own culture and language on the Orissan people.[30] Therefore, any generalization from the perspective of the Gaṅgā valley would be a terrible mistake. The Orissan situation is a brilliant case of regional variation and may act as a corrective to tendencies to generalise about the sub-continent from the perspective of the Gaṅga valley.

Notes

1. See R.C. Majumdar, 'Sources of the Early History of Orissa', in *Journal of Ancient Indian History*, vol. I, pp. 40–1.
2. Analysis based on B.B. Lal, 'Sisupalgarh 1948: A Early Historical Fort in Eastern India', in *Ancient India*, vol. 5.
3. See A.S. Altekar, 'A note on the Kushan Gold Coin', in *Ancient India*, vol. 5, pp. 100–1, and 'A Unique Kushano–Roman Gold Coin of the King Dharmadamodara (?)' in *The Journal of The Numismatic Society of India*, vol. 12, pp. 1–4.
4. *IAR*, 1970–1, p. 30.
5. Description based on *IAR Report*, 1956–7, pp. 30–1.
6. See *IAR Report*, 1972–73, p. 29.

7. *IAR,* 1956–57, p. 31.
8. R.N. Das, 'Gudhela O Khariagarh Pratnatatwika Abiskara', in *Nabajivana* (an Oriya Monthly Magazine), November/December 1974.
9. R.N. Dass 'Adya Lauha Yugare Orissara Sanskriti', in *Paurusha* (an Oriya Monthly Magazine), June 1978, pp. 69–72.
10. R.N. Das, November/December 1974, op. cit.
11. Ibid.
12. Ibid.
13. B.B. Nath, 'Punch-marked coins from Sonepur', in the *Orissa Historical Research Journal (OHRJ)*, vol. I, no. 2.
14. H.K. Mehtab echoed similar sentiments in 1949. What he was lamenting has largely been remedied by successive archaeological discoveries. Strangely not all the available archaeological data is being taken notice of in writing a history of early Orissa. This accounts for the prevaling mistaken beliefs about the early history of Orissa. See H.K. Mehtab, 'Presidential Address, Local History Section', in *IHC Proceedings,* p. 278. I am thankful to my friend B. Pati. a Ph.D. student in History, University of Delhi, for providing this reference.
15. D. Das, *The Early History of Kāliṅga,* p. 254.
16. H. Kulke, 'Early State Formation and Royal Legitimation in Late Ancient Orissa', in *Sidelights on History and Culture of Orissa,* ed. M.N. Das. p. 107.
17. K.A. Chowdhury and S.S. Ghosh, 'Wood-Remains from Sisupalgarh'. in *Ancient India,* vol. 8, 1952, p. 31.
18. See D.P. Patnaik, 'Aryanization of Orissa', in *The Orissa Historical Research Journal,* vol. 7, no. 1, 1958, p. 55.
19. B.B. Lal, op. cit.
20. P. Acharya, 'Ancient Coins from Mayurbhanj,' *The Journal of the Numismatic Society of India,* vol. 2, pp. 123–4.
21. D.C. Sircar, 'Bhadrak inscription of Gana, Regnal Year 8, *Epigraphia Indica,* vol. 29, pp. 169–72.
22. D.C. Sircar, 'Ningondi Grant of Prabhanjanavarman', in *Epigraphia Indica,* vol. 30, pp. 112–14.
23. H. Kulke, op. cit., p. 108.
24. D. Das, op. cit., p. 263.
25. Ibid., pp. 263–4.
26. A.P. Sah, *Life in Medieval Orissa* (AD 600–1200) see Section on Society.
27. D. Das, op. cit.
28. A.P. Sah, op. cit.
29. H. Kulke, op. cit., p. 109.
30. L.K. Mohapatra, 'The People of Orissa,' in *Sidelights on the History and Culture of Orissa,* ed. M.N. Das, p. 29. For details of racial composition and the beginning of cultural evolution in Orissa see the same article, pp. 27–9.

6

Aspects of Early Iron Age Economy: Problems of Agrarian Expansion in Tamilakam

Rajan Gurukkal

ARCHAEOLOGY SHOWS that Tamilakam was more or less a single culture-zone by the first millennium BC, with the diffusion of iron-using people of the black-and-red-ware tradition.[1] Though excavated Iron Age settlements are very few in peninsular India, Iron Age burial relics, often in thin debris of relatively uniform date, are quite widespread.[2] Language, perhaps the archaic Tamil, must have come into being as an important factor of the broad cultural unification during this period. But behind this cultural homogeneity was the isolated existence of uneven material cultures as a historical reality. There seems to have developed no major integration of these unevenly developed people for organised production, though iron technology was widely known then. For a very long period the idea of the Neolithic–Chalcolithic digging stick survived in the form of thrust-hoes made of iron, indicating some sort of stagnancy.[3] Even when ploughshare began to be used it was confined to very few localities of wet-land. Archaeological knowledge of the ancient agriculture of south India is primarily based on the finds of Adichanellur, which give us some idea about the thrust and drawhoes and the actual ploughshares of *c.* 1000 BC.[4] The ancient Tamil works, generally ascribed to the first two or three centuries of the Christian era, depict the same technology of agriculture, which obviously illustrates the alleged snailspace Progress of Iron Age.[5] In the light of evidences in the ancient Tamil anthologies an attempt is made in this paper to offer explanation for the remarkably slow process of agrarian expansion in the Iron Age at its organisational and institutional levels and also how this expansion was ultimately achieved.

The chief source for the present study is the *Ettuttokai* collection excepting *Kalittokai* and *Paripatal* which might be comparatively late.[6] Whatever be their drawbacks as literary compositions based on oral poetry with stock-expressions

*42nd Session at Bodhgaya, 1981.

and stereotypes, the richness of ancient Tamil anthologies in historical details can never be exaggerated.[7] Inspite of editions, classifications and compilations which have put the ancient Tamil works in a big chronological mesh, they serve as invaluable sources of early south Indian life. The most archaic stratum in this literature has definitely much to do with the early Iron Age, and one cannot say that this stratum is absolutely beyond reconstruction. However, such a task is not within the scope of this paper. The focus here is on the material matrix of life and activity reflected in the anthologies, which has not received much attention from the historians.[8]

One need not bother much whether or not the concept of *aintinai* was a mere poetic convention, since the existing physiographic features of Tamilakam can very well substantiate the five fold division of man–nature situations in its historical and anthropological context. There is not much meaning in discerning social evolution in the concept since all situations as marks of uneven development co-existed simultaneously.[9] The thoughts regarding the actual order of the five *tinais* as provided for in the literature are also therefore meaningless.[10] How the *kurinji, palai, mullai, marutam,* and *neital* divisons of nature suited the poetic delineation of human behaviour pattern do not arise here. To us the classification of land and nature involved in the concept alone matters. We only take note of the poets' references to the life and activity in each situation of physiographic importance. It gives a clear picture of five types of terrain, i.e. the hilly backwoods (*kurinji*), the pastures (*mulla*), the patched zones (*palai*), the agrarian tracts (*marutam*) and the sea coast (*neital*) together with their respective economies, viz., hunting and food gathering, stock-rearing and shifting agriculture, plundering and cattle lifting, commodity production and plough agriculture and fishing and salt manufacturing. Hunters and food gatherers were called *kadar* or *vetar;* the cattle keepers as *ayar* or *idayar;* the shifting agriculturists as *kuravar;* the plundering cat tie-lifting people as *maravar, cyinar, kallar,* etc.; plough agriculturists as *ulavar* or *toluvar* and; the fishermen as *valayar, minavar, paratavar* and salt manufacturers as *umanar.* These diverse economies were obviously due to the physiographic differences and the people in each situation constituted a segment. This shows a broad as well as horizontal segmentation of people separated by the physiographic peculiarities and the economic possibilities of each situation. But this was never rigid as situations in nature were often so commingled and overlapping. Both *kurinji* and *mullai* had cultivable slopes, *punam* or *enal* which enabled the *vetar* to take to shifting agriculture as the *kuravar.* In a song of Perumeittiianar about Kumanan, we find a reference to the *vetar* of the Kollimalai doing the slash and burn agriculture (*Pura Nanuru,* 159—hereafter *PN*). In one of the songs of Avvayar there is a reference to the *kuravar* of the Kollainilam doing the slash and burn, probably for cultivation (*PN,* 231). A song of Kuruvur Cattanar clearly refers to the *kuravar* of Kuthiraimalai doing the slash and burn millet (*tinai*) cultivation.

Apart from the above five divisions of physiographic nature, they had a broad agrarian classification of land into *vanpulam* (the miscellaneous non-agrarian region) and *menpulam* (the purely agrarian, *marutam* region).[11] *Vanpulam* included all the hill slopes, arid plains and pastures obviously quite larger than *menpulam* which was exclusively the wet-land plains of paddy cultivation. Cultivable tracts in the *vanyulam* were called *enal* or *punam* where millet and grams grew in abundance. *Vetar* and *kuravar* are mentioned in the anthologies at the clans cultivating *vanpulam*. In the parched zones of *vanpulam* were the plundering clans like *maravar, eyinar, kaflar,* etc. In one of the oft-quoted *PN* songs, we have the four chief clans *tudiyan, panan, paraiyan* and *katampana,* each clan with a magico-religious musical instrument, referred to incidentally, *(PN,* 335) as the people of *vanpulam*. These clans are referred to in the anthologies as dependents, playing some magico-ritual roles, but not in the context of farming. Being inhabited by the clans of such diverse ways of *vanpulam* was one of wild food economy, cattle keeping and subsistence farming. On the other hand, the material basis of *menpulam* was one of advanced plough agriculture. Anthologies refer to *ulavar* or *toluvar* as the tillers of *menpulam.*[12] They knew the technique of harnessing the bullocks (*erutu*) at their necks with a cross-bar (*nukam*) to a ploughshare (*meli* or *nanjil*), obviously iron-tipped, for furrowing.[13] Buffaloes (*erumai*) were also used for ploughing.[14] Tank irrigation *(ayam)* and minor dam (*sirai*) irrigation are mentioned in the anthologies.[15] They ensured the availability of water for agriculture in the required plots of land through the sluices from the tank or through the diversions of harnessed streams. Animal power was widely utilised for various agrarian jobs like threshing, pounding, etc. It is clear that this advanced farming economy of *menpulam* had produced a surplus large enough to support the variety of artisans and craftsmen engaged in works directly or indirectly related to farming. Many of the jobless clans of *vanpulam* depended on the produce of *menpulam* as *iravar* (the beggars) or *kallar* (the looters) or *panar* (the poor bards). The subsistence farmers of *vanpulam* came to *menpulam* for exchanging their hill products for paddy and other goods. The coastal people also came to *menpulam* to exchange their fish and salt for paddy. Paranar refers to the paddy heaped by the coastal dwellers of Kuttuvan's land, who procured it by exchanging their fish in the *marutam* (*PN,* 343). There are references in *PN,* to the bullockcarts of *umanar* loaded with salt going to the points of exchanges in the hinterlands, obviously *menpulam (PN,* 102, 106, 307, 386, etc.).[16] In short, *menpulam* was the nerve centre of contemporary economic life. Here the society was structured on with specialisation of labour. Land was owned by the ruling aristocracy including *vallar,* the scholars (*pulavar,* including brāhmaṇs, the warrior chiefs and merchants). The landed were called *uyarnder,* the high-born and the landless as *ilisinar,* the lowborn.[17] The low born included all the tillers, artisans, craftsmen, and jobless wanderers, and their suburbs were called *puracceri.* We do not know much about the exact relations of production in the *menpulam,* though we have noted that structured division of labour existed there. It appears that the tillers produced and the craftsmen worked for the land owning chieftains, the *pulavar* and the warrior chiefs. The land in *vanpulam* was also owned by the chieftains and their bards and warrior-chiefs. From *PN,* 49 we understand that the owner of land in *vanpulam* was called *natan,* the owner of the land in *menpulam* was called *uran* and; the owner of the *neital* was called *cerpan.*

Reciprocity was the mode of exchange, though paddy and salt at times served as the leading commodities in the field of exchange, with a relative inter-commodity exchange rates centering them. Profit oriented exchanges are not referred to in the anthologies in the context of rural transactions. *Kadam* of *kadani* meaning debt is mentioned in the anthologies.[18] The loan of a fixed commodity to be paid back in same kind and quantity called *kurunumaretirppai* or *kuriyetirppai* was in vogue.[19] *Avanam* or *angadi* were the main organised points of exchanges where standard weights and measures were in use. *Pattanam* or the coastal towns were the centres of long distance trade. Certain weights of gold known as *kadame* and *kalanju* were used as media of exchange in the *pattanam,* perhaps also in certain higher transactions. The exchange points in the hinterland were far removed from the formal centres of exchanges such as *pattanam.* It is clear from certain poems in *PN,* that there was no convenient or safe infrastructure in the hinterland. *PN,* 102, refers to *umanar's* bullockcarts loaded with salt moving through undulated and marshy routes and to *umanar's* retrieving of the wheels of their carts from the mire by filling dry sand, etc. In *PN,* 3, a poet clearly illustrates how scarce the localities of human settlements in the Pāṇḍyan territory were. He says that one had to cross extensive areas of dry land full of fierce *maravar* to reach the Pāṇḍyan fort. Karikilar while praising Mudukudumi says that the Pāṇḍyan fort was surrounded by *menpulam* tracts (*PN,* 6). This shows that often *menpulam* was encircled by large inhospitable zones of *vanpulam.*

Gift giving was the institution through which the resources of both *vanpulam* and *menpulam* were redistributed.[20] The resources were pooled by the chieftains and redistributed among their kinsmen, bards and other dependents. Plunder was the instituted means for pooling the resources. As the recipients of gift (*kodai* or *kodaimai*) there were many scholarly bards (*pulavar*), lesser bards (*panar*), warrior-chiefs and others, who moved around the ruling aristocracy. The chieftains of *vanpulam* were generally short of resources and had to take to plunder as a device of compensation. These chieftains were also depended upon by a large group of wandering lesser bards. Poverty of the chieftains or the land owners of *vanpulam* is clear from certain *PN,* songs. Kapilar in one of his songs in praise of Vel Pari, speaks of the four kinds of yields from the Parampu hills which were bamboo rice, jack fruits, creeper roots and honey. We get an interesting instance in *PN,* 180, of an impoverished chieftain of *vanpulam* calling his blacksmith to prepare an effective spear for plunder-raids when his dependents approach him for help at his all-exhausted state. In *PN*, 127, 327, 328, 329, 330, 331–33, we have clear references to the poverty of the chieftains and land owners of the non-agrarian regions. Instances of giving away even the small quantity of millet reserved for sowing, thought to be a stock expression of poets, interestingly occur only in poems praising the chieftains of *vanpulam*. The chieftains who held sway over *manpulam* were more affluent. Their large paddy farms and huge stock of paddy are referred to in the anthologies. Karikkannanar in *PN*, 353 speaks of a chieftain's hill like paddy heaps. Nannakanar in *PN*, 376 speaks of Oyman's paddy fields and the harvest heaped at his court. Kallatanar in *PN*, 391 refers to Poraiyarrukilan's sky-scraper paddy heaps, Maturai Nakkiranar praises the large crop fields of Tit tan in *PN*, 392. Mankuti Kilar in *PN*, 396 refers to Vettarreliniyatan's paddy fields and paddy heaps. All these mentioned have been lavished on bards as gifts. The institution of gift giving was immanent in contemporary economic setting since the majority of people who lived in the subsistence level had to depend on the gift givers as *iravar*. Certain songs on *PN* show that the lesser bards (*panar*) sang in praise of chieftains of all kinds for food and clothing. *PN*, 376, 382, 398, and 400 are some of the examples which illustrate the acute poverty of the lesser bards. *PN*, 392 and 393 show how badly clothed a *pana* was. Marutan Ilanqkanar in *PN*, 139 refers to the miserable condition of a *virali*, the women folk of the *panar*, who had to live as a head-load labourer. It appears that these poor bards wandered about the courts of chieftains and the houses of land-owners, singing praises and playing their musical instrument, *yal*. But the scholarly bards (*hulavar*) sang in praise of the chieftains for land and gold. Such rich bards were depended upon by the poor. The whole economy was thus based on the institution of gift giving. This in its process involved mutual plunders through which functioned the redistribution of resources in its instituted form.

Plunder-raids being fundamental to the maintenance of contemporary economy all ideas and institutions in the broad superstructure helped the plunder based redistribution function effectively. This paper cannot afford a total survey of all the beliefs and institutions of the people in question. Some of them which had a direct bearing on contemporary economy alone can be touched here. The beliefs such as war begets the chieftain; martyrs would join damsels in the heaven; war as a traditional inspiration of the *maravar;* martial bravery of the sons as a passion of motherhood; cowardice as ignominous and so on glorify wars and involvement in wars. Their totems, musical instruments, ritual dances and songs were all magical and symbolic, capable of stimulating active involvement in wars.[21] Their ethics (*aram*) justified wars and plunders. How institutionalised was war is clear from the descriptions of *vetcci* (cattle raid), *karanttai* (cattle recovering war), *vanji* (chieftain's attack of a territory), *kanji* (defending war), and *tumpai* (getting ready for war) in *PN*. Martial rejoicing was their chief amusement as we find in the institutions like *vakai* (the enthusiastic killing of enemies with clamours), *untattu* (social dining and drinking before and after wars), *perumcorruvilau* (grand rich feast) and, *cirucorruvilavu* (small rice feast) Some of the poetic conventions in *PN*, clearly demonstrate their idealisation of war and war-leaders. *Uvakaikkalulci turai* songs in *PN*, poetise a wife's bursting into tears in happiness at the sight of her husband with many wounds by the sword. *Mutinmullai* turai songs in *PN* idealise the women folk of the *maravar* as brave as their warrior husbands. *Kutinilaiyaraittal turai*, *eranmullai turai*, and *vallanmullai turai* songs in *PN*, are examples of idealising the tradition and family lineages of the warrior-chiefs. In short the ethos of war dominated and moulded contemporary socio-political ideals and institutions.

Destruction of cultivated fields (*kalani* or *palanam)* and settlements was an inevitable part of war. *Malapulavanji turai* songs in *PN*, describe how land was plundered and settlements destroyed in wars. *Eriparandeduttal*, setting fire on the crop-fields and settlements was the sequel to every clash between chieftains. Certain songs in *PN*, show how detrimental the scorched earth policy of wars was to agriculture. In a song of Nettimaiyar, the destruction of crop-fields by the stamping of rough-ridden horses harnessed to the war chariot of Pāṇḍyan Mudukudumi is described. (*PN*, 15). Pandaran Kannanar while praising Colan Perunar Killi, refers to his burning of enemy's *marutam* tracts which knew no forest other than that of sugarcane, (*PN*, 16). Karikkannanar while praising Pāṇḍyan Nanmaran incidentally refers to the destruction of corp-fields by fire as a common atrocity of war, (*PN*, 57). In a song of Kallatanar in praise of Pāṇḍyan Nedunjeliyan, there is a reference to the destruction of land to no use after plundering all that could be plundered from there (*PN*, 23). It is significant to note that at times possession of *marutam* land was also aimed at while executing plundering raids. In *PN*, 297 one poet has described a warrior chief discussing with his fellow warrior-chiefs assembled for an *untattu* before an ensuing *vetcci*, that he would not accept the arid gram growing areas as reward for fighting, but only paddy growing *marutam*. Often the landed people had to support their chieftains in wars. A song of Perumkunrur Kilar in *PN*, while praising a land owner says that the later's land suffers in war and prospers in peace (*PN*, 318). In addition to the chieftain-led wars there were incessant attacks from the non-agrarian tracts by the *maravar*, the *eylnar* and the *kallar* to the agrarian regions.

It appears that the peasants were neither warriors by themselves; nor were they offered sufficient protection by their chieftains. The warrior-power of the chieftains was not often enough to defend the onslaughts. The chieftains mobilised warriors arousing the tribal loyalty in them through *untattu* and *corruvilavu*, wherein the bards sang so as to strengthen the loyalty to the chieftain. Chieftains themselves with words of honour gave drinks with their own hands to the warrior-chiefs intensifying the bond and loyalty. The warriors took a pledge of loyalty (*nedumoli punartt 11*) at the occasion of *untattu*. Most of the *vetcci* and *karanai* songs in *PN*, give us ideas about these matters. It is clear that the organisation of warriors was only at its tribal stage, having no territorial bond or bureaucratic contract. The body of warriors was an ad hoc one raised on demand and never stationary. Its purpose was the conduct of cattle raids and plunder wars, and not the permanent defence of any particular territory. This made the peasants vulnerably exposed to the attacks of all kinds. The passiveness and helplessness of the peasants is incidentally described in a poem of Kurumkoliyur Kilar, who says that the peasants knew no weapon other than plough. They knew no bow other than the rain bow (*PN*, 20).

Some of the poems in *PN*, show an awareness of the danger of wars at the context of agriculture. Songs of *ceviyarivuru* in *PN*, exhort the chieftains to maintain peace. *PN*, 18, makes it clear that the growth of agriculture was the basis of the chieftains' strength and fame. *PN*, 35, advises the chieftain saying that paddy is the basis of his strength and further warns him to leave no ears to intrigues which lead to war. The poem gives stress on the protection of the peasants. The undeniable significance of, agriculture in life was influencing some poets to make use of agrarian imagery even for describing wars. The poetic ideals of *erkaluruvakam turai* in *PN*, provide us with examples for this. In a song of Paranar on Ceran Virkelu Kuttuvan there is a beautiful description of a battlefield in agrarian setting (*PN*, 369). Kallatanar while praising Nedunjelian's martial adventures uses agrarian imagery for describing war, (*PN*, 371). In a song of Aryayar also we find a similar example (*PN*, 392). Other examples are in *PN*, 370 and 373. However, the ideology of peace which had relevance to the agrarian regions could not dominate since the general material milieu nurtured war as an economic necessity.

It was amidst these adversities that the people of *menpulam* had to carry on production. No wonder that advanced farming remained absolutely confined to small pockets of wet-land in the valleys of Kaveri, Vaigai, Tamraparni and Periyar without any remarkable progress till the seventh–eighth centuries. It has been argued elsewhere that the technology of iron ploughshare was known to the people of Tamilakam as early as in 1000 BC, itself. We have seen that it did not make any major advance during the first two or three centuries of the Christian era. In the light of ancient Tamil works it could be argued that the advanced production centres, *menpulam,* were surrounded by large non agrarian regions, *vanpulam,* of uneven economies of the subsistence level. Evidences in the anthologies would have us believe that until an organised agrarian set-up emerged under the initiative of a managerial group from outside, the production field of Tamilakam was caught up in an equilibrium trap. Knowledge of technology alone does not lead to the expansion of advanced production. The availability of the required ecology and terrain also by themselves do not make it. It is again incorrect to argue in the lines of Boserup that population pressure makes it.[22] The expansion of advanced farming requires a managerial group, capable of organising peasants either through coercion or a situation created by the false consciousness of loyalty to a fanatical extent which amounts to coersion in disguise. It was with the arrival of this coercion in disguise that the agrarian scene of Tamilakam began to wrench itself out of the trammels of conflicting interior economic modes. Brahmans with their special status and the ritual primacy took the lead in the task of making organisational and institutional changes in the *menpulam* agrarian set up, through a new ideology of loyalty.

Brahmans had begun to possess wet-land during the days of the theologies themselves. *Padirrup Pattu* mentions the gift of a village called Ohandur, which was famous for a fine variety of paddy, to Brahmans by the Cera ruler Selvakadungo Vali Adan.[23] Kumatur Kannanar, a Brahman bard is mentioned to have received a gift of some 500 villages from his patron[24] Perumkunrur Kilar refers to the numerous villages gifted to Kapilan, another Brahman bard.[25] Avur Mulan Kilar's song in *PN* praises a Brahman land owner called Kauniyan Vinnan Tayan (*PN*, 166). But large scale control of land by the Brahmans, as corporate bodies of *brahmadeyams*, was definitely a feature of the Pallava-Coḷa periods. Considering the special position enjoyed by the Brahmans in contemporary society, one may not be wrong in assuming that their lands must have been comparatively free from the havoc of plundering wars. It is quite reasonable to argue that the Brahmans had a better grip over the peasants under them, who stood for peace, morals and devotion which were lacking in Tamilakam during the pre-Pallava period. The major problem that hindered the advancement of peasant-economy during the major part of the pre-Pallava period was the absence of an effective managerial power which could harness agrestic labour and the required arts and crafts. The chieftains who squandered man-power in plundering wars were not in the material matrix of advanced peasant economy to use coercion for better production. Those land owners who lived as managers of advanced farming, were incapable of making a stable organisation of peasants. It is against this background of the absence of managerial groups capable of using coercion for better production that one has to view the emergence of the Brahmans as corporate bodies capable of large scale peasant integration. The peasant backed Brahman land owners could easily establish themselves as the nuclei of the new monarchy manifested through the ascendancy of the Pallavas, Pandyas, Cera and Coḷas in due course. It is clear that the material basis of the Pallava–Coḷa warrior powers was the Brahaman controlled peasant economy. But once warrior power could render sufficient protection to the peasants it became easier for the Brahmans to venture on large scale colonisation or agrarian land Royal grants of agrarian villages now brought more and more Brahmans to the far south studding the whole wet-land with *brahmadeya* villages. Thus from the long protracted stagnancy the agrarian region, with its acquired managerial force spread widely by the seventh-eighth centuries.[26]

Notes

1. Bridget and Raymond Allchin, *The Birth of Indian Civilization: India and Pakistan Before 500 BC*, p. 232.
2. Arikamedu, J.M. Casal, *Feuilles ce Uikramp.itnam. Kunnattur, Indian Archaeology: A Review*, 1954–55, 1955–56, 1956–57, hereafter *IAR*, Tirukkambeliyur, JAR 1961–62, and Alagarai, *IAR*, 1963–64, are the chief iron age sites. Iron age burial relics are found all over the south, cf. Bridget and Raymond Allchin. op. cit., p. 231.
3. To quote Allchin. 'Certainly the excavated settlements do not give much indication of any major change in the way of life accompanying the arrival of iron. One is left with a feeling of a remarkable conservatism among the population of South India throughout the period." Allchin, op. cit., p. 232.
4. Balakrishnan Nair, 'Adichanallur and the Antiquity of Iron in South India',. *The Problem of Dravidian Origins: A Linguistic, Archaeological and Anthropological Approach*, p. 166ff.
5. The title Sangam commonly used to denote the ancient Tamil works is deliberately avoided, finding it a misnomer. Some of the Western scholars have substituted it as *classical*. George L Hart III, 'Ancient Tamil Literature: Its Scholarly Past and Future,' in Burton Stein, ed., *Essays on South India*, pp. 40–60. Also Burton Stein, *Peasant State and Society in Medieval South India*, p. 64ff. But the term *classical* is more misleading. The term *classical* used in the context of the Hellenic Greece or Mauryan India cannot be used in the context of ancient south India as the level of culture bears no comparison with that of the former. For explanation regarding the unintelligibility of the title Sangam, see K. Kailasapathy, *Tamil Heroic Poetry*, pp. 2–3.
6. George L. Hart III, has referred to his 'Related Culture and Literary Elements in Ancient Tamil and Indo-Aryan', Ph.D. thesis in the article above, note 5, in Stein, ed., op. cit., as the source discussing the chronology of the ancient Tamil works, see Hart, op. cit., p. 60, note 1.
7. George L Hart III, op. cit., Also his *The Poems of Ancient Tamils: Their Milieu and Their Sanskrit Counterparts*.
8. An outline of the economy of the people in ancient Tamilakam is given in K. Siva Thampy, 'Early South Indian Society and Economy: The *Tinai* Concept,' *Social Scientist*, no. 29, December 1974.
9. A discussion regarding the concept of evolution involved in the concept of *Jinai* is given in N. Subrahmanian, *Sangam Polity*, p. 249.
10. On the problem of the order of the five *tinais* inhere is a discussion in cf. N. Subrahmanian, op. cit., p. 249.
11. For reference to *vanpulam*, see *Padirrup Pattu*, 75:8 and *Pura Nauuru*, 395:2. For *manpulam* see, *Pura Nānuru*, ibid., line 2.
12. For *ulavar* see *Akananuru*, 30:8, 37:2, 41:6, 211:5, 266:17, 314:4, 346:5, 366:8; *Narrinai* 60:2, 97:9, 315: 4, 331:1, 340:7; *Padirrup Pattu*, 90:41; and *Pura Nanuru* 13:11, 65:4, 109:3, 230:13, 289:3, 384:8, 395:1. For *toluvar*, *Pura Nanuru*, 24:1, 209:2

13. See *Akananuru,* 244:4, 350:6; *Pura Naura,* 103:1, 179:9, for the idea of cross-bar. The term *meli* occurs in *Pura Nanuru,* 388:11 and *nanjil* occurs in ibid., 19:11, 20:11, 40:1, 56:4, 138:8; and in *Akananuru,* 42:5, 141:5; *Padirrup Pattu,* 119:17, 1115:1, 6:2, 58:17. The term *ulupadai* is also used to mean plough share, *Pura Nanuru,* 35:25.
14. *Akananuru,* 56:3, 91:15, etc., see N. Subrahmanian, *Pre-Pallavan Tamavan Tamil Index, Index of Historical Material in Per-Pallavan Tamil Literature,* pp. 162–3.
15. The term *ayam* is referred to in *Akananuru,* 62:1, 68:2, and the term *sirai;* ibid., 76:11, 200:9, 208:19, 346:9.
16. See *Akananuru,* 37:16, 17:13, 30:5, 119:8, 140:5. 159:4, 169:6, 173:10, 257:17, 295:9. 303:17, 310:14, 329:5, 337:5; and 390:3; Also *Kunmtokai,* 117:4, 1 24:1, 388:4; and *Pura Nauru,* 84:6, 102:1, 116:7, 289:2, 307:7, 327:1, 370:16; and *Narrinai,* 4:7. 138:3, 1 83:5, 254:6, 331:2.
17. See *Pura Nanuru,* 82:3, 170:5, 287:2, 289:10.
18. See ibid., 327:7.
19. Ibid., 333:11.
20. For details of the concept of redistribution see Karl Polanyi, *et al.,* ed. 'The Economy as Instituted Process,' *Trade and Market in Early Empires,* pp. 243–57. In the context of ancient Tamilakam the concept is used in Richard S. Kennedy, 'King in Early South India: As Chieftain and Emperor', *Indian Historical Review,* vol. III, p. 3.
21. George L. Hart III, has referred to the magical element in their musical instruments which were infected with the sacred called *ananku,* see his article in Stein, ed., op. cit., p. 44.
22. Easter Boserup, *Conditions of Agricultural Growth: The Economics of Agrarian Change Under Population Pressures.*
23. The reference is in the *Padikam,* 9 of the 7th *patu* in *Padirrup Pattu.* So it might be later. See Kailasapathy, op. cit., pp. 222–4, for a discussion regarding land and references to it in the Anthologies.
24. IInd ten, *Padirrup Pattu.* This is also a *Padikam* version. See note 23 above.
25. *Padirrup Pattu, Padikam* 9, Perunkunrur Kilar confirms the tradition that Kapilar was given numerous villages as gift by one of his patrons, Ilanceral Irumporai.
26. Burton Stein accepts the tradition of the Kālabra invasion as an interregnum which toppled the three ruling families—Cera, Coḷa, Pāṇdya, for some time. Burton Sein, op. cit., pp. 77–9. To him the Kālabra invasion was the culmination of the non-peasant attacks on the peasants, and he views it in a dichotomy of the urban Jains and the hinterland Brahmans. See cf. Stein, op. cit., pp. 78–79. A detailed discussion on this point is made by him in John F.Richards, ed., 'Kings and Authority in South Asia'. *All the Kings Mana: Perspective on Kingship in Medieval South India.*

    Stein has formulated a concept of brahman–peasant alliance, which was voluntary and peaceful, in order to explain the nature of agrarian integration in early medieval south India. He says that the alliance became strong because of its symbiotic character. See Stein, op. cit., pp. 82–4.

PART 3

Land, Agriculture, Surplus Appropriation and Distribution of Labour

7

Types of Land in North-Eastern India (From Fourth Century to Seventh Century AD)

Sudhir Ranjan Das

A LARGE number of inscriptions of the period between fourth and seventh centuries of the Christian era reveal an elaborate system of land tenure in ancient India. These inscriptions which are mainly copperplate charters while recording grants of land describe various types of land which can be roughly divided into two groups—communal and individual.

Communal land is owned by the whole community of the village or of the locality for the communal benefit. Such land can be classed under two heads—land within the village and outside the village. Of the communal lands within the village mention may be made of *Go-mārga, Go-vāṭa, Go patha, Go-cara,* etc. From these terms it is clear that communal land within the village are particularly associated either with the cattle route or with the grazing fields. Even today in many parts of north-eastern India *Go-patha* and *Go-cara* lands are in existence but they are no longer communal lands. *Go-cara* is undoubtedly, *Go-caraṇa-bhūmi,* i.e., the land where the cattle of the community moves and grazes. Existence of *Go-cara-bhūmi* has been considered essential for an ideal village by the early writers. According to Kauṭilya each village must be surrounded by the *Go-cara-bhūmi,* and it has been laid down that the cowherds 'shall graze the herds in the forest to which are allotted as pasture ground for various seasons.'[1] Similar is the direction given by Manu and Yājñavalkya. Manu says that 'on all sides of a village a space, one hundred *dhanu* or 3 *samya*—throws (in breadth) shall be reserved (for pasture) and thrice (that space) round a town.'[2] Likewise the inscriptions as well refer to '*tṛṇa (yuti) or tṛṇa-puti Go-caraṇa-bhūmi*'. In the Nirmand copperplate of Samudrasena we have, '*sva-sīmā-tṛṇa-kāṣṭha-prasvanayūti*.'[3] In the inscriptions from Camba we however find the mention of *Go-suti* which refers to the land where the cattle is tied.[4] In the inscriptions of the later period also we have the mention of '*tṛṇaputi-go-cara-paryantaḥ*'. *Tṛṇa,* is the general name for grass and *puti* may refer to a particular

*9th Session at Patna, 1946.

kind of grass as it is associated with *tṛṇa*. The constant association of grass, wood, jungles, etc., with the *Go-cara-bhūmi* indicates that such lands are covered with grass, jungles, etc. It is still a common practice with the rural people to take the cattle in an area which is covered with grass, jungles, etc. for feeding the cattle. Such lands are no doubt the *Go-cara-bhūmi* of the earlier days. Our inscriptions do not tell us anything about the ownership of such lands and the taxes to be paid. It seems that these lands belonged to the state which for the benefit of the people used to preserve and maintain such lands.

Besides, there were other communally owned lands lying outside the village. These lands have been described in the inscriptions as *vana, araṇya,* and *jāṅgala-bhūmi.*[5] It is also clear from the inscriptions that the king is the owner of these lands and we often find him granting these lands for converting them into habitable or dwelling places.[6] This is clear from the Tippera inscription of Lokanātha where we have a reference to the establishment of 211 Brāhmaṇas versed in the Vedas in *aṭvai-bhūkhaṇḍa* in Suvvaṅga *viṣaya.*[7] According to Kauṭilya *vana* and *araṇya* are the properties of the king or the state and such lands can be granted to the Brāhmaṇas for the cultivation of *dharma*. How such an *araṇya-bhūmi* is cleared and made habitable for the people has also been described by Kautilya.[8] It seems that Lokanatha's inscription follows closely the principles laid down in the *Arthaśāstra*.

Moreover, in the Maliya copperplate of Dharasena II (571–72) we have the mention of *śiva-padraka* and *bhūmbhusapadraka*, 100 *pādāvartas.*[9] There is a good deal of controversy regarding the meaning of the term *padraka*. According to William *padraka* is a fuller expression of the term *padra* meaning a village, earth or district.[10] Bühler thinks that it signifies the modern expression paḍṛ, i.e., a grazing place.[11] Wilson however contends that it is a common land left uncultivated.[12] Measurement of land as given in the inscription shows that it is a large area and Dr. Saletore thinks that such an extensive area was most probably used for common purpose.[13] Mr. K. Gupta supposes that it refers to a village. In support of his contention he has also quoted certain references in the inscriptions of Jayabhaṭṭa and Daḍḍa where we have the expressions, *padraka-grāma* and *padrakam-eṣa-grāmaḥ.*[14] Dr. Saletore thinks that *padraka* in these cases does not mean a village which is the lowest administrative unit but a still bigger unit in area.[15] He further says that if *padraka* means a common land in a village then there arises difficulty in the expressions *dvesa* and *vaidula* lands referred to in the Nirmand inscription. The passage in question runs as follows—'. . . (the land) including the *dvesa* land (that had been given) by the cultivator Vakkhalika (whose holding was) on the edge of the newly constituted *vaidula* of the village of Sulisagrāma and the *dvesa* land, with *udraṅga* (and) including the edges of its boundaries (that had been given) by a cultivator of the town of Talapura. . . .'[16] Meaning of both these terms is not clear. If *dvesa* land is really a grazing field then it is not certainly a communal land but an individual land as the grant is made by a cultivator. Some take the term vaidula to be a variation of *vidula,* According to Bhagawan Lal Indraji it is 'one of the articles levied from every village in times of war and the grant allows the dome an exception from taking away of arms and ammunitions in times of war.'[17] But this is not quite in accord with the spirit of the statement made in the inscription. If we take these two terms to mean waste lands in the village then there is probably no difficulty in the interpretations of these two terms. It is likely that such lands were originally no man's waste land but became individual land only after being cleared and made cultivable or habitable by a particular individual. Such a supposition is quite in accord with the spirit of the statement made in the inscriptions. *Padraka* may mean a common land in the village used by the people for common purposes and *dvesa* and *vaidula* lands may mean individual waste land. As to the contention of Dr. Saletore it can be noted that we do not get any reference to the mention of *padraka* as a still bigger administrative unit than the *grama* in any inscription. On the other hand, it is more likely that it means common land in the villages owned by the king who made a grant of the same land to a Brāhmaṇa for the maintenance of religious rites and practices.

Of the types of land owned by the individual mention may be made of *vāstu, kṣetra, khila-kṣetra, vapaka-bhūmi, vasika,* etc.[18] In the Damodarpur copperplate of Bhānugupta (533–34) we have reference to three important types of land as *khila-kṣetrasya vastuna.* According to Wilson, *vāstu* is the site for the foundation of a house.[19] It is clear from all the references that *vāstu* is a kind of land which is mainly used for residential purposes.[20] Even today, in Bengal, *vāstu-pūuja* is performed within the area of the home in an elevated place in the cultivated field on the last day of the month of *Pauṣa.* This observance is considered as an indication to the effect that it is a sort of declaration that the land in question belongs to the observer of the rite. In the Baigram copperplate we have a reference to *thai a vāstu.*[21] In some inscriptions of the later period such a land is called *vyābhū,* i.e., land for dwelling but without any boundary. *Kṣetra* is the general designation for all ploughed and cultivated lands from which the coloquial Bengali term *khet* has been derived. Granting of such lands mean only the transfer of the ownership of the land in question. Besides there is another class of land which is, no doubt, cultivated land but is not cultivated. It is often a common practice with the peasants to allow certain land to remain fallow for some time because continuous cultivation for years together may render the field less fertile. Hence after 3 or 4 years of interval such a land is cultivated. This type of land was most probably called *khila-bhūmi. Khila-bhūmi* as described in the inscriptions seems to be barren and unfit for cultivation. The Nandapura inscription gives a description how a *khila-kṣetra* is to be purchased.[22] Even today in Bengal *khila-jami* or *kṣetra* is one which is barren or which is not cultivated, i.e. waste land. In the Gunaighar plate of Vainyagupta we have the mention of *hajjika-khila-bhūmi,* i.e. water-logged waste land which has been also described as *śūnya- pratikara,*[23] i.e.

devoid of any taxation. In the Damodarpur copperplate of Kumāragupta, we have the mention of another class of land called *parc-adaprahatta,* and *khila-bhūmi* is also referred in the same record.[24] According to *Amarakoṣa khila* and *aprahata* are identical, but Halāyudha explains *khila* as a waste land.[25] Though both terms are identical, yet it seems that there is a difference; otherwise these two terms would not have been mentioned side by side. Yādavaprakāśa in his work *Vaijayantī* (eleventh century) says: *Khilamprahaiam sthanusavafyasarenau.*[26] Though it appears (hat *khila* and *aprahata* are the same yet it is clear that the former is no doubt a kind of cultivable land but of inferior quality and most probably allowed the field to fallow for a longer period. This will be clear from the explanation given by Nārada. According to him the land which has not been cultivated for one year is called *ardha-bhūmi* and that which has not been cultivated for 3 years called *khila-bhūmi* and that which has not been under cultivation for more than five years is no better than a forest.[27] In the grant of Jayabhatta we have reference to another kind of land called *vapnka-kṣetram.*[28] The meaning of the term is not clear. Mr. B. Indraji thinks that it was a 'field which by means of irrigation yield a *rabi* crop of rice, etc.' But he has not cited any authority for the same. In the Chamba plate of Yagakaravarman we have mention of *Kolhika-satka bhū, Sabdamgga-nāma kṣetram, Kutika,* etc.[29] Dr. Vogel explains the term *Kothika* as irrigated land. The word is derived from *kuhl* (*a*) meaning a channel. It is the Sanskritised *kolhi* which indicates an irrigated field used for rice cultivation and is regularly found in the vernacular portions of the Chamba title deeds. Bagor bagh means a field. It has been explained as a very fertile land which is meant mainly for cultivation of various important vegetables.[30] As for *Kuṭika* it may be noted that the term *kut* means 'cultivated land lying at a high level, yielding in course of two years only two crops.'[31] Besides, we have also a few reference to terraced land, land full of pits, etc.

In the Baigram copperplate we have the mention of *talavāṭa.* The land which is being purchased is no doubt *vāstu bhūmi* for building house and to live therein. In order to do this he shall also have to find out land and water ways. In Khalimpur plates we have *tala-pāṭaka* which seems to be a variant of *tala-vaṭaka.* Even at present in different parts of north-eastern India the term *vāṭa* is used for the word *patha,* i.e., way or road. *Tala,* no doubt, means below of underneath. In that case *talavāta* may mean water drain or *nala* for the drainage of water. We also find mention of the word *al* in the inscriptions of the eighth century. As the water-drain generally runs along with the way, hence we find mention of *talavāṭa.* In the inscriptions of the 8th century we also have the mention of *satalaḥ soddesa,* i.e. high land and water-drain. According to some *tala* means also waterlogged area.

From this discussion on various types of land it is clear that land was grouped into different types according to the production of the soil and the quality of land. It is highly interesting to note that this description of the different types of individually owned land resemble to a great extent the description of the types of land as given by Abul Fazl in his *Ain-i-Akbari*. He says that the land which was annually cultivated for each crop and was never allowed to fallow is called *Polaj* land. This kind of land was under continuous cultivation and yielded revenue from year to year. This seems to be the same as the *kṣetra-bhūmi* of the earliest days. The land which is cultivated for one or two years is called *parciuti-bhūmi;* when such land is not cultivated for three or four years it is called *chachar-bhūmi* and that which is left uncultivated for five years or for more than five years is called *banjar-bhūmi*. These latter classes of land seem to be same as the *khila-bhūmi* of the earlier days.

Notes

1. Shamasastry, Kauṭilya's *Arihasāstra,* p. 161.
2. Manu, *SBE,* vol. XXV. VIII.8–137, p. 296; Yājñavalkya, II,167.
3. Fleet, *Gupta Inscriptions,* p. 289, 1.10.
4. Vogel, Antiquities of Chamba, pp. 167–8.
5. *Arthasāstra,* p. 54.
6. Fleet, p. 289.
7. *EI,* vol. XV, pp. 307, 311.
8. *Arthasāstra,* pp. 55–6.
9. Fleet, p. 170.
10. Monier-Williams, *Sanskrit–English Dictionary,* p. 585.
11. *IA,* vol. XV, p. 307.
12. *Glossary of Judicial and Revenue Terms,* p. 285.
13. Saletoie, *Life in the Gupta Age,* p. 339.
14. *IA,* vol. XIII, pp. 77–9, 82–4.
15. Saletore, p. 339.
16. Fleet, p. 289.
17. *IA,* vol. XIII, p. 129.
18. *EI,* XV, p. 144.
19. Wilson, op. cit., p. 544.
20. *EI,* vol. XV, p. 144.
21. *EI,* vol. XXI, pp. 81–2.
22. *EI,* vol. XXIII, p. 54.
23. *IHQ,* vol. VI, pp. 56–60.
24. *EI,* vol. XV, pp. 131, 144.
25. *Amarakoṣa,* II. 10.5; *Halayudha,* 2.3.
26. *Vaijayanti,* p. 124.
27. Narada, *SBE,* vol. XXXIII, p. 160.
28. *IA,* vol. XIII, p. 78.
29. *ASIR,* P. 249.
30. Wilson, op. cit., p. 44.
31. *ASIR,* p. 250.

8

The Plough Measure in North India

Pushpa Niyogi

MOST OF the inscriptions of northern India during the period tenth to the twelfth century AD record grants of land for various purposes. In such records there are relevant details about the measurements of pieces of land donated. From the evidence furnished by them it appears that a common standard of measurement was not in use throughout northern India during the period under review. Although it may be possible to bring the different standards of measurement current in different areas to a common base, it may not be safe to rely too much on this process of equation, for it is quite possible that a unit may have been called by a common name but may have conveyed different values in different regions

In this paper we propose to discuss only the plough measure. The plough measure was technically called *hala*. This measure was current in many places as shown by records connected with different dynasties of northern India. Some typical cases of its use may be noted here. In the Dhullā copperplate of Śrīcandradeva[1] of the Candra dynasty of East Bengal (tenth century AD) the term *hala* occurs as a land measure. It also appears in the Reu copperplate grant of Govindacandra[2] of the Gāhaḍavāla dynasty, dated AD 1131, the Rahan copperplate of Govindacandradeva and Madanapāla[3] of the same dynasty, dated AD 1108, the Kadambapadraka grant of Narvarman[4] of the Parmāra dynasty of Malwa, dated AD 1109, in many of the grants of Bhimadeva II,[5] the Palanpur plate of the Cāḷukya Bhīmadeva (VS 1120),[6] the Dohed inscription of the Cāḷukya king Jayasiṁhadeva, (VS 1196),[7] the Bāli inscription of Kumārapāla,[8] the Surat plate of Trilocanapāla, dated AD 1151,[9] etc., in the inscriptions of the Candellas of Jeja bhukti (Bundelkhand), e.g. the Semra plate[10] and the Charkhari plate of Paramardideva,[11] the inscriptions of the Kalacuris of Madhya Pradesh, the Koni inscription of the Kalacuri Pṛthivideva (KE 900), dated AD 1147,[12] the Malhara plate of Jajjaladeva,[13] etc. The use of this measure is also found in the Second Prasasti of Baijnath,[14] etc.

In the Reu copperplate grant of Govindacandra,[15] mentioned above, the term *hala* can be traced in the expression *haladagāṁge*, the meaning of which

*18th Session at Calcutta, 1955.

is, however, not very clear. From the interpretation offered by Dr. Hoernle it may be suggested that *hala* here signifies a plot of cultivable land, measuring in the present case 10 *halas* suitably irrigated.[16]

In some inscriptions the land measuring one *hala* is called *bhū-hala*, e.g. the Bhāṭerā plate of Govindakeśava[17] and a copperplate grant of Mahārāja Yaśovarmadeva.[18]

That *hala* definitely means a plough is clear from the expression *halavāha* which is used in the Bombay Asiatic Society copperplate of Bhīmadeva II,[19] which means that much of land of which could be ploughed with one plough—thus a plough measure of land. The same expression was used by the Paramara king Dhārāvarṣadeva in one of his in inscriptions.[20]

This is clear also that the plough as specified in the Bāli inscription of Kumārapāla[21] means the extent of land that could be traversed in a day by one plough.[22] The same information is furnished in an inscription of Dhārāvarṣa of the Paramāra dynasty, which seems to describe one plough measure of land as being equivalent to an area that could be cultivated with one plough in a day. The Hathal plate of Dhārāvarṣadeva[23] refers to an area of land that could be tilled with two ploughs in a day. These references show in a specific manner that a plough measure of land was conditioned by time factor. It meant only that much of land which could be cultivated with a single plough in one day only.

In this connection it may be noted[24] that the term *hāra* is still used in Gujarat where it means not a land measure but a measure of grain.[25] It is also used to denote current measure of corn in Kathiawar. A suggestion has been made that *hāra* is only another form of word *hala*, and that as the name of a measure the word may have originally been connected with the plough measure, measuring a fixed quantity of grain produced 'by the use of the *hala* or plough'. In short, the suggestion is that, originally the word *hāra* denoted the same thing as a plough measure but later it may have come into use as the name of a measure of grain or corn only.

It seems that *haele* is only a local variation of the word *hala* denoting a particular land measure. The word *hala* in this form is found in the Sānderāv stone inscription of Kelhanadeva,[26] of the Cāhamāna dynasty of Sambhar. Like the word *hara* mentioned above the term *haele* may also be connected with *hala* in which sense Dr. Bhandarkar interprets the former. The inscription in which it occurs mentions that the donor, Ānaladevi, granted one *haele* or *yugaṁdhari* and that some *rathakāras* also granted another *haele* of *yugaṁdhari* which Bhandarkar takes to mean 'jvar corn'. Thus it appears that the term *haele* is used in this record as a measure of corn. If its connection with *hala* is assumed, one *haele* of *yugaṁdhari* will mean one *haele* of jvar corn, which was the yield of a plot of land cultivated with one plough. It is evident, therefore, that in some places what was originally a plough measure had a tendency of being converted into a measure of the yield of the soil. What is actually yielded by a piece of land cultivated with one plough came to be called by some word originally connected with the name of the plough measure such a *haele, hara,* etc. The corn measure thus used represents a definite quantum which is represented by the yield of a piece of land cultivated with one plough, nothing more, nothing less.

It is difficult to say when the word *hala* was first used as the name of a land measure, although it is known to have been in extensive currency in the tenth, eleventh and twelfth centuries. The use of the word *hala* in the sense of a land measure is found in Pāṇini,[27] Patañjali[28] etc. Bāṇa, the author of *Harṣacarita;* [29] shows familiarity with the use of the word in the sense of a land measure as is evident in the passage where he refers to the bestowal by Harṣa of 'a hundred villages delimited by a thousand ploughs'. The passage seems to show that the extent of land given away in 100 villages measured 1,000 ploughs, i.e. as much land as could be tilled with that number of ploughs.

There is difficulty in ascertaining the exact area that could be cultivated with one plough. Soil was of different qualities in different regions; the capacity of the plough depended on the variable character of the soil. As the grades of soils were of different degrees the extent of land indicated by the plough measure could not have been the same everywhere. Then again, the size of the plough may not have been the same everywhere.[30] There may have been different sizes of the plough in the same locality also. Thus the Harṣa stone inscription of the Cāhamāna king Vigraharāja, dated AD 917,[31] refers to a big plough[32] which clearly indicates that ploughs of different types were used. The size of the plough must have been an important factor in the determination of the extent of land cultivated wit its help.

Notes

1. *IB,* vol. III, p. 165.
2. *IA,* vol. XIX, p. 249.
3. Ibid., vol. XVIII, p. 14.
4. *EI,* vol. XX, p. 105.
5. *IA,* vol. XVIII.
6. Ibid., p. 108.
7. *IA,* vol X. p. 158 (1881).
8. *ASR,* pp. 54–5.
9. *IA,* vol. XXXI, p. 255.
10. *EI,* vol. IV, p. 165
11. *EI,* vol. XX, p. 125.
12. *EI,* vol. XXVII, p. 277.
13. *EI,* vol. I, p. 38.
14. Ibid.
15. *IA,* vol. XIX, p. 249.
16. Ibid.

17. *EI*, vol, XIX, p. 285.
18. *IA*, vol. XIX, p. 345.
19. Ibid., vol. XVIII, p. 108
20. Ibid., vol. LX1, p. 50.
21. *ASI*, p. 545.
22. In Pāṇini the area cultivated with one plough is called *halya*, IV.4.97.
23. *IA*. vol. XVIII, p. 193.
24. *IA*, vol. LII, p. 249.
25. Ibid.
26. *EI*, vol. XI, p. 46.
27. IV. 4.97. In Pāṇini the area cultivated with one plough is called *halya*, cf. *dvi-halya*, *tri-halya* cited in *Kāśikā*.
28. *Bhāṣya*, 1.1.72.
29. *Harṣacarita*, English translation, p. 203.
30. A bigger unit is called *parama-hālyu* by Patañjali, *Bhāṣya*, I.1.72.
31. *EI*, II, p. 116.
32. cf. Patañjali's *Bhāṣya*, 1.1.72 *parama-halya*.

9

Classification of Land and Assessment of Land-Tax in Early Medieval Tamil Nadu from 950 to 1300

Y. Subbarayalu

THE AIM of this paper is to underline the complexity of the problem of land-tax assessment in Tamil Nadu from the tenth through the thirteenth centuries by studying some peculiar features least noticed by earlier scholars.[1] These features, rather crucial to the understanding of the problem, are denoted by the Tamil terms *taram, madakku, virivu* and *parappu*. Out of nearly four thousand published inscriptions[2] (the bulk of this belongs to the Coḷa dynasty) belonging to this period only about sixty-five inscriptions provide information about these terms. Most of these sixty-five inscriptions come from the four districts of Tanjavur (Tj). Tiruchirappalli (Tp), South Arcot (SA), and Chengalpat (Cg).[3] There are four inscriptions from Tirunelveli district of the extreme south.

The data relating to the present study comes from the passages containing the description of lands made over to temples and charities. Since lands of a secular character are also described along with the eleemosynary lands in identical terms the description of all lands can be taken into account.

Taram

The idea of classification of land for tax purposes is explicitly known from inscriptions only from the later half of the tenth century as indicated by the term which begins to appear about 950. The basic meaning of the term *taram* is 'grade' or'sort'. When this was used in combination with the auxiliary verbs *chey* meaning 'to do' or *peru* meaning 'to obtain' it meant verbally 'to grade', 'to sort' or 'to classify'. This by extended meaning connoted 'assessment' also.[4] The non-assessed lands were indicated by the term *taram-ili* meaning that has no *taram*.

*38th Session at Bhubaneshwar, 1977.

From the information found in a few inscriptions it may be suggested that there were about twenty different grades of land in certain localities.[5] Whether this whole range of grading was practised throughout the country is not ascertainable. The norms under which the grading was done are also not mentioned. The available irrigation facilities, fertility of the soil and the number of crops raised annually would have formed the basis.[6]

Professor K.A. Nilakanta Sastri has noted that there is inscriptional evidence to suggest that 'the revenue from agricultural lands was periodically reassessed, and the classification of the land revised from time to time in accordance with changes in cropping, fertility and so on'.[7] It is possible to suggest that reassessment should have followed immediately upon reclassification of a land. But such details of simultaneous occurrences are rarely mentioned. What K.A. Nilakanta Sastii had in mind seems to be the gradual enhancement of tax over some years on newly reclaimed lands or on such lands raising long-term crops as the areca-nut crops.[8] When some land was donated for some charity the grade of the land was lowered in order to lessen the tax burden. Thus an inscription dated 1074 (Tp. dt. mentions that a land of fourteenth grade was lowered to the twentieth grade by a *Sabha* for tax purposes.[9] It seems the details of the entire land of each village were kept recorded in a book called *tara-pottakam*.[10] Very few inscription are available to give an idea of the proportionate ratios between different grades and the assessments thereon. An inscription (TP. dt.) of *c.* 1300 mentions that a rate of 60 *kalam (k.)* of paddy per *veli* (v.) was fixed for the lowest grade *kadai-taram*).[11] Another inscription (Tirunelveli dt.)[12] of *c.* 1303 which would have contained rates for the first four grades is unfortunately damaged. The available information suggests that the rate for the first grade was 2.4 times that of the fourth grade both in paddy and money.

Madakku

Madakku as a verb means 'to fold' or 'to club'. It seems in the process of grading when certain plots of land were assigned to a particular grade the actual measurement of that land was converted to the standard unit of the grace. The process of conversion which involved a kind of 'clubbing' was denoted by the verb *madakku*, the converted standard unit was also called *madakku* used as noun. Naturally this conversion resulted in the shrinkage of the original extent in terms of the standard unit. Thus according to an inscription of 1044 from Tp. dt. a land measuring 2.843 *veli* was reduced in grading and standardizing (*taram ittu madakki*) to 0.462 v. The ratio of the original land to the standard land was in this case 6.15 to 1. Only a few instances of this kind are available, but even they show quite a variety.[13] They range between 96.01 to 1 and 4.67 to 1. One inscription of 1247 (SA. dt.) alone gives five instances of five different ratios: respectively 13.09, 28.38, 47.72, 4.67 and 53.35 original units to one standard unit.

Virivu or Parappu

Virivu and *parappu,* used in connection with the classification of land and identical in meaning, are antonyms of *madakku.* They mean 'expansion' or just 'wide area', and seem to have been used to indicate the actual area of a land in contrast to the standardized area of the same. In a few inscriptions the ratio of this actual area to the standard area is given. But here the available ratios are not so different from each other.[14] Broadly they fall into two varieties. Two instances have the ratios of the standard to the actual area respectively as 1 : 1.28 and 1 : 1.25. All the three remaining instances have the ratio as 1 : 5. The contrast between the *madakku* and *parappu* is clearly brought out in an inscription of 1239 from Tj. dt. where it is mentioned that the rate per *mā* (1/20 of a *veli*) towards a local contribution in money called *sabhā-viniyogam* had been fixed at 3 *kachu* in the case of ordinary unit (*parappu*) whereas when it was conveited to the standard (*madakku*) unit the same was fixed at 30 *kachu.*[15]

Distribution

There is some peculiarity in the geographical distribution of the above terms. The term *madakku* is confined to the Tanjavur, Tiruchirappalli and S. Arcot districts, i.e. the *Cola-maṇḍalam* proper. The terms *virivu* and *parappu* taken together are found distributed in the *Cola-maṇḍalam* as well as in the Chengalpat district of the *Toṇḍai-maṇḍalum.* But in the Chengalpat district the term *parappu* alone was used. Since the term *taram* is noticed all over the Tamil area and since the principles underlying the terms *taram* and *madakku* seem to be interconnected, the non-occurrence of the term *madakku* outside the *Cola-ma ṇḍalam* may not signify much, though possible local divergences must be admitted.

Rates

The above information relating to *taram, madakku,* etc. would have been very useful had it been provided with the corresponding rates of assessment. Unfortunately such rates are very rarely mentioned alongside of the details of classification. But the available rates mentioned in the inscriptions containing the classification details provide some idea.

An inscription of 1036 (SA. dt.) give for two lands two rates *(varichai)* respectively of 102.28 *k.* and 245 *k.* The first land was of *virivu* category. The second is not described.[16] (In this inscription the rate for *malvaram* or landlord's share is given as 50 per cent of the *varichai* or assessment rate. This rather puzzling thing is not considered here. The second inscription dated 1215 (Tp. dt.)[17] gives a rate of 60 *k.* for a last grade land. The third inscription dated 1249 (Tj. dt.)[18] gives a rate of 120 *k.* for a classified land (classified grade is not indicated). The fourth inscription dated 1266 (Tj. dt.[19] gives two rates for two different classified lands: 200 *k.* and 78.93 *k.* respectively. The fifth one dated 1257 from Tj. dt. gives three different rates for three different lands (classified but grade not indicated): 370 *k,* 130.37 *k.* and 107.13 /c.[20] The sixth one dated 1259 (SA. dt.)[21] gives a rate of 560 *k.* for a land said to be of *virivu* category. The last inscription dated 1259 (SA. dt.)[22] gives the rates of 765.41 *k.* 830.19 *k.* and 798.59 *k.* for lands raising two crops *(kar-maru)* and 428.01 *k,* 405.61 *k.* and 459.14 *k.* for one-crop *(oru-pu)* land. All these lands are mentioned as *virivu* lands. But from the ratio of conversion (5 : 1) given in the two last-mentioned inscriptions it may be seen that the lands were really of *maclakku* category mistakenly written as *virivu.*

A review of the above rates would suggest that they are too divergent to admit of a general statement. From two Tanjavur inscriptions of Rājarāja I (1014)[23] giving assessment rates from forty different villages it is understood that the rates ranged between 95 and 100 *kalam* per *veli.* The classification details are not given in the said inscriptions. We may assume that the land extent given may be taken as the actual measured area of the lands concerned, i.e. all these lands were of the *virivu* category. We may also assume that cultivation practices did not change so much from the time of Rājarāja I through the thirteenth century as to alter the average yields. In that case, compared to the rates given in the two Tanjavur inscriptions, the rates given above would show that the unusually excessive rates were collected from *madakku* lands. The instances provided in the last-mentioned (seventh) inscription above certainly support this suggestion but for the wrong mention of the appellation *virivu.*

Conclusion

In this paper I have considered only a limited range of the problem of classification and assessment. For instance, the data relating to the survey, the cropping pattern, the total yield of lands, etc., have not been considered, not to mention the large number of tax terms relating to land. This limited study itself has raised some issues to be settled before making a decisive statement regarding assessment. My aim was to stress that the assessment rates given in the inscriptions are themselves of not much use at their face value unless they are correlated with the classification of the concerned lands. Here we may recall a statement of Nilakanta Sastri:[24] 'From an inscription . . . dated 1152, it is seen that some *deva-dāna* land, *apparently of very good quality*, was assessed at 261/4 *kalams* per *mā*, equal to 525 *kalam* per *velī*.' . . . This statement would be rather misleading unless the land is considered as one of the *madakku* category, i.e., the land unit mentioned was not the actual measured area but one converted to standard specificatios.

Notes

1. The best work to date is K.A. Nilakanta Sastri, *The Coḷas*, 2nd edn, pp. 527–9.
2. Unpublished inscriptions are not considered here since the summaries given in the *Annual Report on Epigraphy* do not give the full data relating to the terms under study.
3. The first three districts, Tj., Tp. and SA. comprise the area of the *Coḷa-maṇḍalam* proper which was the central Coḷa area, while Cg forms the central portion of the *Toṇḍamaṇḍalam*, originally the Pallava country, later a part of the Coḷa territory.
4. South Indian Inscriptions (SI1), XIX.378, II.12.3.
5. *SII*, IV, 508.
6. In a paper entitled 'Land Revenue Assessment in Cola Times' contributed to the Felicitation Volume in honour of Father X.S. Thaninayagam, Prof. Noboru Karashima of Tokyo University, has analysed lands from many villages mentioned in two Tanjavur inscriptions of Rājarāja I and an inscription of Virārājendra from *Gaṅgaikoṇḍa-cola-puram* and concluded that there are differences in composition of taxable land and also in productivity among the villages of different localities.
7. *The Coḷas*, p. 529.
8. For instance, *SII*, VI, 438 and *SII*, VII, 412.
9. *SII*, IV, 508.
10. *SII*, XIV, 245. The word is mistakenly read as *tara-yettakam*.
11. *Inscriptions of Pudukkottai (IPS)*, 1929, 170.
12. *SII*, VIII, 454.

	Reference	Ratio	Year
13.	Reference	Ratio	Year
	SII, V. 633.	6.15: I	(1044)
	SII. III, 86.	68.76: I	1187
	SII, VIII, 248.	33.8 :I	1223
	SII, VIII, 206	96.01:I	1238
	SII, VIII, 50.	13.09:I	1247
			28.38:I
			47.72:I
			4.67 I
			53.35:I
	SII, XII, 149.	19.41:1	1248
14.	*SII*, VII, 1031. 1: 1.28	1197	
	SII, VII, 1028.	1: 5.1	1223
	1: 5.0		

SII, XII, 174.   1: 1.25   c. 1250

SII, VI, 35.   1: 5.1   1257

15. *SII*, VI, 50, 1.9.
16. *SII*, IV, 223.
17. *IPS*, 170.
18. *SII*, VII, 1039.
19. *SII*, XVII, 600.
20. *SII*, VI, 35.
21. *SII*. VIII, 55.
22. *SII*, VIII, 56.
23. *SII*, II, 4 and 5.
24. *The Coḷas*, p. 585.

10

Theory of Commendation and Sub-Infeudation in Ancient India (Based Mainly on a Critical Study of the Dudhpani Rock Inscriptions)

Radhakrishna Chaudhary

WITH THE exception of the *Viṣṇusmṛii* (LXIII.1) and the Dudhpani Rock inscription, we have no positive evidence to support the theory of commendation in ancient India. D.D. Kosambi in his brilliant analysis of feudalism has nothing to say on this particular aspect though he has rightly discussed feudalism from above and feudalism from below. In my paper on Feudalism[1] I had touched this problem in a sketchy manner. While certain traits of feudalism in general are seen in Indian system, traces of subinfeudation and commendation of the European pattern are not lacking. Feudalism in India differed from region to region and it is rather difficult to assign any particular feature to this or that aspect of feudalism in this country. The general norm was of course the same everywhere. R.S. Sharma has touched this subject in his *Indian Feudalism* and Dasaratha Sharma has discussed the problem in his paper on *Avalagana* in the *Marubhāratī* (X.84–88). His paper in English language on the same subject is yet to be published.[2]

'Commendan' is described as an ecclesiastical benefice held or the tenure or the grant of a benefice held (in the *Chamber's Dictionary*, it has been described as an act of commending). In the middle ages this practice was in vogue in medievel Europe when the people commended themselves to their lords for protection. Whether the exact replica of the western method was a reality here or not is a matter for enquiry and research since conditions in India were rather different. *Viṣṇusmṛti* (LXIII.1) says: '*atha-yoga-kṣem-ārthānīīśvaram-adhigacchet*', that is, in order to obtain wealth and security one should apply to a lord. We are mainly concerned here with the word security. India, after the decline of the Mauryan empire, had suffered a setback and the condition

*30th Session at Bhagalpur, 1968.

obtaining in north and south were favourable for the growth of fedual elements. Viṣṇu, writing in the third century AD, must have experienced a condition that might have called for security against insecurity.

S.A.Q. Hussaini believes that the institution of commendation in ancient India was from the top and in support of his contention he cites the instances of the early Sātavāhana grants wherein the donees are made the de facto rulers of the donated villages including the right of administering justice and maintaining law and order. Administrative rights are given for the first time in the grants of Gautannputra Sātakarṇi.[3] According to Buddhaghoṣa (fifth century AD) *Brahmadeya* grants carried judicial and administrative rights. The people in the donated areas were thereby commended to the care of the priestly power who had shed their religions functions. We learn from a Tibetan Buddhist text that because of the insecurity caused by the thieves, the people made the strongest amongst themselves their lord.[4] When the donees became rapacious the people felt the burden of their rule and began to seek protection. Hiuen Tsang refers to a practice of surrendering land to landlords in lieu of protection. Kalhana gives an account of the various types of feudal oppressions. Commendation, immunity, forced labour, feudal dues and occasional demands are all found in Indian feudalism and also the established institution of subinfeudation.

Here in this paper we have based our account mainly on the Dudhpani Rock inscription (Hazaribagh district, Bihar). Necessary extracts from the text are quoted below:

Verse 2—There was a ruler, named Ādisiṁha—a second Jarāsandha.
Verse 3—He was the king of Bhramaraśālmalī, Chingata and Nabhutisaṇḍal.
Verse 4—There were three merchant brothers who went from Ayodhyā to Tāmralipti on a business.
Verse 5—While going back home, they refrained themselves and settled permanently.
Verse 12—Ādisiṁha came to this forest for hunting an elephant.
Verse 13—He called the inhabitants of the three villages (localities) and asked them to give him 'Avalagakam' (*Yūyamadyāvalaga- kamasmabhyam*).
Verse 14—The villagers went to Udayamāna (eldest brother among the merchants) and asked him to carry out the behest of the king.
Verse 15—He became a favourite of the king.
Verse 16—Ādisiṁha honoured him by bestowing him a diadem of prosperity (*śrīpaṭṭa*) and at Udayamāna's solicitations assured the people of the village of Bhramaraśālmali of the royal favour.
Verse 17—The villagers of Bhramaraśālmalī told Udayamāna to be their king.
Verse 18—Udayamāna said—let this be so.
Verse 20—When the inhabitants of two villages came and requested Udayamāna he sent two of his brothers to rule.
Verses 21, 22, 23—Dhautamāna and Ajitamāna ruled over Nābhutisaṇḍaja and Chingataas subordinate rulers of Bhramaraśālmalī.

The following points emerge out of the text quoted above. Ādisiṁha was the king of the three villages or to be more appropriate 'Lord'. King's right to live on levy supplies, one of the features of feudalism, seems to have been a recognised practice in Bihar of the eighth century AD and it was as a matter of right that Ādisiṁha ordered the inhabitants to give *Avalagana*. At that lime the three merchant brothers on their way back home were in this region and were thinking in terms of settling permanently in this part of Bihar. While they were there Ādisiṁha came to forest and demanded *avalagana* (meaning not yet clear but translated as presents or supplies). Udayamāna paid that on behalf of the villagers. Whether the villagers requested the king to appoint Udayamāna as a ruler or Ādisiṁha himself did that cannot be ascertained in view of the damaged condition of the text as available at present. Udayamāna agreed to be their king and subsequently his two brothers became his subordinate rulers.

Udayamāna is a merchant but he becomes a ruler by paying *avalagaka* on behalf of the villagers and thereby securing the favour of the lord. He in return and at the request of the two other villages appoints his own brothers as rulers. Thus the epigraph under reference, otherwise unimportant, raises important issues involving some principles of feudalism-like commendation and subinfeudation. Here we find the merchants turning feudal lords. It throws considerable light on the role of traders in the development of feudal society. The epigraph is important in the sense that it states as to how the people of certain villages commended themselves to a merchant prince who afforded the protection by meeting on their behalf a demand made by their lord for a due (*avalagana* or *avalagaka*). With Lord's approval and at the villagers' request the merchant becomes their Rājā.

Avalagaka or *Avalagana* seems to be a type of secular payment.[5] The meaning of the term is not yet clear and we know nothing specific about it. The Sanskrit word *avalagna* does not give us any sense of a tax or presents. Sharma takes it as 'royal dues'[6] in cash or kind and not some kind of feudal service. When Udayamāna undertakes to pay *avalagna*, the lord with the approval of the villagers, instals him as Rājā. We may infer that possibly the villagers were not in a position to pay the *avalagna* to the king and hence they requested the sojourning merchants to pay on their behalf or the merchant paid it on the assurance of his being made the rulers of the villages. What is intriguing here is that the solvent merchant, decides to stay and accepts the requests of the villagers and prefer to turn into a feudal vassal and subsequently convert his two brothers into his subordinate rulers. The position taken by Udayamāna implies a kind of feudal contract between the overlord and the vassal and he, in his turn, appoints his own brothers as vassals. A.L. Basham takes this document as an important source for the study of feudalism in India.

The word *avalagana* or *avalagaka* of the epigraph remains to be explained. Its meaning or interpretation is not yet clear. D.C. Sircar[7] and U.N. Ghoshal describes it as presents or supplies. The term signified several things and among them there is the meaning 'cot' also.[8] Supplying cot to the lord was possibly one of the obligations of the villagers for exemption from the duty of providing 'cots adobe and boiled rice etc.' is mentioned in the Kadamba plate.[9] Literary sources contemporaneous with the Dudhpani Rock Inscription (like Haribhadra Sūri's *Samarāiccakahā* and Uddyotanasuri's *Kuvalayamālā*) refer to *Avalagā* in connection with feudal relationship and it is specially used in relation to the overlord. *Avalagaka, avalagā, avalagana* are almost the same and are indicative of the same meaning. We have in the *Lekhapaddhati-avalagāsad aivāvalokya* (care should be constantly taken). There is a good deal of similarity between *avalagā* and the Gujarati word *Olagā*. *Olage* (in Gyaneśwari *Bhāgavatgītā*, III. 11 indicates personal service. The various terms like *Olagā, olage, ulagi*, etc., are used in the sense of personal or feudal service or even in the sense of military service or attendance on one's own lords. The word is very much in use in south Indian languages like Kannada, Marathi, Gujarati, and also in Rajasthani in the sense of feudal service. *Olagā* has been used in the feudal sense of personal attendance in the twelfth century AD by Śalibhadrasūri whose work *Bharateśara-bābubalarāsa* gives an account of the development of feudalism. *Kāndberdeprabandha* (fourteenth century AD) uses the word *ulagai* in the sense of feudal relationship.[10] The Jain writers of the thirteenth–fourteenth–fifteenth century AD use the term in the sense of feudal relationship.

Avalagā appears to have been a word of southern origin and its origin is traced to the Dravida or Kannada language.[11] It came to northern India with some southern fortune seekers and had come into use in that part of Bihar from where the inscription under reference has been discovered. Though its exact meaning is yet obscure, it is reasonable to suggest that it indicated a type of feudal dues in cash or kind, of feudal service rendered by a tenant to a lord. On the basis of the Dudhpani Rock inscription, it is evident that that the deal between Ādisiṁha and Udayamāna implied a sort of feudal contract. R.S. Sharma has righty observed: 'The inscription exemplifies the feudal practice of commendation and subinfeudation'.[12] Here Ādisiṁha is overlord, Udayamāna lord and his two brothers are subordinates. In my paper referred to above I described *Avalagana* as miscellaneous receipts. The overlord appears to be entitled to receive *avalagana* and whosoever pays it is rewarded in return. Why does Udayamāna pay it? Because the villagers commend themselves to him for protection so he undertakes to pay the *avalagana* and receives the reward from the overlord. According to Dasaratha Sharma, *avalagana* in that context may be described as service to the overlord or military help.[13] The inscription under reference is an example of the development of feudalism in which the lesser chiefs had little more power than the lords though they claimed the proud title of Rājā. Udayamāna, the merchant became a landed noble.[14] Land becomes the dominant form of wealth and chief instrument of economic power. He becomes the founder of the Māna dynasty and instructs his brothers not to act in opposition or separate themselves from the main branch. The villages were assigned to his brothers on condition of personal guarantee of non-opposition and as such feudal tenure in its ultimate form became clear. Here the actual proprietary rights are transferred to Udayamāna and he is honoured with a diadem of prosperity (*Śripaṭṭam*). Ādisiṁha actually invested Udayamāna with power and assured the villagers of his royal favour. When the villagers commend themselves to Udayamāna and give him the sovereignty to rule over them (on having his assurance)—that sovereignty is approved by the king. The feudal procedure is evidently clear here. The vassal-chief system, a chief point of feudalism, is discernible here. It seems to have been a kind of political arrangement conditioned by the contemporary circumstances.

In the post-Gupta period, local units of production were coming into prominence and this factor can be linked up with the weakening of the central authority which adopted the method of paying officials by grant of revenues or in kind. Commercial activities were confined to the enterprising people and they do not seem to have brought any substantial change in the economy of the interior. The powerful vassals practised subinfeudation without any reference to their overlords. Here we see that Udayamāna did it without any reference to Ādisiṁha. He further asked his subinfeudatories to remain loyal to him. The process of subinfeudation, in its broad general sense of beneficiaries themselves making grants,[15] not only continued but increased later on. The grant of land for military or other service was responsible for the origin of feudalism and of a class of vassals.

Notes

1. *JIH*, XXXVIII, p. 392.
2. Vide summaries of papers submitted to the Poona Session of the Indian History Congress, 1963.
3. Sircar, *Select Inscriptions*, pp. 192, 194–5.
4. Rockhill, *The Life of Buddha*, pp. 6–7.
5. cf. *EI*, II, p. 27; R.K. Choudhary, *Select Inscriptions of Bihar*, p. 134 ff.
6. R.S. Sharma, *Indian Feudalism*, p. 36.
7. D.C. Sircar, *Indian Epigraphical Glossary*, pp. 38–9.
8. Bohtlingk and Roth, *Sanskrit Worterbuch*.
9. *EI*, II, p. 344; VI, p. 15.
10. *JIH*, XXXVIII, pp. 105–7.
11. *AIOC*, VII, p. 47.
12. Sharma, op. cit., p. 34.
13. *Marubhāratī*, X, pp. 84–8.
14. *DHNI*, I, p. 349.
15. *EI*, II, no. 8, verse 49.

11

Farm Labourers of Karnataka (Ancient and Medieval Period)

K.S. Shivanna

THE TRENDS in the agrarian system of Karnataka in the ancient and medieval period indicate that there was a continuous growth of the non-cultivating class and institutions. This class was a product of a custom, namely, the issue of land grants free of taxes (on many occasions) in lieu of various kinds of civil, religious and military services rendered to the society of the time, for the perpetual enjoyment of the donees. Village hereditary servants like *Gauda* (headman), *Shanubhoga* (accountant), *Talavara* (watchman), 12 *Ayagars* and Brāhmaṇa landlords living in Agraharas, and institutions like temples (of various sizes) and *maths* constituted a large body of such a non-cultivating class of ancient and medieval Karnataka. The presence of such a class naturally leads us to presume the existence of a group of tenants and labourers. It is not likely that this class actually ploughed the fields and reaped the crops.

Farm labourers were of two kinds—(1) Hired labourers and (2) Serfs. In ancient Karnataka, an estate cultivated not by a land-owner with his own farming stock, but by the labour of others, was called *Kammata*. Inscriptions, belonging to the Cāḷukyan period, from Bijapur and Bellary districts, mention such landed estates.[1] The Brāhmaṇa landlords of Agrahāras also employed hired labourers.[2] Labourers were hired during peak agricultural operations and were given wages in kind by landlords.[3] In south Kanara the hired labourers were known as *Culiyalu* and were different from serfs or *Muladalu*.[4] Unlike serfs, the hired labourers were free to move as they liked. Buchanan found at the end of the eighteenth century that each free male servant hired by the day got two *hanies* of rice in north Kanara. They usually worked from seven in the morning until five in the evening. At noon they were allowed half an hour to eat their food.[5] Vijñāneśvara, in his *Mitākṣarā*, refers to hired labour and its role in agricultural operation. 'They must preserve to the best of their ability', says the law-giver, 'implements of husbandry, such as the hide and the rope of

*39th Session at Hyderabad, 1978.

the plough and the like, otherwise there would not be any ploughing at all.' He says that 1/10 as wage out of the total profits of the landlord should be paid to the hired labourers.[6] This appears to be the theoretical position. But we read in the Hirehadagali plates (Bellary district) that prince Śivaskandarman (third century AD) gave away four *addhikas* along with a plot of land to a certain Brāhmaṇa. Bühler translates *addhilca* as a hired agricultural labour who received half of the produce from the landlord.[7] It may be concluded that the wages of agricultural labourers depended upon local situations and supply and demand.

Hired labourers, on almost all occasions, came from the Śūdra castes who stood in relation to the three upper *varṇas* in the position of helots. They provided the material basis for the non-cultivating classes and institutions of ancient and medieval Karnataka. Inscriptions clearly refer to Śūdras cultivating land in villages.[8] Even when we come across references to non-cultivating classes engaged in agriculture, they could at best be gentlemen farmers who never touched the plough. In this connection it is interesting to recall the injunctions of Manu. Even the Laws of Manu, though inculcating that each of the orders should follow its own calling, allowed considerable latitude in case of necessity. If a Brāhmaṇa could not subsist by teaching the Vedas, he might earn a livelihood as a soldier. Should he fail to get a subsistence by that, he might take up the occupations of Vaiśyas, i.e. commerce or agriculture or the keeping of cattle; and a Kṣatriya, if driven by distress to give up his true calling, i.e. the pursuit of arms, might do the same, *but neither a Brahmin nor a Kshatriya* might till the soil himself.[9] Thus the upper castes were debarred from touching the plough. They might be engaged in agriculture, but must, like gentlemen farmers, employ labourers for manual work. Hence, the supply of hired labourers came from the lowest *varṇa* of the Hindu social structure who were known as *vokkalu* or *vokkaligas* in our sources.

Taluk	*District*	*Date*	*Source*
Hirehadagali	Bellary	third century AD	*EL* II, pp. 485f
Belur	Hassan	AD 1140	*EC*, V, *BI*, 219
Sorab	Shimoga	AD 1141	*EC*, VII, Sb. 253
Kunigal	Tumkur	AD 1157	*EC*, XII, Kg. 1
Sorab	Shimoga	AD 1158	*EC*, VII, Sb. 255
Kurugodu	Bellary	AD 1183	*El*, XIV, p. 277
Sorab	Shimoga	AD 1231	*EC*, VII Eb. 221
Coorg	Coorg	AD 1297	*EC*, I, Cg. 59
Coondapura	South Kanara	AD 1377	*SII*, IX, pt. Ill
Malavali	Mandya	AD 1388	*EC*, III, MI. 20
Koppa	Chikmagalur	AD 1403	*EC*, VI, Kp. 51
Sringeri	Chikmagalur	AD 1408	*EC*, VI, Sr. 25
Bagepalli	Kolar	AD 1430	*EC*, X, Bp. 72
Chamarajanagar	Mysore	AD 1549	*EC*, IV, Chanage 38
Madagihal	Bijapur	—	*EI*, XV, p. 328. n. 2

In addition to hired labourers, serfs were also employed in agriculture by the absentee landlords. They were known as *Kolikas* (Sanskrit), *Holeyalu* and *Muladalu* in Karnataka. Inscriptions of ancient and medieval times of Karnataka history from different places which are given below indicate the widespread existence of serfdom.

Inscriptional evidence indicates that two kinds of forces appear to have shaped the institution of serfdom in Karnataka. First, the creation of a variety of peasant tenures in land, like *Umbali, Koḍagi, Mānya, Sarvamānya, Agrahāra* or *Brahddāya, Devadāya,* and *Maṭhapura.* Secondly, it was the product of low grade economy which existed in different parts of the region, where the ruling classes and absentee landlords were more anxious about the labour supply than the land supply.

The *Hoḷeyalus* were hereditary serfs doing agricultural work and they were regarded as property by the landlords of *malnāḍu* or hilly tracts of Karnataka. There were two classes of serfs: (1) *huttalu* and (2) *mannalu.* The former was a hereditary serf of the family born in servitude and performed agricultural work for the landlord from father to son. The *mannalu* was a serf attached to the soil and changed hands with it.[10] Inscriptions record the transfer of such serfs with the sale of lands.[11] They were sold in *santhes* or weekly fairs as indicated by an inscription belonging to the fifth century.[12] They were also known as *Besavakkalu, Tottu* and *Besavaga.*[13] In the twelfth century a tax was also levied on *Tottu* or serfs.[14] At the end of the eighteenth century Buchanan recorded his impression of the serfs in Canara thus: 'In Canara in the farms of the Brāhmaṇas most of the labour was performed by slaves. These people got daily 1½ *hanay* of rice. A woman slave received 1 *hanay*. Each got yearly 2½ rupees worth of cloth. They were allowed to build a hut for themselves in the coconut garden. They had no other allowance. Out of this income these labourers of farms had to support their infants and the aged people.'[15]

The serfdom of Karnataka was similar to the *Padiyal* system of Kerala, Tamil Nadu and Andhra regions. Dr. Slatter, a western economist, surveyed a few villages at the end of the nineteenth century and published his findings in the first decade of the twentieth century. A resurvey of the selected villages was done by P.T. Thomas and K.C. Ramakrishnan in the 1930s.[16] A brief description of the *Padiyal* system is worth noting here.

The *Padiyal* is a sort of serf on the land bound to toil on it from the time he borrows an amount from the landlord and is tied to it until he discharges the loan. When the land changes hands, the *Padiyal* is transferred with the land as a chattel and the landlord thinks he can get him back if he runs away.

The first loan is usually for his own marriage, and though it is less then Rs. 100/- in most cases and it bears no interest, it is not easily repayable from out of his meagre income. He is given a plot of land to live on where he erects his hut, another plot of about 25 cents to cultivate a crop or two for himself, a quantity of grain varying with his work and the harvest, but generally enough to feed his family, some 'extras' (2 to 3 annas) twice a week for drinking and cash and perquisites on festive occasions amounting to Rs. 10/- per year. There is really little left to save and pay off the original loan, though it would be wrong to say that the rest suffers from want of food.

Under these circumstances it is difficult to accept the views of D.C. Sircar[17] and Lallanji Gopal.[18] D.C. Sircar, while arguing that Indian landlordism is sometimes confused with European, feudalism and feudalism is a misnomer in the Indian context, comes to the conclusion that though landlords in the past ages in India extracted free labour from the tenants, no body was tied to the soil. Likewise Lallanji Gopal positively believes that 'there is no indication that in ancient India cultivators were tied to the soil like the European serfs.' Since there is indication of the existence of serfdom in ancient as well as medieval Karnataka, it is difficult to accept the generalizations of the learned scholars quoted above. It may be argued that though the term serfdom itself arose in medieval Europe, it can be applied without undue extension of meaning to many different regions and times. As a rule serfdom has been rural, flourishing in periods marked by the absence of strong central governments, of organised legal system and of any considerable trade or monetary circulation. It has generally been a feature of feudal societies, including that of India as indicated with reference to Karnataka. Whatever may be the moral and ethical judgements against serfdom of any sort, it certainly provided certain means of livelihood and safeguarded the persons against unemployment and underemployment in feudal societies of the past. There is indeed profound truth in the statement of Toynbee, though made with reference to the Industrial Revolution of England, 'the movement from slavery to freedom is also a movement from security to insecurity of maintenance.'

Notes

1. *EI*, XV, p. 328, n. 2; XIV, p. 277.
2. *EC*, III, Gu. 32.1372.
3. *Bāsaveśvanpurānada-Kathāsangara* (MS), *c.* AD 1600, pp. 109–11.
4. Buchanan, II, p. 227.
5. *Journey Through the Northern Parts of Kanara*, p. 12.
6. *Mitā*, II, 182, pp. 194, 1209–10; p. 1232.
7. *EI*, vol. II, p. 485ff; *Lüder's List*, no. 1200.
8. *EC*, IV, Gu. 32, AD 1372.
9. L.S.S. O'Malley, *Indian Caste Customs*, pp. 122–3, 974.
10. *Mysore Census Report, p. 251; The Mysore Tribes and Castes*, vol. III, pp. 348–9.
11. *EC*, VI, Kp. 51, AD 1403; III, Malavalli, 20, AD 1388; IV, Chamarajanagara, 38; X, Bg. 72, p. 152; *SII*, IX, pt. II, no. 417, AD 1377, *HAS*, no. 5, p. 10 (Reign of Cālukya Vikramāditya VI).

12. *EC*, X, Bp. 72, AD 1430.
13. *KI*, II 37 (AD 1235); *EC*, VII, Sb. 253 (AD 1141), 225 (AD 1158), 221 (AD 1231).
14. *EC*, XII, Kg. 1 (AD 1157).
15. *Journey Through the Northern Parts of Kanara*, p. 12.
16. *Some South Indian Villages—A Resurvey*, pp. 350–1.
17. *Journal of Oriental Institute*, vol. XVI, p. 166ff.
18. *The Economic Life of Northern India, 700–1200*, p. 18.

12

Hālika-Kara: Crystallization of a Practice into a Tax

Y.B. Singh

WITH THE progressive growth of population and fluctuating trade conditions along with the emergence of feudal strongholds several new taxes were levied on peasantry by imperial rulers as well as by their powerful subordinates. The exact nature of a few of such taxes is, however, neither met with in the *Arthaśāstra* of Kauṭilya nor in the Smṛtis. Several scholars have noted this phenomenon and pointed out a number of such taxes on the basis of their mention in contemporary epigraphs. One such term, the *hālika-kara,* is to be noted in the inscriptions of the Uccakalpa rulers who, from all accounts, were the feudatories of the Imperial Guptas.[1]

The term has been variously interpreted by scholars like Ghosal, Maity, Sircar and Jha, though the latter two have pointed out that the exact explanation of the term is uncertain.[2] Thus an attempt is herein made to offer a possible interpretation of the *hālika-kara* in view of certain customary usages handed down to present century.

Ghosal has suggested that *hālika-kara* might have been a tax on plough but it appears that the suggestion, if accepted, is not free from certain difficulties.[3] Since *hāli* has also been explained as a measure of land it cannot be equated with plough without doubt in the present context.[4] Maity suggests that the term refers to that tax which was realised on an area under one plough.[5] But assessment of tax on the basis of such computation is unheard of during the entire revenue administration of ancient times, for a strong pair of bullocks would cover up more than eight to twelve acres of land whereas an ordinary one could hardly plough more than five. During the Mughal period such assessments, no doubt, were known in areas which had not been properly surveyed.[6] But as suggested by Jha references to taxes on plough and on the area which could be cultivated with the help of one plough do not mean conclusively that *hālika-kara* stood for either.[7]

Prior to a consideration of the exact nature of this particular type of tax its etymological meaning may also be taken into consideration. *Hāli* is obviously

*43rd Session at Kurukshetra, 1982.

a large plough, whereas *hālika* refers to the ploughman.[8] Both are derived from the root *hala* which means 'to plough'. All these meanings refer either to a plough or to a ploughman engaged in the act of ploughing. Since excessive emphasis has been laid in all texts on increasing agricultural production the role of the ploughman has all along been very important. Kauṭilya specifically lays down that no arable land should be left uncultivated.[9] Etymologically, since the term *hāli* refers to a large plough, obviously it was required in breaking land freshly cleared for cultivation. This echoes very well the sentiments of Kauṭilya who suggests several measures for increasing the area of arable land, e.g. clearing of forest and, what is more significant, of all sorts of labour for that purpose.[10] It would thus appear that the large plough *(hāli)* and the ploughman *(hālika)* behind the plough are connected with this particular type of tax.

If the above etymological meaning has any bearing on the nature of tax, the following suggestion may be offered. The *hāli* may be equated with one of the types of *viṣṭi* tax and treated as an equivalent of the *hari* system. *Hari* and *begari* are practices known from very early times. Pāṇini in two different contexts refers to *hālika* conveying the sense of a bullock and elsewhere to the bullock driver.[11] It is interesting to note that Prof. Agarwala had equated the word *hali* with *hari* which is current in Avadhi language even nowadays.[12] *Hari* denotes the employment of all bullock teams under the field of a landlord for cultivating his *sir* lands without any payment. The practice gained wide currency throughout northern India and has continued even to this day. The landlords used to call upon all their tenants to plough their land, that is, for one day. In fact all the plough teams of the village cultivators were forced into such exactions and this could rightfully be called a type of special tax.[13]

The *karindas* of the landlords declared a fixed date for such service by the cultivators of the entire village whose teams of oxen were thus forced into tillage. In case a peasant had only one bullock he was asked to team it with another such party. Those who were engaged in cultivation and had no bullocks at all were forced into manual labour in the fields. They had to clear fields of all weeds, grass, roots etc., and also do spade work in areas where bullocks and plough teams could not possibly reach. The *hari* system has been in vogue all through the years and is perhaps reminiscent of an earlier practice which goes back even to the days of Pāṇini. That the system became more common in Madhya Pradesh can be easily surmised from certain natural conditions obtaining therein.[14]

The pressure of population resulted in clearance of more land for agriculture in that province where people were encouraged to settle down to such pursuits.[15] The landlords had their own state farms which they could not possibly cultivate with their own plough teams. They hit upon the idea of extracting such work from all cultivators new and old alike in order to enhance their agricultural production. Another inscription mentioning the term under discussion has the word *hālika-kara-sametaḥ* which is further corroborative of the practice of allowing the donee the right to exact such customary employment of plough teams of the village for the cultivation of his land.[16]

It is interesting to note that such plough help was known to Kauṭilya who recommends employment of all type of farm labour in founding and setting new villages in areas cleared for the purpose.[17] He even goes on to recommend employment of slaves and prisoners for the cultivation of crown land.[18] Want of plough could hamper such tillage and naturally all plough teams would have been pressed into service for such purpose. It is possible that each such plough team may have been allotted a fixed area for such tillage and the term *hali* may have gradually come to signify a fixed measure of land from this practice; otherwise it simply means a large plough.[19] Later when land was freshly cleared at the instance of the feudals such teamwork became necessary to cultivate the enhanced land of the landlords. It did not matter whether the feudatory himself maintained sufficient teams of oxen for cultivation of the increased area or not. For, he could fall back on the practice which had crystallized from a tradition into a tax at least by the time of the Imperial Guptas.

Notes

1. J.F. Fleet, ed. *Corpus Inscriptionum Indicarum,* III, pp. 132, 134: *EI,* XX. p. 127.
2. D.C. Sircar, *Indian Epigraphical Glossary,* p. 125; D.N. Jha, *Revenue System in Post-Maurya and Gupta Times,* p. 56.
3. U.N. Ghosal, *Contribution to the History of Hindu Revenue System,* p. 213; L. Gopal, *The Economic Life of Northern India,* p. 54.
4. D.C. Sircar, op. cit., p. 125; *EI,* XXIV, p. 336; cf. L. Gopal, op. cit., p. 17.
5. S.K. Maity, *Economic Life of Northern India in the Gupta Period,* p. 63.
6. Richard Burn, ed., *The Cambridge History of India,* vol. IV, Mughal Period, p. 454: Irfan Habib, *The Agrarian System of Mughal India, 1556–1707,* p. 198.
7. D.N. Jha, op. cit., p. 56.
8. M. Monler-Williams *Sanskrit–English Dictionary,* p. 1293; V.S. Apte, *The Practical Sanskrit-English Dictionary,* pp. 1025–6.
9. R. Shamsastry, *Kautilya's Arthasastra,* p. 46.
10. Ibid., pp. 129–33.
11. V.S. Agrawala, *Pāṇini Kālīna Bharatavarṣa* (Hindi), pp. 156, 200.
12. Ibid.
13. For the information regarding the currency and detail of this practice till the Zamindari abolition in U.P., I am indebted to the present Taluqdars of Shahmau (Raebareli), Pali (Sultanpur), landlords of Sohwal Saloni, Bhawanipur (Faizabad), Budhauli (Bareilly), and to my teacher Prof. J.P. Misra (Lucknow) and Laloo Saheb, Taluqdar of Gaura, Raebareli.
14. The decay in trade and rise of new powerful families brought, mounting pressure upon land and thus we find establishment of capital cities of these feudals in forest tracts particularly in areas included in present day M.P. Forests were cleared for the purpose of agriculture. The contention is supported from the available land

grants found in abundance in the aforesaid regions. Since the economy of such upcoming states was based on agriculture even the construction of water reservoirs and use of scientific equipment like *arghat* (Persian wheel) were taken into account for the purpose of irrigation by the rulers. For the extension of the old villages see my paper, 'A Possible Explanation of the Term Padra or Padraka', presented at Bodhgaya Session of *IHC*, in Section V.

15. Ibid., Kr. Narsingh Narayan Singh, the landlord or Rajavapur (UP) who had friendly relations with the ex-ruler of Khanidhana, a princely state of MP, has been kind enough to inform that even till recently states having more forests encouraged tenants to indulge in agriculture by providing irrigational facilities etc. For example, Balrampur (Gonda, U.P.) had tube-wells for this purpose since the early decades of the present century.
16. *EI*, XIX, p. 127.
17. R. Shamsastry, op. cit., pp. 45–6.
18. Ibid., pp. 129–30.
19. D.C. Sircar, op. cit., p. 125; S.K. Maity, op. cit., p. 68.

PART 4

Crafts Production and Craftsmen

13

Artisans in Manu

Rajeshwar Prasad Singh

EVER SINCE Sir Willian Jones gave to the world the first English translation of the *Manusmṛti* in 1794 and V.N. Mandlik published all the famous commentaries on the subject in 1886, it has served as a valuable source for the historians of our own times for reconstructing the history of early Indian polity, society, economy and jurisprudence. Though mainly concerned with elaborating moral precepts and legal topics in a more systematic and rather sophisticated style than the early law-books,[1] the *Manusmṛti* is a source of most of our direct information for the period *c.* 200 BC–AD 200. Manu's provisions which are generally theoretical can be better appreciated against the general background of the period marked by constant foreign invasions and the rise of numerous indigenous dynasties. This was also a period of flourishing trade between India and the outside world which contributed immensely to mercantile activity. The penetration of the foreign people like the Bactrian Greeks, the Śakas, the Parthians, the Kuṣāṇas, and so an, in northern, western and north-western India, which is attested to by the law-book of Manu itself,[2] gave rise to social convulsions. The precepts of Manu, therefore, were formulated in such a way as they would keep the producing masses within the bonds of their assigned duties.

Types of Artisans

The term 'artisan' is generally used in the sense of one who is possessed of practical skill in a particular trade or profession such as a 'handicraftsman', a 'mechanic', etc.[3] Although the law-book of Manu makes just incidental references to artisans, a large number of craftsmen can be listed from its provisions. It is significant that some sixteen verses from chapter III to XI mention such terms as stand for artisans, craftsmen, mechanics, practical arts, handicrafts, mechanical works, etc.[4] The expression *kārukarmāṇi, sîlpāni vividhāni*[5] itself suggests that during this period there were a large number of

*32nd Session at Jabalpur, 1970.

artisans who practised various arts and crafts. Even the *Arthaśāstra* or the early Buddhist texts do not inform us of so many kinds of artisans as we find during this period.[6]

Karmayoga, that is, the performance of work including production of all sorts of commodities by skilled labour, is one of the seven lawful modes of acquiring property as outlined in Manu.[7] The text further states that *śilpa* or mechanical arts is one of the ten modes of subsistence.[8] We can deduce about twenty-five types of artisans from the provisions of Manu. These artisans can be placed in two broad divisions, namely, general artisans and metalworkers.

If we take into account the contemporary Buddhist and Jain texts as well as the epigraphic evidence, many other types of skilled labourers can be added to the list of craftsmen computed on the basis of Manu. The Buddhist texts like the *Mahāvastu* and the *Milindapañho* enumerate thirty-six and seventy-five kinds of workers, respectively.

The types of artisans to be enumerated on the basis of the *Manusmṛti* may tally with those given in the Buddhist texts mentioned above and Jaint text *Pannavana.*

Weavers

Weaving, one of the most ancient crafts of India, was a flourishing trade during the period under discussion. Manu's provisions suggest that weavers (*tantuvāya*),[9] who constituted a very important section of artisans, were proficient in the art of weaving all types of clothes made from materials such as cotton, flax, wool, silk, etc.[10] Of all the materials necessary for spinning thread and weaving clothes, cotton was naturally most commonly used. Manu also refers to clothes made of cow-hair or that of other animals such as goat, sheep, etc.[11] According to Kulluka Manu's reference to *kutapa*[12] denotes a soft blanket from Nepal. From this we may infer that Nepal was an important centre of wool weaving.[13] As regards the term *ksauma,*[14] generally translated as flax, Kulluka explains it as a cloth made of *atasī* fibre, that is, linseed fibre, which was used as one of the materials for textile industry in ancient India.[15] Hemp (*śaṇa* and *bhāṅga*), generally translated as jute, was also used for making textiles.

The fact that the weavers during this period had attained a very high degree of proficiency in their craft is attested to by some passages in Manu which speak of excellent clothes[16] and different measurements for weighing them.[17]

On the basis of the Buddhist evidence it can be pointed out that implements like spindle, loom, shuttle, etc., were generally used by the weavers during this period. Thus textile industry seems to have made considerable progress, and there were a large number of weavers particularly in the Mathura region, who owed their affluence to this trade.[18]

Tailors

The mention of tailor (*tunnavayah*)[19] and of garments,[20] *aṁśupaṭṭas,*[21] robes of state,[22] etc., clearly shows that tailoring was an important occupation during the period under discussion.

Dyers and Washermen

That dyers and washermen formed another important occupational group is evident from several provisions of Manu.[23] Though artisan (*kāruka*) and washerman (*nirṇejaka*) figure separately in a passage,[24] yet as the latter is treated as an artisan in the Buddhist texts of the period, and as he is very closely associated with the professional skill of a dyer, both should be placed in a single occupational group. We may just have some idea of materials used for washing clothes at that time. Silk and woollen stuffs were to be purified or washed with alkaline earth, blankets with *ariṣṭa* fruit and linen cloth with a paste of yellow mustard.[25]

Carpenters

Manu gives about eighteen references to wood and objects made of this material which clearly show that woodcraft, a flourishing trade during the Mauryan period, had made further progress in later times. Manu's provisions show that a large number of articles of daily use such as plough, sword (*sphya*), cart, chariot, utensils, pestle, mortor, bed, seat, carriage drawn by camel and asses, etc., were made by the artisans engaged in the profession of woodwork.[26]

The specific mention of the usefulness of several kinds of trees and the provision for imposing fines on those who destroyed them[27] suggest that carpentry was a very important craft. The provision of observing penance for stealing wood and trees[28] further strengthens the point.

Leather-workers

Manu incidentally refers to leather-workers[29] and objects made of leather[30] such as shoes, tattered garments, utensils, etc.[31] The mention of three categories of leather-workers, namely, the *carma-kāra*, the *dhigavana* and the *karavara* show that leather-work had become an important craft during this period.[32]

Architects

We have direct references to architects[33] and articles used in masonry such as bricks, stones, chaff, potsherds, cinders, pebbles, sand,[34] etc. With further advance in the field of architecture, which is evident from the monuments of the period, masonry had become another important profession which gave employment to a large number of people.

Sculptors and Stone-cutters

Manu's provisions relating to stones and articles made of them[35] show that sculpture and stone-cutting had made considerable progress.

As a matter of fact, the aesthetic and artistic value of the period find expression in two branches of practical arts, namely, architecture and sculpture.

Potters

From frequent references to earthen pots such as vessels and utensils in Manu[36] pottery seems to have been one of the flourishing trades during this period.

Oilmen

Manu's provisions regarding oilmen,[37] oilseeds like sesamum, mustard[38] and oil[39] suggest that oil pressing was an important occupation of a section of artisans. It is not known whether any special progress was made in the manufacture of oil, but the *Divyavaddna* evidence of oil-wheel[40] and Manu's reference to oilcake[41] give us an idea of the art of oil-pressing.

Salt-makers

As salt is one of those essential commodities which is consumed by cent per cent population, it suggests that there must have been a large number of artisans following the profession of salt-making during this period. This inference can be drawn from Manu's provision regarding salt.[42]

Sugar-makers

Manu's rules relating to molasses[43] show that sugar-making also was an important occupation.

Perfumers

The law-book of Manu lays down several rules in which perfumes[44] also figure on one pretext or the other, which clearly shows that perfumers constituted a separate class of artisans.

Wine-brewers

The text specifically mentions three kinds of wine and three materials from which it can be manufactured.[45] Wine-brewers (*Śauṇḍika*)[46] distilled liquor from three materials, namely, molasses, ground rice (*paisty*) and *madhuka* flowers.

Chemists and Druggists

Manu's provisions regarding drugs and medicines,[47] herbs and roots,[48] etc., suggest that many persons may have specialized in the art of manufacturing various kinds of drugs. Since Manu assigns medical practice to the Ambasthas (X.47), one of the mixed castes, and prohibits Brahmanas from dealing in medicinal herbs (X.87), the medical profession was stigmatised.[49]

Basket-makers

That basket-makers or workers in bamboo and cane formed one of the important sections of handicraftsmen is evident from the mention of the term *venakara* and objects made of bamboo and cane such as winnowing baskets and vessels.[50] It is obvious that a large number of workers were engaged in this profession.

Rope-makers

The mention, though not frequently, of rope[51] along with cotton, silk, wool, etc., shows that there must have been a sizeable section of people subsisting on the profession of rope-making.

Workers in Conch-shell, Ivory, Bone and Horn

Manu's provisions concerning conch-shell, horn, bone, ivory and objects made of these materials[52] clearly show that there were craftsmen who had attained proficiency in this class of trade. Specimens of objects made of them have been found at several places in northern and western India.[53]

Makers of Musical Instruments

The *veṇas*, one of the mixed castes, performed the work of playing drums which suggests that they were also connected with the profession of making musical instruments. Manu refers to musical instruments and sound of music[54] which show that there must have been several types of musical instrument-makers.

Metal-workers

The *Manusmṛti* speaks of precious metals (*taijasanam*),[55] base metals (*kuphya*)[56] and metallic ores (*dhatunam*),[57] treasures buried underground and mines of metals, etc.[58] Manu's provisions concerning metals can be corroborated by a Buddhist evidence of the period which enumerates eight crafts associated with the working of metals[59] such as gold, silver, iron, brass, copper, tin, lead, and precious stones. From the mention of ways of removing impurities from metallic ores by melting them in fire and by cleansing them with alkaline substances, ashes, acids, water, etc.,[60] we may have some idea of various metallurgical processes during the period under review. All this shows considerable advance and specialization in metallurgical works.[61]

Goldsmiths

Out of about thirty-five to forty passages in Manu bearing on metals some sixteen or so refer to gold and goldsmiths in one context or the other. Among all categories of artisans the goldsmith[62] and gold[63] occur most frequently in the code of Manu. It further mentions technical names of different qualities of gold.[64] This was because of the fact that gold occupied the first place among all metals in order of purity,[65] and that in a period of far more developed money economy when gold coins first appeared in India[66] on a large scale. As Manu's provisions show, the procurement and preservation of gold seem to have been a subject of much concern (or the ruling elite. Manu enjoins that metals belong to him who takes them from the conquered, and that the king should strive to gain what he has not yet gained, and what he has gained with the help of his army, he should protect and augment it.[67]

In a period of flourishing trade and money economy, it became imperative for various ruling houses to adopt a numer of measures to procure and control gold. Several provisions of Manu well illustrate this point. Manu ordains that by speaking falsely in a case concerning gold the witness kills both the born and the unborn, and that the act of stealing the gold of the Brahmana amounts to the crime of slaying a Brahmana which is one of the five great sins.[68] The law recommends severe expiations for stealing the gold of a Brahmana.[69]

It was the goldsmith who was proficient in the art of minting gold coins and that of manufacturing weights and measures for weighing gold and silver. Manu states that all kinds of weights and measures should be duly marked and re-examined once in six months, and that the king should cut a dishonest goldsmith to pieces.[70] Manu's provision that one commodity mixed with another one, or a commodity less than the proper quantity or weight cannot be sold[71] also reflects the gold hoarding mentality of the people during this period.[72]

Manu also mentions silver, silver coins, articles sold by the weight of silver, technical names of different qualities of silver, etc.,[73] which shows that working in this metal was another important craft associated with mineral products. There may have been a separate section of smiths working in silver or this work fell generally under the jurisdiction of goldsmiths in the same way as we find it today.

Jewellers

Jewellers other than goldsmith too seem to have constituted a section of artisans working in gems, pearL precious stones, etc.[74] Mention has been made of various kinds of ornaments, accoutrements and robes of state fitted with jewels[75] which suggests that there must have been several categories of jewellers.

Other Metal-workers

Manu's provisions speak of metals other than gold and silver such as brass and vessels made of it,[76] copper and technical names of different qualities of this metal,[77] etc. Tin, lead and pewter also find mention in Manu in one context or the other,[78] which shows that there were many artisans well versed in the technique of melting these metals and making objects of them which were used mostly by the common people in their day-to-day life. As regards copper, it has been suggested that at no other time in ancient Indian history do we find so many copper coins as during this period.[79]

That metal industry had made considerable progress during this period is also evident from Manu's provisions regarding pledge and deposit of articles between the creditor and depositor,[80] which may have covered mostly the ornaments made of gold, silver, etc.

Blacksmiths

Since the *Periplus* mentions Indian iron and steel as imports into the Abyssinian ports, technological knowledge about the working of iron had made considerable progress in post-Maurya times.[81] The blacksmiths seem to have been among the busiest metal-workers in Manu, who were concerned with making objects of iron such as agricultural implements, arms, ornaments, etc.[82] Iron objects excavated at Taxila and other places in northern and western India show that agricultural implements and tools of craftsmen such as spade, axes, adzes, sickles, and various articles of domestic use like nails, cramps, hooks, knives, etc., were made from this metal.[83]

Armourers

Manu's provisions speak of arms and weapons several times[84] which show that there must have been specially trained armourers among the blacksmiths who owed their affluence to this trade in period of constant foreign invasions and internal political upheaval. Weapons such as arrowheads, spears, javelins, etc., belonging to this period have been discovered at many places in northern and north-western India.[85] The text also refers to makers of bows and arrows.[86]

Technique of Production

Like other literary sources of the period, the *Manusmṛti* too is not very helpful in providing information about technique of production. In a varṇa-divided society like India the producing masses had neither any incentive in the shape of adequate rewards nor the facility of education to improve the technical methods.[87] Many of the objects found in the Taxila region reflect Graeco-Roman influence.[88] But there is no doubt that the growth of foreign trade and commerce on an unprecedented scale during this period gave impetus to the producing skill of artisans. It was the fingers, muscles and mental abilities of artisans which sustained the entire social fabric.

Varṇa Distinctions and Artisans

In the whole range of classical India the term *varṇa* stood for the organisation of society into four main professional classes; and as the producing sections of society mostly belonged to the two' lower orders, Manu's provisions can be generally applied to them. Manu ordains that the Śūdras may take to the avocations of artisans to maintain themselves if they are unable to secure livelihood through their servitude to the three upper *varṇas*, and if the lives of their wives and sons are at stake.[89] Manu further lays down that Śūdras should follow various mechanical occupations and practical arts from which the twice-born are better served.[90]

But these two passages by no means suggest that craftsmanship was open exclusively to the Śūdras.[91] The Vaiśyas also, who accounted together with the lowest order for the overwhelming majority of producing masses, must have practised many of these crafts, as this is evident from some seven provisions relating to the duties and functions of the Vaisyas. Since Manu lays down in unequivocal terms that if a Vaiśya is unable to subsist by his own assigned duties, he may take to the occupations of the Śūdras,[92] it seems that distinctions between the functions of the two lower orders were being gradually obliterated[93] during this period. It is likely that some of the well-to-do Vaiśyas following mechanical occupations employed Śūdra artisans under them on daily wages. Thus it may reasonably be argued that since the Vaiśyas and Śūdras constituted the warf and the woof of the producing sections of society, their mechanical persuits cannot be defined separately.

Since Manu's provisions concerning socio-economic and politico-legal disabilities relate mostly to Śūdra artisans, they accounted for the overwhelming majority of craftsmen. Besides, Manu enumerates a number of mixed castes which either arose from dissimilar sex unions or all of them were backward aboriginal tribes who retained their traditional occupations even when they were assimilated into the brahmanical fold.[94] Some of them such as the *ayogava* took to carpentry,[95] and the *dhigvana* and the *karavara* worked in leather.[96] The *pandusopaka* worked and dealt in cane and the *venas* made musical instruments like drums.[97]

Lastly, a number of provisions in Manu by way of restricting the Br"ahma. nas from taking to mechanical occupations[98] show how they were unworthy to sit in the company of the sacrifices to the gods and the manes if they worked as oilmen, as makers of bows and arrows and as architects.[99] Manu ordains that those, Brāhmaṇas who take to the occupations of craftsmen shall be treated as Śūdras in a court of law.[100] This clearly shows that as this was also a period of socio-economic crisis[101] on account of the penetration of foreign peoples far inside the country, even distressed Brāhmaṇas had to take to practical arts for their livelihood. Manu, therefore, ordains that the king should carefully compell the Vaiśyas and the Śūdras to perform the functions assigned to them; for if these two *varṇas* deviated from their duties, they would throw the whole world into confusion.[102] In view of a critical situation the upholders of traditional social laws and usage had to define clearly and precisely the rules pertaining to the lawful activities and functions of the four *varṇas*.[103] The precepts of Manu were therefore formulated in such a way as to keep the producing masses within the bonds of their assigned duties.

Socio-economic Status

In a brahmanieal scheme of society as outlined in Manu, artisans belonging to the lower orders had a far more degraded social status. But K.V.R. Aiyangar's view that in Manu's scheme of things equality in a civil sense is a myth because human needs and powers emphasise inequality,[104] is equally a myth. For, it was the Vaiśyas and Śūdras who possessed the requisite technical knowledge and experience of production, which the members of the higher orders lacked.[105] Although Manu states that the hand of artisan is always pure (*nityaṁśuddhāḥ kāruhastāḥ*, V.129) the Brahmanas were prohibited to take the food of tailors, goldsmiths, blacksmiths, basket-makers, armourers, distillers, dyers and washermen, etc.[106] The food of a goldsmith was supposed to impair the longevity of a Vedic student, that of a leather-cutter his fame, and that of other artisans his offspring and physical strength.[107] Thus Manu's precepts reflect the attitude of holding manual and skilled labour in contempt. The members of the upper classes were prohibited to deal in the articles produced by artisans.[108] A greedy man of a higher *varṇa,* who stole gems, pearls, coral or any other precious things, is condemned to take birth among the goldsmiths.[109] If the higher caste people work in mines and execute great mechanical works, they cause the loss of their own castes.[110] These laws of Manu clearly show that the artisans suffered from many social disabilities. Many of the crafts which were held in high esteem in early times thus came to be regarded as socially degraded during this period.[111]

As regards their economic status in view of the growth of arts and crafts during a period marked by the disappearance of the all powerful state control, the artisans seem to have gained considerable independence which led to some improvement in their socioeconomic status.[112] The development can be attributed to the increase in the number of guilds which may have weakened the direct control of the state over artisans.[113] There were artisans called *rāja-śilpins,* who were employed by the king. For, Manu ordains that the king's fort should remain equipped with artisans and other necessary tools.[114] But the majority of artisans were independent workers who either carried on their occupations at their own places or visited the houses of their customers.[115]

There were a large number of artisans organized in guilds who functioned both as producers and small trades. Manu, unlike other literary and epigraphic sources of the period, though does not discuss the constitution, powers and functions of the guilds of artisans, enjoins the king to honour their customs and usage.[116] Manu's provisions seem to have been aware of various producing groups which performed their work through the bonds of their guilds. As for example, the rules of agreement concerning the execution of a particular work between the employer and the employee,[117] and the provisions of imposing fines amounting to six *niṣkas* of gold and one *śatamāna* of silver on the breaker of an agreement[118] well illustrate this point. Adhya thinks' that Manu's provisions concerning officiating priests and their sacrificial fees (VII.206.11) relate to the working of private concerns in accordance with some sort of partnership.[119] It may be pointed out that despite the growth of towns and cities and the increase in the number of artisans and their guilds at this time, the law-book of Manu does not make adequate mention of this development. This probably due to the fact that the attitude of the law-givers was not in as much favour in towns as in villages.[120] The main reason for this negligence on the part of the *smṛtikāras* seems to have been the softening of the rigours of the caste-system to the more liberal atmosphere of the port and inland towns.[121]

The epigraphic and Buddhist records of numerous benevolent donations by the guilds of artisans to religious institutions, particularly to Buddhist monks, and to charitable cause during this period clearly show that many of them constituted the affluent section of society. The rule of Manu that a Brahmana in distress may accept gifts even from despisable men,[122] the Ś''udras, and in its justification the mention of the example of Bharadvāja accepting in abnormal circumstances a gift of many cows from the carpenter Bhridhu, fit in well with the epigraphic evidence of donations to Buddhist monks by the artisans.

Some of the passages in Manu suggest that this was a period also marked by the eruption of social tensions between the upper and lower *varṇas*. Manu forbids a Śūdra to collect any wealth, even though he may be in a position to do so, because a Śūdra who, has acquired wealth, gives pain to Brāhmaṇas.[123] The property of the Śūdras should be regarded as the property of the demons (*asuras*).[124] Manu further lays down that the two lower orders should pass their misfortunes by their wealth,[125] which cannot apply to ordinary slaves and *karmakāras* who worked under their masters in the hope of getting their daily bread. All these provisions rather suggest that a considerable number of Śūdra artisans had grown rich by pursuing various crafts in post-Maurya times.

Manu repeats the old precept that artisans and other Śūdras who subsist by manual labour, shall work one day per month for the king.[126] While the Vaiśya agriculturists and traders have to give one-eighth of their grains and one-twentieth of their profits on gold as tax, Śūdra artisans and mechanics would have to work for the king in lieu of taxes.[127] All this amounts to forced labour that the artisans had generally to perform in lieu of taxes.

But several categories of artisans seem to have been taxed as a few provisions of Manu suggest. It is laid down that a weaver who receives ten *palas* of thread shall return eleven *palas* of cloth, and in default, he shall have to pay a fine of twelve *palas*.[128] Probably these were taxes in kind levied on the produce of well-to-do weavers.[129] Similarly, from the provision that the king may take one-sixth part of skins, of objects made of cane, of earthen vessels and of stone,[130] it may be inferred that articles produced by artisans were to be taxed. Although Medhātithi and Kulluka explain these taxes in kind in the sense of 'from the profits made on' the above-mentioned articles,[131] we may reasonably presume that this provision must have applied to artisans working in these trades.

Legal Status

The precepts of Manu do not allow artisans to appear as witnesses in civil cases.[132] Kulluka adds that as these people are always occupied with their work and as they can be won over by bribery they cannot appear as witnesses in a court of law.

Obviously, the artisans mostly belonging to the two lower orders were not on par with the higher *varṇas* in the politico-legal spheres. In the matter of award of punishments and imposition of fines, etc., there was naturally a big gulf of difference between the two higher and lower *varṇas*.

Regulation of Productive Activities

Apart from the customs and usage of guilds of artisans which guided their productive activities, there must have been a number of laws, as Manu's provisions tend to show, promulgated by the ruling elite to regulate the working conditions of artisans. For, Manu lays down that persons who act improperly by showing their proficiency in mechanical occupations, shall be punished by the king.[133] This shows that there were people who pretended to be at home in various crafts, although actually they lacked the requisite knowledge in those trades. Manu further states that those washermen who either weakened the fibres of clothes or handed them over to those who were not their owners, or indulged in lending clothes to persons other than their legitimate owners, were to be duly fined.[134] A weaver who violated prescribed rules had to pay a fine of twelve *paṇas*.[135]

As the houses or shops of artisans, particularly those who produced costly articles, were full of their artefacts, they were to be provided with adequate protection. Manu explicitly enjoins that the shops of artisans shall be guarded at the instance of the king (if and when necessary), by stationary and patrolling soldiers and spies to keep away thieves.[136]

Thus, despite their socio-economic and politico-legal disabilities and abilities, artisans constituted a very important section of society in a period marked by the growth of trade and commerce between India and Rome, between India and western and central Asia and east and South-East Asia, on an unprecedented scale. The period under discussion may not have witnessed any far-reaching improvement in the technique of production because of constant foreign invasions and internal political vicissitudes, which affected the rigours of the *varṇa* ideals and, in turn, compelled the upholders of traditional social laws to formulate severe rules to keep the producing masses within the bonds of their assigned duties. But the functioning of various producing groups through the bonds of their caste associations or guilds held society together and gave stimulus to mercantile activity in particular, and continuity and consistency[137] to a period of plitical and social upheaval in general.

Notes

1. *Classical India*, ed. W.H. McNeill and J.W. Sedlar, p. 136.
2. X.43–44.
3. For details, *see The Shorter Oxford English Dictionary on Historical Principles*, vol. I, ed. C.T. Onions, 3rd edn.
4. III.64; IV.219; V.116, 129; VII.75, 138; VIII.65, 102; IX.239, 265; X.99, 100, 129; XI.64.
5. X.100.
6. R.S. Sharma, *Light on Early Indian Society and Economy (LEISE)*, p. 74.
7. X.115.
8. X.116.
9. VIII. 397.
10. II.41, 44; IV.66; V.120; VIII.326; X.87; XI.167, 169; XII.64.
11. II.44.
12. V.120.
13. G.L. Adhya, *Early Indian Economics (EIE)*, p. 71.
14. V.121.
15. Adhya. *EIE*, p. 73.
16. VII.222.
17. VIII.397.
18. Sharma, *LEISE*, p. 75.
19. IV.24.
20. IV.66, 188–89.
21. V.120.
22. VII.222.
23. IV.215, 216, 219; X.87; XI.66.
24. IV.219.
25. V.120.
26. IV.46; V.117; VII.220, 222; VIII.285; XI.202.
27. VIII.285.
28. XI.167.
29. IV.218; X.36; XI.167.

30. V.119; VIII.289, 328.
31. IV.66; VI.6; VIII.289.
32. Sharma, *Sudras in Ancient India (SIAI)*, p. 206 n. 2.
33. III. 163.
34. VIII.50
35. V.III; VII.132; VIII.100; XI.168.
36. IV.65; VII.122, 132; VIII.289, 327.
37. III.158.
38. IV.188–89; VIII.133–34.
39. X.88.
40. Sharma, *LEISE*, p. 75.
41. XI.93.
42. VIII.327.
43. VIII.326; XI.167.
44. VII.219; X.88; XI.169.
45. XI.95.
46. IV.216; IX.215.
47. VIII.326; IX.293.
48. XI.169.
49. A.N. Bose, *Social and Rural Economy of Northern India*, vol. II, p. 249.
50. V.119; VII.132; V.117; VIII.327.
51. XI.169.
52. V.121.
53. Adhya, *EIE*, p. 81.
54. IV.64; VII.225.
55. V.III.
56. VII.96; XI.67.
57. VI.71.
58. VIII.38–39; XI.64.
59. *Milindapañho* tr. T. W. Rhys Davids, *SBE*, p. 331.
60. V.III, 114; VI.71.
61. Sharma, *LEISE*, p. 75.
62. IV.215, 218; IX.292; XII.61.
63. IV.188–89; V.113; VII. 130, 206; VIII.99, 113, 220, 321; XI.120.
64. VIII.131, 134, 135, 220.
65. Adhya, EIE, p. 60.
66. P.L. Gupta, *Coins*, p. 20.
67. VII.96, 99, 101.
68. VIII.99; XI.55, 102.
69. XI.100 103, 251.
70. VIII.403; IX. 292.
71. VIII.203.
72. Adhya, *EIE*, p. 61.
73. V.113; VIII.136, 137, 220, 332; XT.168.
74. V.III.VII.218; VIII.100; XI.168; XII.61.
75. VII.219, 220, 222.

76. V.114; IX.65.
77. V.114; VIII.136; XI.65.
78. V.114.
79. R.S. Sharma, 'Indo-Roman Trade' (being a review of G.L. Adhya *Early Indian Economics*), *Economic and Political Weekly*, 20 May 1967, 91–8.
80. VIII.144–50.
81. Sharma, *LEISE*, p. 15.
82. IV.215; V.114; IX.293; X.198.
83. Adhya, *EIE*. pp. 51–52.
84. IV.215; V.117; VII.75, 222; IX.293; X.88.
85. Adhya, *EIE*, p. 52.
86. III.160.
87. R.S. Sharma, *Some Economic Aspects of the Caste System in Ancient India*, p. 20.
88. Adhya, *EIE*, p. 50.
89. X.99.
90. X.100.
91. IX.326–33.
92. X.98.
93. Sharma, *SIA*, p. 177.
94. Ibid.
95. X.48.
96. X.36, 49.
97. X.37, 49.
98. III.64.
99. III.158, 160, 163–64.
100. VII. 102.
101. Sharma, *SIAI*, pp. 176–7.
102. VIII. 418.
103. Romila Thapar, *A History of India*, p. 121.
104. *Aspects of Social and Political System of Manusmriti*, p. 93.
105. Sharma, *Some Economic Aspects of the Caste System in Ancient India*, p. 26.
106. *Manu.*, IX.214–17.
107. Ibid., IX.218–19.
108. X.36–92.
109. XII.61.
110. XI.66–67.
111. Chitra Tiwari, op. cit., p. 17.
112. Sharma, *SIAI*, p. 218.
113. Sharma, *LEISE*, p. 74.
114. VII.75.
115. Adhya, *EIE*, p. 82.
116. VIII.41, 46.
117. VIII.215–17.
118. VIII.220.
119. *Early Indian Economics*, p. 82.

120. Amita Roy, *Villages, Towns and Secular Buildings in Ancient India, c.* 150 BC–c. AD 350, pp. 50–1.
121. Sharma, *SIAI,* p. 219.
122. X.107.
123. X.129.
124. XI.20.
125. XI.34.
126. VIII.138.
127. Ibid., X.120.
128. *Manu.,* VIII.397.
129. Sharma. *SIAI,* p. 179.
130. VII.132.
131. *The Laws of Manu,* ed. Buhler, *SBB,* vol. XXV, p. 237.
132. VIII.65.
133. IX.259, 262.
134. VIII.396
135. VIII.397.
136. IX.266.
137. Romila Thapar, *AHI,* p. 109.

14

Urban Occupations and Crafts in the Kuṣāṇa Period

Kameshwar Prasad

CONTEMPORARY SCRIPTURAL and epigraphic evidence gives an idea of urban occupations and crafts during the Kuṣāṇa period in India. The crafts and the persons associated with them seem to be of two types, those engaged in productive works, like carpenters, smiths, potters, weavers, etc., and others like washermen, barbers, garland-makers and so on. Majority of them depended on towns for their existence. Contemporary literary works like the *Jātakas*, the *Milindapañho*, the *Lalitavistāra*, the Buddhist *Avadānas* (*Mahāvastu*, *Divyāvadāna*, *Avadāna Sataka*), the dramatic works of Aśvaghoṣa (*Buddhacarita* and *Saundarānanda*), the *Saddharama Puṇḍarīka*, the *Jaina Sūtras*, the *Kāmasūtra*, the *Mṛcchakaṭika* of Śūdraka, the early law books of Manu, Yājñavalkya and Viṣṇu also contain interesting information on the subject.

Since most of these texts were composed between the first and fourth centuries of the Christian era, the data available in these sources may be ultilized for the Kuṣāṇa period (AD first–third). Moreover, the *Aṅgavijjā*, a Jaina Prakrit text, originally compiled in the Kuṣāṇa period and improved upon in the Gupta period,[1] contains a detailed account of crafts and occupations. The 'Karmayoni' *adhyāya* of this text mentions five kinds of professions, i.e. government officers, trade and commerce, agriculture and animal husbandry, arts and crafts, and work on daily wages or labour.[2] Of these five kinds of occupations, except agriculture and animal husbandry, others found a congenial ground in towns. The text gives a long list of professionals and craftsmen.[3] But by far the best evidence supporting the existence of some of these occupations and crafts is provided by inscriptions and archaeological material. Some of the inscriptions of the Kuṣāṇa period refer to persons like superintending engineers (*navakarmikāḥ*),[4] actors (*śailākāḥ*)[5], perfumer (*gandhika*),[6] goldsmith (*suvarnakdra*),[7] big merchants (*seṭṭhi*),[8] leader of caravans (*sārthavāha*),[9] servant or priest,[10] cloakmakers (*pravarika*)[11] and so on. Similarly, the material

*38th Session at Bhubaneshwar, 1977.

discovered from Kuṣāṇa horizons over a widely dispersed area in the shape of pottery, terracotta objects and figurines, metal, stone, ivory and bone objects, plaques and sculptural pieces, beads, etc., confirms the prevalence of potters, smiths, sculptors, weavers, tailors and similar other craft groups in the Kuṣāṇa period.

Such crafts could flourish well in urban centres only. In fact, whereas agriculture, cattle rearing and other small crafts, connected with land, forest and animals, with limited scope and localized markets, were the chief features of rural economy, urban economy was dominated by the large number of professionals and craftsmen who earned more and produced for a wider consumption and circulation. In rural set-up artisans were not as skilled as in towns. In village artisans and craftsmen worked as part-time workers when they were free from agricultural pursuits. But urban craftsmen were more skilled, manufactured articles for wider consumption, because they worked as full-timers. This created a specialized class of artisans and craftsmen like weavers, lapidarists, smiths, jewellers, etc., in towns.

Urban crafts and occupations may broadly be put under the following heads:

1. service class; 2. independent professionals; 3. amusement class; 4. persons connected with the working of clay; 5. workers in textile industry; 6. carpenters; 7. smiths; 8. lapidarists; 9. workers in glass; 10. bone and ivory workers; 11. makers of perfumes; 12. liquor and oil manufacturers; 13. tanners; and 14. other miscellaneous occupations and crafts.

The Service Class

This class consisted of state officers, armymen and a large number of attendants attached to the royal court and elite, which find mention in the contemporary literature, notably in the *Aṅgavijjā*.[12] It appears from these works that a large section of urban population depended on services offered by the state as well as rich persons. However, the Kuṣāṇa epigraphs do not convey much information about royal officers. They record only officers like *kṣatrapa*, *mahākṣatrapa*,[13] *daṇḍanāyaka* and *mahādaṇḍandyaka*.[14] Of these, *kṣatrapa* and *mahākṣatrapa* were civil officers whereas others acted as semi-military officers.[15]

Class of Independent Professionals

In this category may be placed merchants, prostitutes, physicians, lawyers, barbers, washermen, tailors, astrologers, etc. They generally carried on their business individually and independently, though sometimes they were employed by the state and attached to rich persons also. Particular mention may be made of merchants, *gaṇikās*, physicians, lawyers, and scribes. Merchants constituted the back-bone of urban economy. Their trading activities and fabulous wealth form a recurrent theme in contemporary literature, particularly the *Jātakas* and the *Mṛcchakaṭika*. The word *seṭṭhi* (modern *sethi*) finds place in a Kuṣāṇa inscription also.[16] Similarly there are innumerable references to *gaṇikās*, their wealth, character, charming qualities, proficiency in song music and dance, tact of alluring customers and the types of persons who visited them. Some of them carried their profession independently, others ran brothels, while still others were attached to royal courts and came to be known as courtesans. In the *Jātakas* Benares is referred to as a famous seat of prostitutes.

From the *Saddharama Puṇḍarīka* we come to know that physicians were not only adept in curing diseases but also prepared medicinal herbs with equal proficiency[17] The *Aṅgavijjā* mentions different types of physicians, e.g. *Vejja Kāyategicchaka* (healers of the body), *Salakatta* (surgeon), *Salaki* (eye-surgeon), *Bhūtavijjika* (witch doctor), *Komārvicha* (physician for children) and *Visithika* (poision doctor).[18] Manu reserves the occupation of the physicians for the *Ambaṣṭhas*,[19] There are a few references to layers in the *Jātakas* and the *Kāmasūtra*.[20] Scribes were other important professionals inhabiting towns. The discovery of a large number of Kuṣāṇa inscriptions and seals suggests the existence of scribes. Literary references also suggest the existence of scribes. For example, Yājñavalkya advises the king to protect his subjects from the *Kāyasthas*.[21] The word *Kāyastha* denotes two meanings according to *Mitākṣarā* on Yājñavalkya; accountant as well as scribe. Teachers and barbers, referred to in contemporary literature, may also be placed in this class.

Amusement Class

Contemporary evidence suggests that many persons adopted public entertainment as a profession. Literary texts are full of references to Musicians and musical instruments,[22] dance and drama performed by professional dancers and actors. They earned money by performing public or private shows and received encouragement from the urban population. Some of the Mathura and Gandhara sculptures depict scenes of musical instruments and dance.[23] The actors of Mathura going as far as Benares to perform dramatic plays are noticed in the *Mahāvastu*.[24] The high status acquired by the actors becomes clear from a Kuṣāṇa epigraph which records the setting up of a stone slab in the place of the abode of *Dadhikarṇa*, by the boys, chief among whom was Nandibala, the sons of the actors (*Śailālkaḥ*) of Mathura, who are praised as Chandaka brothers.[25] Professionals like jesters, wrestlers, etc., may also be placed in this class. The *Kamasūtra* even refers to *viṭa*, *vidūṣaka vaihāsika* and *pithamarda*. These persons were known as *upanāgarkas* and were advised to earn their bread with the help of *nāgarakas* and *guṇikās*,[26] Thus urban growth produced a class of professionals who subsisted on such acts of entertainment as dance, drama and music.

Persons Connected with the Working of Clay

Both literature and archaeology suggest the flourishing condition of potter's crafts. The word *Kumbhakāra* finds mention in the *Aṅgavijjā*.[27] A guild of potter's is referred to in one of the inscriptions from western India.[28] The potters prepared pottery of diverse shape and use, human and animal figures, toy carts, toys, bricks, tiles, heads and other miscellaneous house hold objects. Kuṣāṇa pottery and terracotta figurines depicting typical Kuṣāṇa features, costume and coiffure have reported from a number of town sites in Pakistan (Sakistan Dheri, Taxila), and India (Mathura, Srāvasti, Kauśāmbi, Rajghat, Vaiśāli, Kumrahar, Chirand, etc.). The discovery of pottery from these urban sites implies local manufacture in towns or in their vicinity, because unlike the 'NBPW' the 'red ware' of the Kuṣāṇa period was not a deluxe ware which could have been an item of trade. Moreover, potters' dabbers and stamps discovered from some of these sites[29] (Taxila, Kurukshetra, Noh, Mason, Rajghat, Kauśāmbī, Kumrahar, etc.) also suggest the local manufacture of pottery in towns.

Textile Industry

It was one of the most important and flourishing industries of the period. The fine Indian muslin formed an item of foreign trade and was as much popular as Chinese silk in the Roman world. The *Jātakas* refer to tailors, weavers, washermen, and *Kāsī* cloth manufactured in Benares.[30] Cotton thread spinners, dyers, dye manufacturers, and cloths of various kinds are noticed in the *Milindapañho* and *Mahāvastu* also.[31] Archaeological evidence bearing on textile industry is sparse, but some epigraphs attest to the existence of weavers and dyers.[32] Moreover, the terracotta and sculptures of the Kuṣāṇa period depicting elaborate costumes and coiffure also point to the development of this industry.

Carpentry

Carpentry was another important craft. The extensive use of timber as a building material, household furniture, chariots and boats, made the profession of carpenters prosperous. There are many references to carpenters and to wooden objects in *Lalitavistāra, Mahāvastu* and other texts. The *Aṅgavijjā* refers to several kinds of boats, apparently made of timber. There were *nava pota, kottimba, salika, tappaka plava, pindika, kandevelu dati,*[33] etc. However, archaeological evidence for carpenters craft is lacking apparently on account of the perishable nature of material in which they worked, but some epigraphs do refer to carpenters. Thus an inscription of Kanaka's twelfth regnal year records a dedication by a Lady who belonged to the carpenter (*Vaddhakirt*) class.[34]

Metal Industry

Mining and metallurgy thrived under the Kuṣāṇas. This included working in ordinary and precious metals like iron, copper, bronze, tin, lead and gold. Silver seems to have been a rare metal. The use to which metal was put was apparently for manufacturing household utensils, weapons, ornaments and coins. Literary sources suggest different craftsmen in each of these metals. For example, iron smith or *lohakāra* is mentioned in the *Aṅgavijja,*[35] copper and bronze smiths in the *Milindapañho*[36] and goldsmiths (*suvarṇakaro*) in the *Saundarānanda.*[37]

Although archaeological evidence for the working in metals is not very encouraging as most of the material remains have been destroyed by time and weather, a few inscriptions and objects discovered during excavations indicate the knowledge of metallurgy during the period. Thus *lohakāra* and *maṇikāra* find mention in the Mathura Kankali Tila Jaina image inscription of the year 20 of Kaniṣka's reign.[38] *Suvarṇakāra* is also mentioned in Kuṣāṇa inscriptions.[39] Archaeological excavations have also brought to light many metal objects, copper and gold coins from Kuṣāṇa sites. Iron slags, furnace and crucibles from some sites,[40] and a golden standing human figurine in the Kuṣāṇa–Mathura style from Vaiśali,[41] indicate the prosperous condition of the metal work during this period.

Lapidary

Stone comes only next to pottery and terracotta in number and object like household utensils, architectural objects, ornaments, statues and beads were made of ordinary and semi precious stones. Stone was used for engraving inscriptions also. Such objects have been discovered in course of excavations from Kuṣāṇa levels which suggest the flourishing condition of stone industry.

Glass Industry

Some references to glass and lead are found in contemporary literature. Thus the *Milindapañho* refers to *Sisakara.*[42] The makers of lead sheets or *Sisapiccatakāra* are mentioned in the *Mahāvastu.*[43] The articles made of glass were beads, bangles and mirrors. Such objects have been brought to light by archaeological excavations. Glass finger-rings, bangles, vessels, glass tiles of first–second centuries AD and a large number of beads were found at Taxila[44] The discovery of as many as 392 'flans' of grey-coloured glass, for making beads from a jewellers' shop at Sirkap,[45] suggests local working in glass. Glass bangles and beads are reported from other Kuṣāṇa sites like Hastināpura, Kauśāmbī, Rajghat, Kumrahar, Vaiśālī, Sonpur, Buxar, Chirand also. Besides, a glass factory site, belonging to the Kuṣāṇa times and notably the period of Kaniṣka was noticed at Kopia, near Maidaval in the Basti district of Uttar Pradesh.[46] The fine colour of these glass objects and their low specific gravity suggest that Indians had good knowledge of the chemical side of glass technology.[47]

Bone and Ivory

The working of bone and ivory also developed during the Kuṣāṇa times. These were used for manufacturing domestic objects, luxury goods and weapons. Some of the important bone and ivory objects were combs, hairpins, bangles, dices, handles of mirrors, decorative pieces, small boxes for cosmetics, arrowheads, short daggers, harpoons, styluses and similar objects, some of which have been reported from the Kuṣāṇa levels of excavated sites in India. The best specimens of ivory work are represented by the finds at Begram and Taxila.[48]

Perfumery

The *Jātakas* refer to the process of making perfume.[49] Incense, essence and excellent unguents are mentioned in the *Lalitavistāra*[50] also. The *Milindapañho* mentions dealers of perfumes as inhabitants of towns. Both cosmetic makers (*prasādhaka*) and perfumers (*gandhika*) appear in the *Aṅgavijjā*.[51] Perfumes and cosmetics were very popular amongst the *nāgarakas* who could afford to spend on such items. Some inscriptions from Mathura record the endowments of *the gandhikas*,[52] which attest to the prosperity of this class.

Liquor and Oil Manufacturers

Liquor and oil industry also thrived during this period. From literary references it appears that liquors and oils had become the commodities of common consumption. Different types of drinks and oils, shops where they were sold and the persons employed in them are noticed.[53] The vedic *Soma* continued to be used, but some new varieties were also discovered. The *Ācārāṅga Sūtra* and the *Angavijjā* contain interesting lists of fruit juices, drinks and oils. The *Kāmasūtra* also speaks of the art of preparing *sharbats* and drinks. Kinds of liquor, oil and their dealers are mentioned in the law books too.[54] The drinking scenes noticed in the Gandhara art[55] also suggest the popularity of drinks which was a natural consequence of growth of urban life.

Leather Industry

References to leather industry are also preserved in contemporary literature. The *Jātakas* refer to leather *jerkins,* big sacks, ropes, straps, etc. A cobbler is referred to as making shoes.[56] Leather was used in musical instruments also. Other references also, suggest similar use of leather.[57]

Miscellaneous Occupations and Crafts

Apart from professions and crafts listed above, contemporary literature mentions some others also. Some of these were garland-makers, bow, comb, and basket-makers, ferrymen and boatmen, jewellers, betel-leaf sellers drivers, of carts and charioteers, *sārthavāhas,* vendors of prepared food, butchers, fowlers, fishermen, corpse-burners, etc. It seems that persons connected with almost all aspects of human life earned their livelihood in towns.

An important feature of urban economy as noticed from the law books of the period is that most of the artisans and craftsmen belonged to the lower strata of the varṇa-ridden society.[58] Moreover, it appears from Manu that some of the mixed castes pursued important crafts. Thus we are told that *āyogava* practised wood work, the *dhigvana* and the *karavara* worked in leather, the *pandu-sopaka* worked in canes, the *margava* or the *dāsa* subsisted by working as boatmen. The *veṇās* played on drums and the *sairandhra* was skilled in attending on his master. The *maitreyaka* rang bell at the appearance of dawn and praised great men. Most of these mixed castes were untouchables and they lived outside brahmanic settlements.[59] However, there is nothing to ascertain how far these scriptural regulations were in force. It is quite possible that the advent of foreigners like the Greeks, Śakas, Parthians and Kuṣāṇa, displacement of existing population, establishment of new settlements, and increased mobility, might have loosened the shackles of the *varṇa* system.[60]

Another important feature of the period seems to be the considerable increase in the number of artisans and crafts during this period. Whereas the Jātakas, *Painnavana Sūtra* and the *Dīgha Nikāya* mention only 18 and 24 kinds of guilds, the *Mahāvastu* and the *Milindapañho* refer to as many as 36 and 74 types of artisans and crafts. With the increased number in arts and crafts, specialization in crafts and localization of industries also become apparent. From literary and epigraphic evidence it appears that Taxila, Mathura and Benares flourished as industrial centres in northern India during this period.

Generally artisans and craftsmen worked as individual entrepreneurs, but side by side joint entrepreneurship also existed. Although guilds of artisans and craftsmen are seldom mentioned in Kuṣāṇa inscriptions, epigraphic evidence from western India and the law books suggest the existence of a large number of guilds which acted as a stimulus to the growth of crafts andindustries during the Kuṣāṇa period.

Notes

1. V.S. Agrawala,'Introduction to Angavijia' in Munishri Punyavijayaji ed., *Aṅgavijjā*, p. 94.
2. *Aṅgavijjā*, XXVIII, 20, p. 159.
3. Nearly forty-five types of professionals which included trader (*Vavahārin*), naval architect (*udakayaddhaki*), goldsmith (*suvarṇakāra*), ironsmith (*lohakāra*), bronzesmith (*kaṁsakāra*). dyer (*suddharajaka*) and perfumer (*gandhaki*), eight kinds of professionals who earned their livelihood by tongue, sixteen varieties of metal workers, eleven classes of merchants, three types of weavers, six kinds of physicians and eight types of illusionists are mentioned. See Motichandra. 'Introduction to Angaviija', ibid., pp. 35–55. The information gathered from the *Aṅgavijjā* on urban occupations is further supplemented by the *Silappadikāram*, a work of about second century AD, which forms part of the Sangam literature and contains valuable material on crafts, occupations, trade and town life of the Tamils during the early centuries of the Christian era. See V.R.R. Dikshitar trans., the *Silappadikāram*, Bk. I, canto V.24–39; 40–58.
4. D.C. Sircar, ed., *Select Inscriptions Bearing on Indian History and Civilization, (SI)*, I, nos. 27, 43; Sten Konow, ed., *Corpus Inscriptionum Indicarum (CII)*, II, p. 28; *Annual Report Archaeological Survey of India—Frontier Circle*, p. 20.
5. *EI*, I, no 18.
6. *IA*, X, III, no. 21; *EI*, X, p. 68.
7. *EI*, XIX. p. 16.
8. Ibid., p 1.
9. Ibid., p. 1.
10. *IA*, XXXHI, no 13, p. 102.
11. *EL* XIX, no. 1, pp. 65–6.
12. E.B Cowell, ed , *Jātaka*, I.4 105; II 155, 220; III.318, 421; V.531, 544; J.J. Jones trans.. *Mahāvastu*. *SBS*, XVI-XVIII, p. 34; H. Kern trans., *The Saddharama Pundarika*, *SBE*. XXI, IV, p. 17, 19 22; XI 43-4ff; E.H. Jhonston, trans, *The Saudarananda of Aśvaghoṣa*, VI 35; IV.26rf; G Bühler, *The Laws of Manu*, *SBE*, XXV, VIII.215–17; J. Jolly, tr., *The Institutes of Viṣṇu*, *SBE*, VII, V.153; *Aṅgavijjā*, XXVII.
13. *EI*, VIIIa.
14. *CII*, p. 145.
15. R.S. Sharma, *Aspects of Political Ideas and Institutions in Ancient India*, p. 222.
16. *EI*. I, no. 1, p. 381.
17. *SP* V. 44, p. 130; VII.8, pp. 130–1.

18. *Aṅgavijjā*, p. 161.
19. *Manu.*, X.47
20. *Jātaka*. II.155; Devadatta Sastri, ed., *The Kāmasūtram* (in Hindi), VI. 1.9.
21. *Yājñavulkya*, XXX.336.
22. *Jātaka*, I 59, 60; II.327; VI.544; *Mahāvastu*, II, p. 375, III, p. 443: *SP*, II.29, 89–91; *Kāmasūtra*, III. I. 16; *Aṅgavijjā*, p. 160.
23. B.N. Puri, *India Under the Kuṣāṇas*, pp. 95–6.
24. *Mahāvastu*, II, p. 169.
25. *EI*, I, no 18, p. 390.
26. *Kāmasūtra*, pp. 149–50.
27. *Aṅgavijjā*, p. 160.
28. *Lūders List*, no. 1137.
29. John Marshall, *Taxila*; II, p. 424: *IAR*, 1960–61, p. 39; 1967–68, p. 52; 1970–71, p. 31; 1971–72; p. 42; *MASI*, 74, p. 74; A.S. Altekar and V.K. Mishra, *Report on Kumrahar Excavations*, 1255–51, p. 129.
30. *Jātaka*, I.38, 80; IV.542–43.
31. *Milinda.*, I.2, p. 3; 1.33, p. 27; V.4, p. 210; *Mahāvastu*, I, pp. 191, 245, 255ff.
32. *EI*, I, no. 5, p. 384; *Lūders list*, no. 1135.
33. Motichandra, op. cit., pp. 38, 47.
34. *EI*, IX, no. 2, p. 239.
35. *Aṅgavijjā*, p. 163.
36. *Milinda.*, II 3.14, p. 96; V.4, p. 210.
37. *Saundarānanda*, XV, 68–69; XVI.65–66.
38. *EI*, 1. no. 4, p. 383; XXI, p. 391.
39. Ibid., X, no. 12, p. 118; XIX, no. 6, p. 68.
40. Noh (*IAR*, 1970–71, p. 62), Puranaquila (ibid., p. 19). Hastinapura (*AI*, nos. 10–11, p. 97); Kausambi (*MASI*, 74, p. 103) and Chirand.
41. B.P. Sinha and S.R. Roy, *Vaisali Excavations, 1958–62*, p. 195.
42. *Milinda.*, V.4, pp. 120, 331.
43. *Mahāvastu*, III, pp. 112, 444, see also P.L. Vaidya ed., *Divyāvadāna*, pp. 142, 433.
44. Marshall, op. cit., pp. 650–742.
45. M.G. Dikshit, *History of Indian Glass*, pp. 39, 153.
46. *AI*. p. 17.
47. N.P. Dwivedi, *Indian Ivories*, pp. 87–89; Marshall, op. cit., chs. XXXII- III; *AI*, no. 4, pp. 79, 81.
48. *Jātaka*, III.408; IV.454, 481; VI.538.
49. pp. 77, 134ff.
50. V.4, p. 120.
51. Motichandra, op. cit., p. 47.
52. *EI*, I, no. 7, p. 385; II, no. 16, p. 202.
53. III.1.6.
54. *Manu.*, III.180; *Yājñavalkya.*, III.48; *Viṣṇu.*, V.83, 100.
55. B.N. Puri, op. cit., pp. 95–97.
56. *Jātaka*, III.324, 336; V.514 and VI.538.

57. *Milinda.* V.4, p. 210; *Mahāvastu,* III, pp. 11–3, 444; *Manu.,* VIII. 289, X. 49; *Yājñavalkya.,* VIII.82–8; *Viṣṇu.;* VI.16; LI.8.
58. *Manu.,* X.81–116; *Viṣṇu,* II.10–14.
59. R.S. Sharma, *Ś"udras in Ancient India,* pp. 206–7.
60. Ibid., p. 219.

15

Leather Workers in Ancient and Early Medieval India

Vivekananda Jha

LEATHER WORK is one of the earliest occupations of India and was a flourishing craft in the Vedic period.[1] The most commonly used word for leather or hide in the *Ṛgveda* and later Vedic texts is *carman, mla* signifies tanning[2] and the leather worker is represented by Carmamna.[3] Leather containers for wine, meat, curd and water, besides straps for yoking chariots, whiplashes, slings, bowstrings and shoes manufactured from leather are mentioned.[4] References to such processes as wetting the hide,[5] stretching it with pegs[6] and rolling it up[7] are made. The use of *go* occasionally as a synonym of *carman*[8] reflects the extensive use of cattle hide in addition to hides of boar, black antelope, deer, etc., during the period. The Carmamna also appears among the numerous victims at the *puruṣamedha* (symbolic human sacrifice) in the *Vājasaneyi Saṃhitā*[9] and the *Taittirīya Brāhmaṇa*[10] along with the *jyākara*[11] or maker of bowstrings.

According to Carl Darling, Buck, the terms for tanner and hide in the principal Indo-European languages have a common origin.[12] This fact and the manufacture of a wide variety of useful and essential leather goods of daily use indicate that far from originally belonging to the non-Aryan stock,[13] the Carmamna was a member of the Aryan community or *viś*. The Ṛgvedic society does not reveal any sharp class division and although a large number of occupations had come into existence in the later Vedic period, these had apparently not yet petrified into castes in the modern sense, marked off from each other by rules pertaining to endogamy, hierarchy and restrictions on food and social intercourse.[14] Surely the profession of leather worker was quite dignified at this stage and the Carmamna did not evoke contempt nor communicate impurity through touch or contact. This would suggest, as R.S. Sharma rightly emphasizes, that impurity did not accrue merely from the nature of a particular work which remained unchanged even in later times.[15]

The material perspective changed considerably during post-Vedic times and this had its impact on the development of castes, their rating in various

*40th Session at Waltair, 1979.

religious texts and actual social position. The period witnessed the growth of cities,[16] thriving trade and commerce[17] and commodity production by artisans in principal towns on an unprecedented scale.[18] Quite a few of these urban artisans were organised into guilds which took care of their interests. They were economically much better off than artisans scattered in villages and catering locally to the needs of a predominantly agrarian economy. Of course the state envisaged by Kauṭilya was a veritable leviathan[19] which sought to regulate every economic activity including that of the guilds. The *Arthaśāstra* furnishes ample evidence for increased division of labour and specialization in crafts and prescribes specific areas within the fort walls for residential accommodation of different categories of workers. Hides are considered important enough to be constantly stored in the city and replaced by and replenished with fresh supplies,[20] and workers in hides are enjoined to be settled along with workers in wool, yarn, bamboo, armours, weapons, shields and śūdras in the western quarter.[21] Although the segregation involved was mainly functional, the *varṇa* element cannot be completely missed here. It seems that through his uninterrupted association with manual work, from which the higher *varṇas* were progressively moving away and for which they were developing increasing aversion, the leather worker had by now lost his one time vaiśya status, and Kauṭilya looked upon him as a segment of the hereditary śūdra *varṇa*. There is not the slightest evidence in the *Arthaśāstra,* however, of any ritual impurity being attached to the craft of the leather worker or of his being a socially tabooed person.

The disappearance of the powerful Mauryan state did not entail general commercial decline. Trade with Rome grew and reached its peak during the first two centuries of the Christian era, making western Deccan under Satavahana rule an immensely prosperous region. The number of crafts and artisans swelled further during the period[22] and the influence and authority of guilds increased. Among the traditional eighteen guilds[23] figures the guild of leather workers,[24] who formed an important category of artisans, especially in urban areas. Commodity production of a wide variety of leather articles[25] must have contributed to their material well-being and leather workers are found bestowing gifts to Buddhist monks and monasteries[26] and tax to the king.[27] There is no reason to suspect that they suffered annoying caste prejudices or that their social status was low.[28]

Artisans in rural areas (*grāmśilpins* of Pāṇini's *Aṣṭādhyāyī*)[29] probably did not enjoy an equivalent economic position. They are asked to render a day's work for the king every month in lieu of taxes,[30] which shows how materially vulnerable they were. Taboos on the pursuit of an artisan's profession by a Brāhmaṇa,[31] accepting food offered by him,[32] inviting him to a funeral meal[33] and allowing him to act as a witness[34] appear in brahmanical legal texts, the leather worker is specifically mentioned in these contexts.[35] Not only, however, are these taboos—which fall short of untouchability—restricted to Brāhmanas, the leather worker is also tagged with an assortment of people including artisans such as a carpenter, a blacksmith, a goldsmith, a weaver, a dyer, an oilman, a cane worker, a distiller of and dealer in liquor and others such as an actor, a Śūdra, a usurer, a physician, a woman in her courses, a eunuch, a king and even some Brāhmaṇas. The accent in these provisions still seems to be on the profession rather than on the caste of the leather worker, and though regarded as no better than a Śūdra the bias against him is not acute. Manu's reference to the Karavara[36] and the Dhigvana[37] as two mixed castes of leather workers besides the Carmavakartin[38] or leather cutter, however, underscores not only the importance of the craft in his time but also its crystallization into more than one caste. It is possible that unlike the Carmavakartin, the Karavara and the Dihgvana had non-Aryan tribal roots[39] and they were rated lower, though not considered untouchables. The Anuśāsana Parva mentions the Carmakāra as a caste and the Karavara as its mixed progeny through a Niṣāda woman.[40] The leather worker appears as Padukṛta and Carmakāra in the *audvavarga* of the *Amarakoṣa*,[41] which perhaps throws light on the formation of two subcaste groups of makers of shoes and makers of leather respectively.[42]

Such appearance of taboos in relation to the leather worker, through not verging on untouchability, is a feature of the contemporary Buddhist and Jain literature as well, and its coincidence with growing class division and economic disparity in society is significant. Thus the *Vinaya Piṭaka* includes the craft of the leather worker in the list of five low occupations (*hinasippāni*), others being those of Nalakara (bamboo worker), the Kumbhakāra (potter), the Peśakāra (weaver) and the Nāhapita (barber).[43] The treatment of four of these as ordinary crafts in the *Dīgha Nikāya* and the exclusion of the craft of the leather worker from this list[44] imply a sort of consensus about the tabooed nature of this calling.[45] To seek merely economic factors for this prejudice may not be quite appropriate. The manifest reason for Buddhist abhorrence for the craft of the leather worker was its connection with flaying cattle, and this was entirely in keeping with the cherished norms and values of an influential social segment[46] which downgraded the Rathakāras[47] simply because they built chariots for war which it hated. This prejudice by itself, however, was not enough to make the leather worker socially untouchable. References to Rathakāras taking up leather work[48] betoken occupational mobility among the followers of allied or subsidiary occupations.

From a tabooed section for whose untouchability there is no direct evidence up to the Gupta period,[49] the leather worker became a distinctly untouchable caste in early medieval period. Parāśara is the first lawgiver to place the Carmakāra midway between the Śūdra and the Caṇḍāla; unlike the Śūdra, the Carmakāra causes pollution through touch or contact, though its degree is only half of that incurred from the Caṇḍāla.[50] Since the context is the prescription of penance for persons belonging to the four *varṇas* in whose house a Caṇḍāla woman is envisaged as staying unknown, the leather worker had slowly become untouchable even for a Śūdra.[51] Carmakāra is one of the seven *antyajas* in the well-known identical list of Atri[52] and Yama,[53] and *antyaja* certainly means an untouchable here. Aṅgīras brackets the Carmakāra with Rajaka, Naṭa, Dhīvara and Buruda and enjoins sipping water as expiation for a twice-born (*dvija*), who has touched one of these.[54] The leather worker is tagged with Rajaka, Vyādha, Sailusa and Veṇujīvī in the *Āpastambasmṛti* and *candrāyāṇa* and *prājapatya* penances are laid down for a Brāhmaṇa eating their food.[55] The *Vedavyāsa-smṛti* includes the Carmakāra in its list of twelve *antyajas* and other beef-eaters, talking with whom requires expiation through bath and seeing whom should be followed for purification by a look at the sun.[56] It is true that even Bṛhaspati refers to beef-eating by labourers and artisans in the middle country,[57] and in view of his physical handling of the carcasses of cattle, skinning them and manufacture of leather goods, the Carmakāra may have been among artisans who took beef,[58] but Vedavyāsa's is the first known provision in brahmanieal legal texts explicitly treating beefeaters as untouchables. B.R. Ambedkar was definitely wrong in attributing the origin of untouchability to beef-eating,[59] for this social phenomenon appeared in relation to the Caṇ. dāla and a few other sections several centuries ago (at least in the period of the *Dharmasūtras)* when there is no such stipulation of severe social consequence of beef-eating.

Vijñāneśvara in his *Mitākṣarā* commentary on a verse of the *Yājñavalkyasmṛti*,[60] quotes Madhyamāṅgīras to differentiate between *antyavasāyins* represented by the Caṇḍāla, Svapaca, Kṣatr, Magadha, Suta, Vaidehaka and Ayogava and the seven *antyajas* occurring in Atri and Yama and including the leather worker; sexual relations with women of the former category are said to entail more severe penance. Although the equation of the Kṣatr, Magadha, Suta, Vaidehaka and Ayogava with the Caṇḍāla and Svapaca is misleading and seems to have been prompted by orthodox regard for *pratiloma* theory, there is no doubt that the leather worker was generally regarded as superior to the Caṇḍāla and Svapaca.

One interesting development of the period was that unlike in the past, the Carmakāra himself is brought within the purview of the *varṇasaṁkara* theory. Thus Uśanas speaks of him as the offspring of a Śūdra from a Kṣatriya girl,[61] and, again, of Vaidehaka and Brahmanic extraction.[62] Vaikhānasa agrees with the latter derivation. This suggests an increasing arbitrariness with regard to the *varṇasaṁkera* theory. To emphasize his low ritual status, the leather worker is included in the list of *asat* (impure) Śūdras and *adhama saṁkaras* (low mixed castes).[63] Even the Jain *Jambudvīpa-prajñapti* refers to *cammayaru* (shoe-maker) as an untouchable caste.[64] Alberuni mentions the leather worker as a category below the Śūdras marrying exclusively among themselves and staying outside settled villages and towns.[65]

There can hardly be any doubt about the fact that the early medieval period was marked by an intensification of the practice of untouchability and the swelling of the ranks of untouchables by the incorporation of several new castes. The leather workers were one of them. Undoubtedly the contempt for occupations of primary production, especially those of an unclean nature, had grown among the higher *varṇas*, who showed abnormally strong notions of purity and pollution during the period. It cannot be denied that the material milieu of the period—the decline of trade and commerce and urban life, the growing agrarian character of society and the emergence of a closed local economy[66]—played a significant role in the growing tendency towards segregation and social exclusiveness and the extension of touch–taboo which encompassed the leather workers. The redeeming feature of the social situation was the discordant note struck by sections like the tantrics who ignored caste considerations and welcomed even the lowest within their fold. Also perhaps the intensity of the phenomenon varied from region to region.

Notes

1. *Carmanya* in the *Aitareya Brāhmaṇa,* V.32, signifies leather work.
2. *Ṛgveda,* VIII.55.3.
3. Ibid., VIII.5.38. According to A.A. Macdonell, the dental n may stand for *l* in Carmamna, *Vedic Grammar,* p. 34, fn. 1; cf. 249, fn. 4.
4. A.A. Macdonell and A.B. Keith, *Vedic Index of Names and Subjects,* I, pp. 233, 257; S.K. Das, *The Economic History of Ancient India (From the Earliest Times to the Invasion of India by Alexander the Great),* 2nd edn., pp. 54, 139.
5. *Ṛgveda,* I 85.5.
6. *Śatapatha Brāhmaṇa,* II.1.19.
7. *Śvetāśvatara Upaniṣad,* VI.20.
8. *Ṛgveda,* X.94.9; VI.75.11; VIII.59-5, etc.; *Atharvaveda,* 1.2.3.
9. XXX 15. The Carmamna is dedicated to Sadhyas (*sadhyebhyascarmamnam*).
10. III.4.13.1.
11. *Vājasaneyi, Saṁhitā,* XXX.7; *Taittiriya Brāhmaṇa,* III.4.31. The Jyākara is dedicated to the deity Karma, *Karmane Jyākaram*. The making of bowstrings had already become a specialized craft.
12. *A Dictionary of Selected Synonyms in the Principal Indo-European Languages,* cited by R.S. Sharma, *Śūdras in Ancient India,* p. 27.
13. Jaimal Rai, *The Rural Urban Economy and Social Changes in Ancient India, 300* BC to *600* BC, p. 190.
14. cf. P.V. Kane, *History of Dharmaśāstra,* II, pt. I, 2nd edn., p. 44.
15. *Śūdras in Ancient India,* p. 48.
16. According to R.S. Sharma, urbanization ushered in northern India, specially in the middle Ganga basin, in the sixth century BC, reached its peak in the first and

second centuries AD and continued up to the sixth century, 'Iron and Urbanization in the Ganga Basin', review Article on A. Ghosh, *The City in Early Historical India*, I, no. 1. Ghosh rules out the contribution of Harappa culture to this phase of urban development in the north.

17. As Romila Thapar points out, cities in this period were not only important commercial centres and seats of a flourishing cash and market economy, but also, unlike the temple cities of Bronze Age civilization, the nuclei of the affluent and the natural habitat of the *Setthi-guhapatis*, the immensely wealthy traders and financiers, *Ancient Indian Social History: Some Interpretations*, pp. 43–4.
18. cf. D.D. Kosambi, *The Culture and Civilization of Ancient India in Historical Outline*, pp. 125, 152, 184.
19. It was the main land-clearing agency, by far the greatest landowner, the principal owner of heavy industry and even the greatest producer of commodities, Kosambi, op cit., p 145.
20. *Arthaśāstra*, II.4.27–28.
21. Ibid., II.4 13.
22. *Mahāvastu*, III, 442tt; *Milindapañho*, p 331; *Pannavana*, 1,61; *Aṅgavijjā*, Appendix V, pp. 349–50, cited by S.C. Bhattacharya, *Some Aspects of Indian Society from c. second Century* BC *to fourth Century* AD, p. 3.
23. *Jātaka*, VI, 1.427.
24. Ibid., R.C. Majumdar, *Corporate Life in Ancient India*, 3rd edn., p. 15; S.K. Das, op. cit., p. 242.
25. T.W. Rhys Davids and William Stede, ed, *Pali-English Dictionary*, p. 262; J.C. Jain. *Life in Ancient India as Depicted in the Jain Canon*, p. 103; S.K. Das, op. cit., pp. 226–27; Jaimal Rai, op. cit., p. 116.
26. H. Lüders, *A List of Brahmi Inscriptions from the Earliest Times to About* AD *400 with the Exception of those of Asoka (Appendix to Epigraphia Indica)*, X, no. 1273. Cammakāra Vidhika, who along with his son Nāga and relatives presents the gift of a slab with a filied vase *punaghadakapata*, is said to be the son of a teacher *(Upajhaya)* Nāga. This shows that there was a considerable occupational mobility at that time.
27. cf. A Pallava inscription of AD 446 from southern India *EI*, XXIV, Inscription no. 43, 16.18–19. A charter of Siṣṇusena of Gujarata (AD 592) mentions the Padakuras along with the Chimpakas (dyers of clothes) and the Kolikas (weavers) who had to pay as tax half the money that would be the price of things produced by them according to the rate prevalent in the land, *EI*, XXX, no. 30, I, 72 D.C. Sircar, *Studies in Political and Administrative System in Ancient and Medieval India*, and D.N. Jha, (*Revenue System in Post-Maurya and Gupta Times*) interpret Padakara as a shoemaker. G. Rai, however, translates Padakara as a producer of things and goods, 'Forced Labour in Ancient and Early Medieval India', *IHR*, III, no. 1, p. 21.
28. Christoph von Furer-Heimendorf's theory that it was the city-life which first bred the most acute caste consciousness that slowly percolated to villages (Foreword to Stephen Fuchs, *The Children of Hari: A Study of the Nimar Balahis m Madhya Pradesh, India*, pp. vii-viii), is patently untenable; cf. Suvira Jaiswal, 'Some Recent Theories of the Origin of Untouchability: A Historiographical Assessment'. Paper read at the Indian History Congress, 1978, pp. 2–4.

29. VI.2.62. Pāṇini refers to skinning *tvacayati,* III.1.25 and a few leather articles (*carmano'n,* V. 1.15), V.S. Agrawal, *India as Known to Panini,* 2nd edn., p. 234. Bṛhaspati defines *silpin* as one able to work on gold, silver, thread, wood, stone or leather, and acquainted with articles to be manufactured with such materials, XIV.27.
30. *Gautama Dharmasūtra,* Y.31; *Vasîṣṭha Dharamsūtra,* XIX.28; *Manusmṛti,* VIII 138; *Viṣṇusmṛti,* III.132.
31. *Baudhāyana Dharamasūtra,* 1.5.10.24.
32. *Āpastamba Dharmasūtra,* 1.6.18.18; *Gautama Dharmasūtra,* XVI1.7.
33. *Gautama Dharmasūtra,* XV.18.
34. Nārada's list of incompetent witnesses (1.117-87) includes a few artisans.
35. *Vasîṣṭha Dharmasūtra,* XIV.3; *Manusmṛti,* IV 218; *Viṣṇusmṛti,* LI.8; *Nāradasmṛti,* 1.185. That shoes were no longer regarded as particularly clean is proved by Gautama's injunction that a *snātaka* (a Vedic student from Brāhmaṇa *varṇa*) wearing them shall neither eat nor worship gods, IX.45. No impurity is implied in Āpastamba's provision (1.2.7.5) that a *snātaka* should avoid such objects of comfort as shoes, umbrella or chariot. S.K. Das refers to ritual shoes and giving of dry skin bags as sacrificial fee earlier, op. cit., p. 140.
36. X.36.
37. X.15, 49.
38. IV.218.
39. This view is reinforced by Manu's ordaining for Dhigvana's stay outside villages near famous trees and burial grounds, on mountains and in groves (X. 49.50).
40. 48.26. Carmaśilpī appears in Bālakāṇḍa and Carmacchedaka in Ayodhyākāṇḍa, S.K. Das, op. cit., p. 140.
41. II. 10.7.
42. cf. B.N.S. Yadava, *Society and Culture in Northern India in the Twelfth Century,* p. 39.
43. IV, 6-7; N. Wagle, *Society at the Time of the Buddha,* p. 135.
44. I.51.
45. Padakāra, synonymous with Cammakāra in Jain texts, fares no better. J.C. Jain, op. cit., p 103.
46. Vivekananda Jha, 'Stages in the History of Untouchables', *IHR,* II, no. 1, 28.
47. Vivekananda Jha, 'Status of the Rathakara in Early Indian History', *Journal of Indian Hsitory,* III, pt. I, 42, 43.
48. *Jātaka,* IV.172; VI. 151; *Petavatthu Commentary,* III.1.13.
49. According to both R.S. Sharma, *Ś"udras in Ancient India,* pp. 262–63, and B.N.S. Yadava, op. cit., p. 49, the leather worker was not an untouchable up to the Gupta period.
50. VI.40, 44.45.
51. The facade of treating the leather worker as a Ś"udra is, however, maintained in the *Vaijayantī* of Yādava Prakāśa and *the Abhidhāna Cintāmaṇi* and *Desînāmamālā* of Hemacandra Yadava, op. cit., p. 39.
52. Verse 199.
53. Verse 33.
54. *Rajakaṁ carmakāraṁ ca nataṁ dhīvarhmeva ca; burudaṁ ca tathā spṣṭvā śudhyedācamanāddvijaḥ,* verse 17.

55. XI.32; X.13.
56. I.12-13.
57. *Madhyadeśe karmakārāḥ śilpinaśca gavasināḥ, cited by* R.S. Sharma, *Śudras in Ancient India,* p. 258.
58. Taboo on beef-eating in orthodox *varṇa* society has been strong indeed and the defilement and degradation resulting from beef-eating for large sections of people have been substantial. As Andre Beteille observes, in no other society is the backwardness of such a large section of the population so closely associated with inherited status; even when a Harijan caste abandons beef-eating, it rarely succeeds in freeing itself entirely from its traditional stigma, *Castes: Old and New,* pp. 6, 91.
59. *The Untouchables,* pp. 103, 153, 159.
60. III.260.
61. Verse 4.
62. Verse 21.
63. *Bṛhaddhanna Purāṇa,* III.13; *Brahmavaivarta Purāṇa, Brahma Khaṇḍa,* ch. X.
64. Cited by Yadava, op. cit., p. 42.
65. E.C. Sachu, ed. and tr., *Alberuni's India,* 1.101.
66. B.N.S. Yadava, 'Problem of the Interaction between Socio-Economic Classes in the Early Medieval Complex', *IHR,* III, no. 1, p. 44; Vivekananda Jha, 'Position and Status of Bamboo Workers and Basket Makers in Ancient and Early Medieval Times', paper read at the Indian History Congress Session, 1978, pp. 15–16.

16

Some Crafts of Ancient Bengal (Textile)

Annapurna Chattopadhyaya

THE VILLAGES of ancient Bengal have been mostly self-sufficient and self-contained primary units, in respect of both agriculture and crafts, meeting the day to day requirements of their inhabitants. Both literary and epigraphic records of early periods bear ample testimony to villages and peoples of ancient Bengal producing all kinds of agricultural and industrial articles for both internal consumption and export to other countries. In the present paper, an attempt has been made to throw some light on the textile industry, the most important rural craft of ancient Bengal—a craft which was practised by the indigenous tribal communities of the region such as the *Vaṅgas, Puṇḍras, Niṣādas, Śavaras. Chaṇḍālas, Kirātas* and others who now belong to the lowest order of the Hindu society.

Amongst the various crafts of ancient Bengal the most important was, of course, that of textiles of cotton and silk. Cloth and garments (*vāsas*) are, no doubt, described in the Vedic and other early Indian texts; but nowhere does Bengal figure as a great manufacturing centre of textiles.[1] It is only from the *Arthaśāstra* of Kauṭilya that we have a graphic account of the textile products of ancient Bengal.[2] In the works of both Pāṇini and Patañjali there are specific references to raw materials for cloth-making and to various kinds of textile.[3] It is significant to note that the various textile products mentioned by Kauṭilya have been named after the centres of their production. Kauṭilya has made specific references to a variety of such products as *kārpasika, dukula, kṣauma, patrorṇa* and *kauseya*.[4] Manu also, while describing the consequences of stealing, speaks of different kinds of cloth, such as, *kauseya, kṣauma* and *kārpāsa*. Again, when entailing taboos on the Brāhmaṇas regarding selling of articles in times of need, Manu refers to woven cloths from *śaṇa* (hemp), *kṣauma*, and *kambala* (rug) made of sheep's hair.[5] In the *Amarakoṣa* all these varieties of fabrics have been elaborately enumerated as *kṣauma, kārpāsam, kauseya, patrorṇa, dukula*[6] etc. Kālidāsa refers to *dukula, kauseya; vāsa*, etc.[7]

*41st Session at Bombay, 1980.

Of cotton fabrics, i.e. *Kārpāsika,* those produced in Vaṅga and six other regions have been mentioned as the most excellent ones (*Madhura .... vaṅgakān Kārpāsikam śreṣṭhamiii).*[8] Seven countries producing cotton cloth are considered best, and Vaṅga is one of them. That Vaṅga was a great centre manufacturing fine cotton farbics is also proved by the testimony of the *Mānasollāsa* which furnishes a long list of fabrics for the use of the king along with the places of their origins. In this list of places figure Vaṅga and Kaliṅga of eastern India.[9]

The *dukula* textile was made of a kind of silk. On the basis of texture and colouration the *dukula* variety of textiles, was stated to be of three types, namely, *śveta, śyāma* and *suvarṇa,* i.e., white, dark, and red or golden colour, produced in different parts of Bengal and the adjoining regions. Thus, the most pleasing, soft and white coloured *dukula* was produced in Variga country, soft and *śyāma* (dark or green in colour) like that of the surface of a gem in Puṇḍra country and soft and red in colour like that of the Sun in Suvarṇakuḍya, i.e., in South, East and North Bengal or Kāmarūpa or Burma or Suvarnadvīpa (*Vaṅgakam śvetam snigdham dukulam Pauṇḍrakam śyāmam maṇisnigdham, sauvarṇakuḍyakam sūryavarṇam maṇisnigdhodakuvanam, Caturasravanam, vyamisravanam*).[10] It has been further pointed out that red *dukula* was woven with wet mixed yarns.[11] Three types of *dukula* have also been distinguished on the basis of techniques of weaving; (1) *maṇisnigdhokavanam,* (2) *chaturasravanam,* (3) *vyamisravanam, i.e*, mixed texture or made with yarns of different colours.[12] An interesting point that emerges from the description of Kauṭilya is that all these types of *dukula* fabrics have been actually named after the centres of their production as *Vaṅgaka, Pauṇḍraka* and *Sauvarṇakuḍyaka* and the quality and nature of each have also been enumerated. The identification of Suvarnakuḍya is a matter of dispute. It is generally taken to be Kāmarūpa but Sastri argues in favour of its identification with ancient Karṇasuvarṇa, in the district of Mursidabad, which is still famous for the production of fine varieties of *resam* or silk cloth.[13] In this connection, it is significant to note that, as in ancient times, even today cotton and silken fabrics are called after the centres of their production, such as Mursidabad-silk, Vishnupuri-silk and Tangail, Dhanekhali and Amarshi cotton fabrics.

The *Kṣauma* is a coarse variety of linen mixed with cotton, or made of flax.[14] In the *Amarakoṣa, kṣauma* and *dukula* have been made synonyms. It is stated in the *Amarakoṣa*: '*Kārpāsam vadaram praktvam dukuladyañca balkalam dhautatasaravastram patrorṇam kṣaumiti puṭṭavastra*'.[15] The most famous variety of this textile has been specifically called *Pauṇḍraka* (*Pauṇḍarakañca kṣauma vyākhyātam*).[16] It follows accordingly that the best *dukula* linen was produced in Puṇḍra country only.

The *patrorṇa* linen (washed *kauseya)* was manufactured from leaves as the name denotes. This is made of yarn of thread obtained from the spider's saliva. In the *Harṣacarita* it is described as *lālātantujai,* i.e., made of yarn of saliva or of spider's thread.[17] It is further learnt from the *Artkaśāstra* that *nāgavṛkṣa* (a kind of plant being a resort of serpents), *likuca,* coral tree, i.e. *Artocarpus Lakucha, vakula (Mimusops Elengi)* and *vaṭa (Ficus Indica* or *Ficus benghalersis)* trees are the primary sources from which fibres or yarn were extracted (*nāgavrkṣa Likuco-vakula-vāta*).[18] This description of Kauṭilya is also confirmed by Kṣīraswāmī, the commentator on the *Harṣcarita.* While commenting on *patrorṇa* Kṣīraswāmī says: *"Lakucavaṭādipatreṣu kumilalorṇakṛtam patror. nam)".*[19] But Kṣīraswāmī speaks of *lakuca* and *vaṭa* plants only. Kauṭilya further refers to different colours of these fabrics, such as, *pītā* or yellow from *nāgavrskha,* wheat-colour from *likuca, śveta* or white from *vakula* and butter-colour from *vaṭa* and other (*Pītika nāgavṛkṣiku godhumavarṇa laikuco śvetavakulo śeṣanāvanītavarṇa).*[20] The *patrorṇa* fabrics used to be manufactured in different places of the country, such as Magadha, Punḍra and Suvarṇakuḍya *(Māgadhika Pauṇḍrika Sauvarṇakuḍyaka ca patrorṇaḥ.*[21] It has also been clearly stated that the most excellent variety of *patrorṇa* was produced in Suvarṇakuḍya (*tasam Sauvarṇakuḍyaka śresṭha*) which may be identified with Kāmarūpa (Assam or Burma or *Suvarṇa-dvīpa* or *Karṇasuvarṇa.*[22] In this context, it may be noted that the red silk-cotton tree grew largely in Assam. The Nowgong copperplate grant of Balavarman of the 10th century AD refers to *Suvarṇavaṭa-vṛkṣa* and also of *Śālmalī-vṛkṣa* denoting red silk-cotton tree, i.e., *Bombaz Malabaricum.*[23] But it has been already pointed out that, according to Sastri, Suvarṇakuḍya was no other place than Karṇasuvarṇa in Mursidabad district where the aforesaid plants abound and where even today a fine variety of silk is produced.[24]

Another variety of fabric has been called *kauseya,* i.e., silk cloth manufactured from the aforesaid plant fibres (*taya kauseyam).*[25] From the description given in the *Arthaśāstra* it would appear that *Kauseya* linen was manufactured by fibres obtained from silk worm. Besides, Bāṇa in his *Harṣacarita* refers to some other kinds of fabrics like *aṃśuka, (vastra* in general, and *muslin* as translated by Cowell and Thomas), *netra* (short silk garment) and *vadam* (cotton cloth).[26] But the *Amarakoṣa* speaks of it as a synonym of *amsuka.*[27] *Kārpāsam vadaram,* i.e., of cotton is also to be found in the *Amarakoṣa.*[28]

It would be thus evident that out of several kinds of fabrics described by Kauṭilya at least four, i.e., *dukula, kṣauma, patrorṇa* and *kauseya* were varieties of silk-cloth made with yarn produced by worms. It is generally believed that silk was introduced in all countries from China. But the way Kauṭilya speaks of *Cinapaṭṭa (taya kauseyam cīnapaṭṭa cīnabhūmija vyākhyātaḥ)*[29] does not justify such a contention. In the first place, it is to be noted that in China, *resam* (silk) was produced from *tnut*-plant, i.e., mulberry (mulberry work), but in India i.e., in Magadha, Puṇḍra and Suvarṇakuḍya, *resam* was obtained from a number of trees enumerated above, excluding of course mulberry plants. Second, Chinese *resam* is white and it is to be dyed, if necessary. But in Bengal, *resam* of different colours is obtained from the leaves of various trees as described (i.e., from the leaves of various trees on which worms are reared). It naturally follows that *resam* cultivation in Bengal or India might have an indigenous origin. In a later period, i.e., after Kauṭilya, *resam* cultivation might have begun in other parts of India as well. An interesting reference in this context is to be found in the Mandasor inscription of the fifth century AD wherein we are told that traders in *resam* from Saurashtra established trading settlements in Mandasor.[30]

From the account given by Kauṭilya in his *Arthaśāstra* it would be quite evident that the villages of north, south and east Bengal were well-known for manufacturing varieties of textile. This is also clearly borne out by the testimony of the *Periplus of the Erythraean Sea* (the first century AD) and the *Natural History* of Pliny (the first century AD). The *muslins* called the *Gaugetic*, the finest and the most delicate of all fabrics, are not only mentioned but highly spoken of and appreciated by these treatises.[31] It has been said that 'a piece of Muslin was to be drawn through a finger-ring'. These fine *muslins* were also known under such names as *Textile Breeze, Evening Dew* or *Running Water*. In the Roman empire these *muslins* were called *ventus* textiles or *nebula*. Kālidāsa also refers to a very fine cotton and silk cloth which can be blown away by breath (*niḥśvāsahaya*).[32] This certainly refers to *muslins*. Even Hiuen Tsang speaks of various materials of which textiles were made, and in I-tsing's account there is a reference to the Buddhist monks wearing silk cloth.[33] Here, a particular reference may be made to the *Rāmcarita* of Sandhyākaranandi as well, wherein *lakuca, śrīphala, nāgakeśarī* and *vakulu* plants supplying raw materials for linen have been mentioned. The *Rāmcarita* also refers to 'variegated costly garments and youthful heavenly courtesans wearing their veritable apparels.'[34] Besides, instill later works like Sridhara's *Saduktikarṇāmṛta* and the *Caryyāgīti* there are poetic descriptions of raw materials and weaving of textiles.[35]

Besides, some Arab geographers and merchants like Sulaiman Ibn Khordabah and others from the ninth to the eleventh century AD, made several references to the various kinds of excellent textiles of Bengal.[36] Marco Polo, Ibn Batu tah, the Chinese writers Wang-Ta-Yuan and Fei-Hsin, Ma-Huan of the fourteenth and fifteenth century AD and Barbosa of the sixteenth century AD have referred to Bengal producing very fine cotton cloth.[37]

Besides all these references, the inscriptions from the fifth century onwards obtained from different parts of Bengal contain some casual mention of textiles. The Deopara inscription of the eleventh century AD refers to Lord Siva being dressed with a piece of variegated silken garment (*Citra Kṣauma*) in place of elephant's hide.[38] Not only that, the same inscription refers also to the cultivation of cotton, and cotton seeds (*Kārpāsa-vīja*).[39] It is further stated that cotton seeds were so familiar to the people that one could easily recognise pearls from their similarity with seeds of cotton.[40]

Literary texts contain references not only to textile products but also to raw materials and techniques of their manufacture. This would be evident from the *Caryyāgīti* of the tenth–eleventh century AD and *Saduktikarṇāmṛta* of the eleventh–twelfth century AD. In the former, there is a vivid description of the blossoming of cotton flowers and their cleaning with *dhuni* (bow) and also of spinning yarn.[41] Weaver's loom made on bamboo has been also referred to in the said work.[42] In the *Saduktikarṇāmṛta* we have a specific reference to the spinning of yarn from cotton-flower by a poor Brahmin lady in the following words:

Kārpāsathipracayanicita nidhana (or *nirdhana) śrotriyānām*
Yeṣāṁ vatyapraxitata kuṭiprāṇganata vabhūvuḥ.

In another śloka we have: Vāsamsukṣaṁ vapasi,[43]

From the above survey it may be reasonably contended that different regions of ancient Bengal excelled in producing textiles, cotton and silk of all kinds.

In this context, it is interesting to note that from indeterminable time some indigenous tribal communities of ancient Bengal like the *Puṇḍras, Vaṅgas, Śavaras, Niśādas, Kirātas, Caṇḍālas, Puliadas, Doms,* and others who settled long before the coming of the so-called Aryans in Bengal, attained great excellence in various sorts of crafts and industries including textiles. It would be evident from literary records that textiles produced by each of these communities have been also named after them. A reference to such names as *Vaṅgaka, Pauṇḍraka,* etc., has been already made. These are all generic names denoting also the regions of south, east and north Bengal. That the *Puṇḍras, Pulindas, Śabaras, Kirātas* and others were great experts in textile manufacture is evident from the references in the *Mahābhārata, Periplus of the Erythrean Sea, Caryyāpadas,* and so on.[44] The modern *Kirāntis,* generally identified with the ancient *Kirātas,* are experts in spinning, weaving, and dying cloth.[45]

A consideration of the ethnic characteristics of these people like the *Puṇdras, Niṣādas, Śabaras, Caṇḍāla* and others, excepting the *Kirātas,* would reveal that they belonged originally to the Australoid racial stock.[46] The Australoid affiliation of these peoples is further supported by the study of a few Bengali words denoting raw materials for textile products and manufactured fabrics, such as *kārpāsa* (cotton), *Śālmalī* (silk-cotton), etc. The Bengali words *kapas* and *simul* are said to be of Anstro-Asiatic origins. Not only that, even words like *pāṭ* (jute) and *parpaṭa (paṭṭavastra)* are of Austric derivation.[47] As to the *Kirātas* it would appear from the available evidences that they belonged to another ethnic stock, namely the Mongoloid.[48]

On the whole it would appear that the textile manufactures of ancient Bengal were the veritable contributions of the Australoid and the Mongoloid peoples. Besides textile manufacture, other rural crafts like those of clay, wood, metal, sugar, salt, stone, bamboo, ivory, conch, lac, shell, etc., are also the creations of the non-Aryan tribal communities of ancient Bengal. These peoples not only formed the very substratum of the Bengali people but also of the language and different traits and complees of the Bengali culture.

Notes

1. Macdonell and Keith. *Vedic Index*, vol. II, p. 291; Majumdar, ed., *The Vedic Age*, p. 393.
2. Shamnsastry, *Kautiliya's Arthaśāstra* Eng. trans, ch. XI, pp. 83–84; Basak. *Kautilāya Arthaśūtra*, pp. 52–3, 117–18.
3. *Aṣṭādhyāyī*, V.24; 3.158; IV.3.134; VII.3.5; VI.282; 1V.2.82; Agrawala, *India as Known to Paṇini*, pp. 248, 211, 214. Patañjali, *Mahābhaṣya*, IV.1.55; V.1.3; 1.1.11; V.13; V.2.4; 1.55; 1.2.43; Puri, *India in the Time of Patañjali*. pp. 103, 128, 134,185.
4. Shamasastry, op. cit.
5. Shyamakanta Vidyabhushan, *Manusaṁhitā*, XII, 64; X, 87.
6. Tarkaranta, *Amarakoṣābhidhānam*, p. 158.
7. Upadhyaya, *India in Kalidasa*, p. 198.
8. Samasastry, op. cit., p. 84.
9. *Mānasollāsa*, III, 107–20, Majumdar, ed., *The Struggle for Empire*, p. 518.
10. Basak, op. cit., p. 52.
11. Shamasastry, op. cit., p. 84.
12. Ibid.
13. Sastri, *Vanglar Prachin Gaurav* (in Bengali), p. 14.
14. Basak, op. cit., p. 117; Ray, *Bangalir Itihas*, p. 176.
15. Tarkaratna, op. cit.
16. Shamasastry, op. cit., p. 84; Basak, op. cit., p. 117.
17. Kane, *Harṣacarita*, Ucchvāsa, IV, notes, p. 55.
18. Shamasastry, op. cit.
19. Kane, op. cit., p. 55.
20. Basak, op. cit., p. 55.
21. Ibid.
22. Ibid.
23. *JASB*, LXVI, pt. I, p. 285.
24. Sastri, op. cit., p. 14.
25. Shamasastry, op. cit., p. 84; Basak, op. cit., pp. 53, 118.
26. Cowell and Thomas, *Harṣacarita*, p. 125.
27. Kane, op. cit., p. 55.
28. Tarkaratna, op. cit., p. 97.
29. Shamasastry, *Arthaśāstra*, Eng. trans, p. 84.
30. Fleet, *Gupta Ins.*, p. 86.
31. Schoff, *The Periplus of the Erythrae m Sea*, p. 47; Majumdar, *The Classical Accounts of India*, pp. 308, 338.
32. Upadhyaya, *India in Kalidasa*, pp. 198–99, 270.

33. Watters, *Yuan Chwang's Travels in India,* vol. I, pp. 147–8. 151, 287, 340. Beal, *Buddhist Record,* pp. 67–8.
34. Majumdar, Basak, et al., *Ramacharitam,* pp. 87, 93.
35. *Saduktikarṇāmṛta* of Srīdharadāsa, 2/84/6, 2/136/5, 5/31/2; Banerji, *Saduktikar-nāmṛta,* pp. 87, 93; Dasgupta, *Bauddha-dharma-o-Charyyagiti,* p. 123.
36. Majumdar, ed., *The Age of Imperial Unity,* p. 404; Ray, *Bangalir Itihas,* p. 178.
37. Marco Polo, vol. II, p. (115; Majumdar, *Struggle for Empire,* p. 16, Majumdar, *The Delhi Sultanate,* p. 644; Hussain, *The Rehla of Ibn Battuta,* p. 235; Gibb, *The Rehla of Ibn Batuta,* p. 267; Bagchi. *Extracts from Three Works Relating to Bengal; Ma-Huam, Visvabharati Annual,* vol. I, p. 127.
38. Majumdar, *Inscriptions of Bengal,* vol. III, verse 31, pp. 45, 49, 55, 56; Mukhopadhyaya and Maity, *Corpus of Bengal Inscriptions,* pp. 248–9, 255–7.
39. Ibid.
40. Ibid.
41. De, *Charyyagiti,* p. 118; Dasgupta, *Bauddha-dharma-o-Charyyagiti,* p. 123.
42. Ibid.
43. Banerji, *Saduktikarṇ-aṃrta,* p. 393; Kay, *Bangalir Itihas,* p. 180.
44. Tarkaratna Panchanam, *Mahābhārata,* Sabha Parva, 26–28, 30, p. 242, Schoff, *The Periplus of the Erythraean Sea,* p. 266. Chatterji, *Kiratajana-kriti,* p. 21; Majumdar, De, *Charyyagiti,* p. 118; Dasgupta, *Bauddha-dharma-o Charyyagiti,* p. 123.
45. Mitra, *Tribes and Castes of West Bengal,* 1951, p. 223.
46. Chanda, *The Indo-Aryan Races,* pp. 4–5, 7–8. *Mahābhārata,* XII, 59, 94–97; *Viṣ-nupurāṇa,* 1.13. *Bhāgavaṭa purāṇa,* IV. 14.44; *Padmapurāṇa,* II.27. 42–43; Cowell and Thomas, *Harṣacarita,* p. 230.
47. Sur, *History and Culture of Bengal,* p. 27.
48. Tarkaratna Panchanan, *Mahābhārata,* V.584; *Rāmāyaṇa,* Kiṣkindhākanda, 40, 27. 28: Vasu, *Social History of Kamarupa,* p. 92; Chatterji *Kiratajanakriti,* pp. 20, 23.

17

Basic Industries in Northern India on the Eve of Turko-Afghan Conquests

B.P. Mazumdar

On the analogy of European history it was presumed that the period between the eighth and the twelfth century was a dark age in India. Valuable researches into the dynastic history of the North and the South have filled up the blank in the political history of India left by earlier historians of India from the death of Harṣavardhan to the invasion of Muhammad Ibn Sain. But mere details of the wars and conquests of the rival princes ruling simultaneously in the different parts of the country cannot dispel the idea of the general backwardness of India during the aforesaid period. It is presumed that India was mainly an agricultural country with a feudal type of socio-political organisation. This idea, however, is proved to be erroneous when we make a close study of the technical literature produced during the age. Two outstanding works on such technical literature are Bhoja's *Yuktikalpataru* and Vāgbhata's *Rasaratnasanniccaya*. The former was written in the tenth century and the latter is believed to be a compilation of the thirteenth century. Like Vātsāyana's *Kāmasūtra* and Kauṭilya's *Arthaśāstra*, these two are a compendium of the knowledge gathered by previous writers in the field of the technique of production of industrial goods. They reveal a surprising state of manifold activities in the production of producer's goods. These works also supply valuable data on the production of consumer's goods. The technical processes described by these works could not have been possibly undertaken by small-scale farms. Minute subdivision of labour is presupposed in the production of many of those commodities, especially of the metallurgical goods. Many men must have been required to work under a common management, if not under the same roof. We cannot, however, expect production in middle ages on a scale similar to that prevailing today because of the lack of power resources. Still the production of many goods by the complex roundabout processes, described in these works, must evoke both admiration and astonishment, when we remember that it was not before the middle of the eighteenth century that England showed the way in the production of machine-made goods to the West.

*10th Session at Bombay, 1947.

(a) Metallic

Iron came to be used on a pretty large scale, and for a greater variety of purposes. Utbi in his *Tarikhi-Yamini*[1] informs us that on both sides of the city of Mathurā 'there were a thousand houses, to which ideal temples were attached, all strengthened from top to bottom by rivets of iron'. But Indian blacksmiths did not manufacture pegs and rivets only. They are known to have produced beams also. About 239 beams ranging upto 17ft long and up to 6" × 4" or 5 × 6 inches section have been counted in the Gunduchabari at Puri. This Puri temple was built c. AD 1174. Graves[2] gives a detailed record of those beams—95 beams at lintels of doors, and 114 below the temple. He has also measured the length, breadth and height of the beams at the lintels of doors in outer compound wall, inner and outer doors of the temple, and pillar plates. Iron beams are to be seen in the Bhuvaneswar temple which was constructed in the seventh century AD and also in the Koṇārka temple.[3] In the Koṇārka temple Stiriling[4] in 1824 counted 9 beams and Graves 29 beams. Dr R.L. Mitra noted the length of beams to be 21 ft with average cross-section 8 inches by 10 inches. But Graves found the largest beam being 35 ft long and 7 to 7½ inches square weighing 6000 lbs.

It may be mentioned in this connection that even today when India has made considerable progress in metallurgical skill, large beams are not being produced in sufficient quantity to meet even the most urgent needs of the government and educational institutions. The finds of these beams are not the only evidence of acquaintance of the North Indians with iron and steel, but literary works like *Rasendrasārasaṁgraha,* Tantric work of the thirteenth or fourteenth century, the *Yuktikalpataru* of Bhoja, the *Rasaratnasamuccaya* refer to the varieties of iron. The *Rasendrasdrasāṁgraha* quotes a passage from the *Yuktikalpataru.* Bhoja relates relative qualities of iron. *Krouñca* iron is twice better than *Sāmānya* iron, *Kaliṅga* iron 8 times better than *Krauñca* iron, *Bhadra* iron hundred times better than *Kaliṅga* iron, *Bajra* iron one thousand times better than *Bhadra, Pāndi* iron again hundred times better than *Bajra, Niraṅga* iron ten times better than *Pāndi* and *Kāntha* iron million times better than *Niraṅga* iron. These gradations of iron distinctly refer to pig, cast and wrought iron. But the author of the *Rasaratnasamuccaya* is more precise in describing the characteristics of each quality of iron. *Munda*[5] or cast iron has been classified thus: *Mṛdu* or easily malleable but unbreakable and glossy, *Kuntha*[6] which expands very little after hammering, and *Kadāra*[7] which is breakable. *Tikṣṇa* or steel has been classified into six varieties—*Khara,* Sāra, *liṛnnālu, Tarabhatta, Vājira* and *Kālalauha. Kania*[8] has also different varieties: *Bhrāmaka* or iron which moves all other iron, *Cambaka* and *Karṣaka,* i.e. magnetic iron, *Drāvaka* or iron which at once melts, *Romakāntā,* i.e. iron which when broken shoots forth hair-like filaments. So these characteristics of iron and steel significantly point out that the manufacture of iron reached a high stage of development and the workers were acquainted with the science of metallurgy. Sir P.C. Ray[9] brought in several evidences from Sanskrit books regarding the process of killing iron. The Kashmir manuscript of *Vṛnda* prescribes that iron iṣ to be lighted first and then 'macerated in the juice of the emblic myrobalan and trewia nudiflora add exposed to the sun, and again to be macerated in the juice of certain other plants and then to be rubbed in a mortar.'[10] Cakrapāṇi of the eleventh century AD prescribes a better method. After the bar of iron is rubbed with impalpable powder, as described by Vṛnda, it is then heated to fusion point and plunged into the decoction of the myrobalans and roasted repeatedly in a crucible. The *Rasaratnascimuccaya*[11] informs us that if a piece of iron is rubbed with cinnabar weighing one-twentieth of the weight of that iron, lemon juice and sour gruel, and roasted in a covered crucible forty times, *Kantam, Tīkṣṇam* and *Mundam* are killed. *Tīkṣ. na* iron can also be powdered if it is repeatedly heated and plunged into water.[12] The medieval blacksmiths were so expert in melting, iron that fine powdered iron could pass through linens.[13]

Crucibles, words and swater-vessels were manufactured from iron. The making of the *Jāranāya Yantram* has been mentioned in the *Rasārṇava*[14] and *Ranaratnasamuccaya.*[15] Iron crucibles were twelve digits long. Regarding the ingredients for crucibles, Vāgbhata[16] recommends: 'Earth which is heavy and of a pale colour, sugar or earth from an ant-hill or earth which has been mixed with the burnt husks of paddy, fibres of hemp plant, charcoal and horsedung pounded in an iron mortar and also rust of iron, are to be recommended for crucible-making.' The Edilpur plate[17] of Keśavasena mentions 'water-vessels of iron.'

Weapons of war such as arrowheads, spearheads and swords have been mentioned by a host of medieval Muslim historians. Manufacture of swords is an old industry of India. Utbi[18] says that the soldiers of Brahmanpal, the son of Anandpal used white swords, blue spears and yellow coats of mail. White swords evidently mean that the best steel[19] was used in the manufacture of sword, which when swung appeared to be only a flash of light, a radiant whiteness. Nizami in his *Taj-ul Manasir*[20] has given a more vivid picture of Indian swords used by the soldiers of Gwalior. 'That sword was coloured of caerulean blue, which from its blazing lustre resembled a hundred thousand Venuses and Pleiades, and it was a well tempered horse-shoe of fire, which with its wound exhibited the peculiarity of lightning and thunder; and in the perfect weapon the extreme of sharpness lay hid, like (poison in) the fangs of a serpent, and (the water of the blade) looked like ants creeping on the surface of a diamond.' This is not a mere poetic hyperbole. The elaborate description of the processes of manufacturing arms and weapons found in Sanskrit technical literature proves the truth of the statement made by Nizami. It is a well-known fact that industrial skill is developed and perfected by the localisation of industries. Certain localities specialised only in the making of swords. Thus

Yuktikalpataru[21] states that Benares, Magadha, Nepal, Saurāṣṭra and Kaliṇga had a reputation for producing swords. According to Sārangadhara[22] who flourished in the thirteenth or fourteenth century, Khati-Khattara, Rishi, Vanga, Surpāraka, Videha, Madhyamagrāma, Vedieśa, Sahagrāma, and Kāliñjara were the centres for manufacture of swords. The best swords were of Benares, Saurāṣṭra, Rishika and Aṅga and the swords of Kalinjar could stand the test of time. A comparative study of the works of different periods shows that some localities developed their skill in course of time, while others fell into decay. Thus according to the *Yuktikalpataru,*[23] the swords of Aṅga were light, dirty and blunt-edged, hut in course of next three hundred years, i.e., by the thirteenth century when Sārangadhara[24] is supposed to have written his work, the Aṅga swords became famous for their sharpness, strength and excellent handle. The decadence of Magadha in the medieval age is well known and a reference to the bad type of swords produced here, by Bhoja[25] in the tenth century, illustrates the decay of once famous industrial city, Bhoja in the chapter on *Khaḍgaparīkṣa* dealt on the method of distinguishing between bad and good swords by the sound produced by swords. Sārangadhara[26] devotes nine *ślokas* on swords of good quality and nine on bad quality. That sword which '*āhate yatra madhurodhvaniḥ samuyajātelpūjyaḥ sa khaṅgo nṛpateā śatru sañcayanāśana.h*' is worshipped by kings and that which is '*tiryag yasya bhaveccihṇamapi sarvvāṇgagocaram/khaṅgāmaṁtaṁ nṛpatir-dūradeve vivarjayet*' should be thrown away by the king. Other weapons[27] of war were bows and arrows, *ardhacandra, nārāca* and *paraśu.*

Copper

India is deficient even today in copper but the people in middle ages made the best possible use of this precious metal. They had presumably no knowledge of the copper ores of Chota Nagpur, but they utilised the resources of Nepal and also imported it from foreign countries. That is why Vāgbhaṭa says that copper could be had from mines and also from extraction of other minerals. The best copper ore was that of Nepal[28] and other mines were located in the Mlecca countries.

Sulphide and sulphate are two compounds of copper. Vṛnda says that *parpatitāmram* or sulphide could be prepared artificially. 'Sulphur, copper and pyrites are to be pounded together with mercury and subjected to roasting in a closed crucible.'[29] But in the eleventh century we learn from Cakrapāṇi that the compound could be prepared in a pure state. He writes: 'Take a thin leaf of Nepalese copper and embed it in powdered sulphur. The substances are to be placed inside saucer-shaped earthenware vessels and covered with another. The rims are luted with sugar or powdered rice-paste. The apparatus is heated in a sand-bath for three hours. The copper thus prepared is pounded.'[30]

Copper could be extracted from blue vitriol by heating with organic substances and borax in closed crucible. *Rasārṇava* and *Rasaratnasamuccaya*[31] prescribe the following formula: 'Take blue vitriol one-fourth of its weight of borax and soak the mixture in the oil expressed from seeds of *pcngamia-glabra* one day only and then place it in a covered crucible and heat in the charcoal fire—by this process an essence is obtained from it of the beautiful appearance of coccinella insect.'

Copper could also be extracted from *makṣika* which has been identified with pyrites and *vimala*. In *Rasārṇava*[32] the following formula is prescribed for extraction from *makṣika*. '*Makṣika* repeatedly steeped in honey, oil from *ricinus communis*, urine of cow, clarified butter and extract of bulbous root of *musa sapientum* when gently roasted in a crucibe yields an essence in the shape of copper.' The formula for the extraction of copper from *vimala* has been given in *Rasaratnākara*, *Rasārṇava* and the *Rasaratna-samuccaya*.[33] '*Vimala* digested with alum, green vitriol, borax and watery liquid extracted from *moringapter*, *musa sapientum* and finally roasted in a covered crucible in combination with the ashes of schrebera-swiet, yields an essence in the shape of *Candraka*.'

Just as copper could be prepared artificially from pyrites, blue vitriol or borax, so other substances like bell-metal, *vartaloham* could be prepared from mixture of copper and tin and zinc. *Rasarainasamuccaya*[34] prescribes eight parts of copper and two parts of tin for making *Kāṁsa*. *Vartalohan*.[35] could be produced from mixture of *kāṁsya*, copper, *pittala*, iron and lead.

Mica

Besides iron and copper other metals were also pressed into service. Mica in which India has got almost a world mdnopoly was utilised for medicinal purposes. A close study of the *Rasaratnasamuccaya*[36] reveals three varieties of mica, namely, *pinākam*, *nāgamaṇḍukam* and *vajram*. Their colours were either white or red yellow or black. That mica whose layers could be easily detached were preferred. The speciality of mica as known to them was that mica did not combine with mercury. But that which could take up mercury was used with other metals and administered in medicine.

Mirrors

The artistic excellence and ingenuity of Indian workers in metals is nowhere better illustrated than by their production of mirrors, from brass. The polish on the brass was so brilliant that faces could be reflected on it. There is no definite mention of glass mirrors in medieval literature. But it can be gathered from the *ślokas* that mirrors were manufactured from eight minerals.[37] Mirrors were known by different names—*Bhavya*,[38] *Vijaya*[39] and *Pauruṣa*.[40] According to *Vīramitrodaya* mirrors were made of bell-metal. There were two current varieties—*Sapāda,* which has stand at the back of it, and *Sanāla* which has stand on the lower side of it.

(b) Transport

Transport facilities are essential for the industrial development of a country. The medieval Indians could not indeed invent railways or steamships, but they did not depend entirely on the slow and costly method of transporting goods by roads on the back of animals. Large-scale production necessitated transporting of heavy goods by rivers on boats. Boat-making, therefore, was much more important for industry and commerce of the country than today.

Boats were usually classified into four categories,[41] e.g. light, soft and pieceable wood belongs to Brahmanic class; light and yet strong and not easily pieceable belongs to the Kṣatriya class; which is soft and yet heavy belongs to Vaiśya class and which is strong and heavy is Śūdra. For boats Bhoja recommends the Kṣatriya wood. Bhoja mentions about twenty types of boats according to size—ordinary ones are Bhīmā, Kṣudrā, Madhyamā, Capalā, Patalā, Bhayā, Dīrghā, Patrapuṭā, Garbharā and Mantharā[42] which are not sea-going; the special ones are Dīrghikā, Tarini, Lolā, Gatvarā, Gāmini, Tarī, Jaṅghāla, Plāvinī, Dhariśī, Veginī.[43] Of these Bhīmā, Bhayā, Garbharā Lolā, Gāminī, Plāvinī were troublesome.[44] Elaborate descriptions of painted rooms have been given by him.[45] There were also boats meant for fighting on seas. Such sea-going vessels have also been referred to by Medhātithi and also in a copperplate inscription of Dharmapāla.[46]

Besides these basic industries numerous references are found regarding the existence of textile, wooden, jewellery and other consumers' goods. These are too well known to be described in this brief article. The conclusion which forces itself on the mind of a student of socio-economic organisation of this period is that the wealth of India was derived as much from industrial production as from the agricultural one. The vast wealth which attracted the invaders from beyond the Hindukush could not have been produced by a mere agricultural community. History abounds in instances of a highly developed industrialised community being overthrown by rude, sturdy and unsophisticated invaders from abroad. As the Western Roman Empire fell into the hands of the Visigoths and Lombards, the Byzantine Empire was overthrown by the Turks and the Gupta Empire by the Hūṇas, so also the principalities in medieval India succumbed to the attacks of the less civilised Turko-Afghans. But the conquest of India by the Turko-Afghans could not be completed in course of a century or two. The explanation for this long-drawn conflict lies in the vast industrial resources of the country. These enabled the fighting classes of India to give a stiff, though isolated, resistance for centuries to the invaders.

Notes

1. Elliot and Dowson, vol. II, p. 44.
2. *Journal of the Iron and Steel Institute,* vol. LXXXV, no. 1,1912, pp. 200–2.
3. Koṇārka—the black pagoda of Orissa.
4. *Asiatic Researches,* XV, p. 330.
5. *Rasaratnasamuccaya,* Bk. V, *ślokas (śl.)* 71–72.
6. Ibid.
7. Ibid.
8. Ibid, *śl,* 84–89.
9. *History of Hindu Chemistry.*
10. Ibid., pp. 59–60.
11. *Rasaratnasamuccaya,* V, *śl,* 113–14.
12. Ibid., *sl,* 107–8.
13. Ibid., 134–37.
14. *Rasārṇava,* Bk. IV.7.
15. *Rasaratnasamuccaya,* Bk. X, 5–6.
16. *IB,* 128.
17. *Agni, P.,* 21, 245.
18. Elliot and Dowson, II, p. 33.
19. *Yuktikalpataru, sl,* 24.
20. Elliot and Dowson, II, p. 227.
21. *Yuktikalpataru,* p. 170, *sl,* 24–29.
22. *Sāraṅgadharapaddhati,* cd. Peterson, *sl,* 4672–79.
23. *Yuktikalpataru,* p. 170, *śl,* 27.
24. *Sāraṅgadharapaddhati, sl,* 4676.
25. *Yuktikalpataru.*
26. Ibid., *sl,* 4658, 4666.
27. *Yuktikalpataru, Athāstrayukti, sl,* 28–29.
28. Book, V, *sl,* 44
29. Ray, op. cit., I, p. 58.
30. Ibid., p. 62
31. *Ras.,* II, 133–34.
32. *Rasārṇava,* VII, *sl,* 12–13; *Rasaratnasamuccaya,* II, 89–90.
33. *Rasārṇava, Rasaratnasamuccaya,* II, 103–4, *Rasaratnākara,* II, 35–36.
34. V.205.
35. Ibid., X, *śl,* 212–16.
36. II.5–14.
37. *Yuktikalpataru:* अय वितानलक्षणम्, *sl,* 10.
38. Ibid., *sl,* 6.
39. Ibid , *sl,* 8.
40. Ibid., *sl,* 8.
41. Ibid., अय निष्पादपानोद्देश:, 83–86.
42. Ibid., *śl,* 92.
43. Ibid., *śl,* 97.
44. Ibid., *śl,* 94, 100.
45. Ibid., *sl,* 9, 19, 20–23.
46. *Gauḍa-lekhamālā,* p. 14.

PART 5

Aspects of Exchange in Early Indian Economy: Trade, Organization of Traders, Interest, Coinage

18

Trade and Commerce from Pāṇini's Asṭādhyāyī

Vasudeva S. Agrawala

PĀṆINI IS acquainted with a wide sphere of trading and commercial activities of the people. He mentions both money economy and barter, traders and trade routes, sale and purchase transactions, shops and saleable commodities, taxes on trade and profit, and also refers to banking and loans.

Vyavahāra

Trade and commerce are implied in the general term *vyavahāra* (II.3.57). The essence of all trade activities is graphically expressed in the term *kraya-vikraya* (IV.4.13), i.e. sale and purchase transaction. *Paṇa* was used as synonym of *vyavahāra* (II.357) which is explained by *Kāśikā* as constituting *kraya-vikraya.* It appears that *vyavahāra* had reference to the wider sphere of export and import activities, viz., commerce, whereas *paṇa* denoted sale and purchase of articles in markets and shops as indicated in the term *paṇya* meaning saleable goods (IV.4.51).

Traders

Merchants are referred to as *vaṇik* (III.3.52) and as *vaṇija* (VI. 2.13). These words seem to have been applied to traders without distinction of caste, although it may be presumed that a large percentage of trade volume was controlled by the Vaiśyas. There must have been several categories of merchants according to the nature of their business and the manner of financing trade propositions. For example, an ordinary shopkeeper who made a living by selling and buying things was called *kraya-vikrayika* (IV.4.13), whereas a merchant who financed business with his money was called *vasṇika* (IV.4.13), much more

*5th Session at Hyderabad, 1941.

important were those who carried on commercial activities in a corporation or *saṁsthāna* from which they were known as *saṁsthānika* (IV.4.72). This appears to be but another name for a *sārthaka* or *sārthavāha* frequently mentioned in the *Jātakas* as merchants pooling their resources to equip united caravans of several hundred wagons. Pāṇini also refers to persons whose nature of business connected them with forest thickets (*kaṭhina*) and with the operation of mines and seams (*prastara . . . vyayaharati,* IV. 4.72).

Pāṇini refers to the practice of traders deriving their names on the basis of articles in which they dealt, and secondly from the countries frequently visited by them on business errands (*Gantavya paṇyam vaṇije.* VI-2.13). The second factor, viz., the naming of merchants from the names of countries to which they would habitually go to transact business, is indicative of an interprovincial commerce existing in a flourishing state. The three examples in *Kāsîkā,* viz., *Madra-vaṇija, Kāśmira-vaṇija, Gāndhārīvaṇija,* provide a glimpse of that inter-provincial hegemony in the domain of commerce to which references are found in ancient literature. The *Jātakas* supplement the details by saying that merchants from the eastern country preceded on trading missions to remote destinations in the north-west of India. Indeed, the principle of nomenclature envisaged in Pāṇini's rule can operate more naturally in the cases of only those merchants who do business with distant countries.

Business Methods

Business was transacted in specified markets and shops known as *āpaṇa* (III.3.119, *etya tasmin-āpaṇānta ityāpaṇah Kāsîkā*) and the articles of trade were called *paṇya* (III.1.101, *paṇitavya*). It was necessary that the articles meant for sale should be properly displayed in shops which were then called *krayya,* i.e. saleable (*Krayyas-tadarthe,* VI.1.82). There were certain regulations of trade which must have been observed in respect of articles pronounced *krayya.* For example, a *paṇya-kambala* is stated to be of a certain standard, weighing a *kambalya* measure of wool. Generally *paṇya* seems to be a term of wider application than *krayya.*

The Sūtra *Tena krītam* (V.1.37) 'purchased with that' points out to a well-established practice of sale and purchase of goods in consideration for a fixed price paid by the buyer to the seller. There is a reference in Pāṇini to standard currency in gold, silver and copper which was the normal medium of exchange. Wealth measured in terms of current gold coins called *niṣka* is referred to (V.2.119). The system of barter also prevailed. The article purchased in the market usually derived an epithet from the price paid for them. A considerable variety of such names is reflected in the *Aṣṭādhyāayī;* thus we find mention of articles for which the price paid was one *niṣka* (V.1.20), two *niṣkas,* three *niṣkas*

(V.1.30), one or one and a half *viṃśatika* coin (V.1.32), one *śatamāna* (V.1.27), one *kārsāpaṇa,* or a thousand *kārsāpaṇas* (V.1.29), one *śāna* coin or a *pāda* or a *māṣaka* of copper (V.1. 34–35) and so on in sub-multiples and multiples of various denominations. The exact significance of Pāṇinian coinage has already been discussed[1] and it is enough to point out here that articles of many descriptions ranging in price from a small copper pice to a thousand or more silver rupees were the subject of sale and purchase transactions in market places.

Earnest-money

In making stipulations of sale and purchase it is customary for the buyer to pay something in advance as earnest-money which is considered as a guarantee of good faith. The seller is bound by it as much as the buyer, for, if he has accepted earnest money for a certain article, he becomes bound to deliver it only to the first buyer. Pāṇini refers to this custom as *satiyapayati* (III. 1.25) or *satyakaroti* (V.4.66) which is explained by *Kāsîkā* as 'giving a pledge to purchase' *mayaitat kretavyamitit tathyam karotia.* In a third Sutra Pāṇini refers to the earnest-money as *sātyaṁkara* (VI. 3.70) which corresponds to Hindi (##) or part of the settled price paid in advance.[2] In the village economy the system of *satyapa. na* is extended even to hired workers as confectioners engaged to work for a marriage feast.

Capital and Profit

The motive of earning profit (*lābha*) is found at the root of all business dealings. Pāṇini draws a clear distinction between the capital invested called *mūla,* and the gross profit earned thereby *mūlena anamya* called *mūlya* (IV.4.91). He prescribes another meaning for *mūlya* in the same Sutra which states that *mūlya* is that which is equivalent to the capital invested (*mūlena samam,* (IV.4.97), which amounts to saying that *mūlya* is that which is good for the price paid. The first meaning of *mūlya,* viz. sale price inclusive of profit, is justified from the point of view of the *mūla* or cost price of the seller, and the second meaning from the point of view of the buyer who judges the fairness of a transaction in securing equivalent 'value' for the price paid *mūlena samam.* Reference is also made to a custom by which a transaction was named by the amount of profit earned from it (*Tadasmin vṛddhyāya-lābha śulkopada diyate,* V.I. 47), on which the *Kāsîkā* cites *pañcaka, saptdka, satya* or *satika,* and *sahasra,* i.e. a deal resulting in a profit of 5, 7, 100, or 1,000 silver rupees. There is a statement in the *Arthaśāstra* placing the profit of a middle man at 5 per cent.[3]

Vasna

It is an older word than Panini. In the *Ṛgveda* and later *Samhitās* it denoted the 'price' paid for anything or its 'value', or the thing as an object of purchase, 'ware'.[4] Pāṇini discusses the implications of *vasna* in three different Sūtras (IV.4.13; V. 1.51; V.l.56) and the meaning uniformly suggested appears to be value or sale price realised: In the first instance *vasnika* trader is contrasted with *krayavikrayika* (IV.4.13); the former was a person interested in the profits of the sale-proceeds only, and not concerned with sale and purchase, while the latter was engaged in conducting actual business transaction. Thus a *vasnika* trader owned only a financial interest (*vasnena jīvati*) in the *vyavahāra* carried on by others. Second, the Sūtra *So'syamsa-vasna bhṛtāyaḥ* (V. 1.56) seeks to regulate the designation of a *vasnika* trader in accordance with his *vasna* or share in the sale proceeds. For example, one entitled to a thousand rupees as his share in the value realized was called *sahasra,* which is conceivable only in the case of joint or corporate business. Third, a *vasnika* merchant is distinguished from a *dravyaka* (V. 1.56), the former being the name of the trader who 'carries away, conveys or brings' (*harati, vahati, avahati,* V.1.50) the *vasna* or the sale-price, and the latter of the merchant who did the same with respect to merchandise or goods (*dravya*). The distinction of meaning may be clearly understood by applying *dravyaka* to a trader on his outward journey conveying merchandise for sale, the epithet *vasnika* to the merchant on his homeward march returning with the sale proceeds. It is strange that *vasna* does not occur in the *Arthaśāstra* where it is replaced by the more popular word *mūlya.* Its use appears to have dropped out in the post-Pāṇinian period as Patañjali uses it only once independently of S''utra explanation in the sense of price (*anyena hi vasnenaikam gāṁ krinati, anyena dvau, anyena trin, Bhāṣya,* I.95).

Taxes on Trade

The general name *śulka* seems to refer to the taxes on trade in the form of customs, excise, and octroi charges Pāṇini lays down that the amount of *śulka* paid gives a name to the consignment in relation to which it is paid (V. 1.47), and as specific examples of octroi payments he mentions half-a-*kārṣāpaṇa* called *Ardha* (V.I.48) and also *Bhāga* (V. 1.49). The custom barrier known as *śulkaśālā* was one of the important sources of income to the state, the proceeds of which were called *śaulkaśālika* (stock example on IV.3.75. *Thagaya-sthānebhyaḥ*. Pāṇini makes a general reference to taxes levied in the eastern part of India amongst which Patañjali includes also toll taxes as exemplified in the illustration *avikatoraṇaḥ* which shows that one ram was the tax levied on a flock of sheep (VI.3.10, *Karanamni ca Pracam haladau: Bhāṣya,* III.144). It would appear from other illustrations cited in the *Kāśikā* that in the north of India

(Udīcam) one animal or cattle head was charged for one herd of cattle (*yuthapaśu*); other such taxes mentioned are *nadidohani*, one pailful of milk paid at river ferry; *driṣadimāṣakaḥ*, a *māṣaka* coin collected per hand mill; *mukuṭe kārṣāpaṇam*, one *kārṣāpaṇa* coin raised per head; *hale dvipādika*, two *pāda* coins realised per ploughshare, which seems to have been a tax on agriculture. Patañjali considers these to be names of taxes current in *loka* or society.

Trade-Routes

Reference is found in the *Aṣṭādhyāyī* to the existence of roads leading from one city to another (IV.3.85) which were marked into well-defined stages (II.3.136). Kātyāyana mentions a full complement of trade routes leading through forests *(kāntārapatha)*, Jungle- thickets (*jāṅgalupatha*) or trade-routes connected with land (*sthala patha)* and others which were used for riverine and sea-borne trade *(vāripatha)*. He also teaches that goods imported along these particular routes were known by the respective route names. The *Kāntārapatha* seems to be the name of the prominent trade-route leading across the great forest-belt of Central India which as we know from Buddhist literature once connected Kosambi with Pratiśṭhāna and Bharukaccha. In the same context are mentioned *ajapatha* and *śaṅkupatha* which appear to be routes leading via mountainous country (V. 1.77) *(Bhāṣya*, II.358). He also makes the important statement that liquorice (*madhuka*) and pepper *marica* were imported by the trade route known as *Shtalapatha*. But most important of all is the reference by Pāṇini to the great arterial trade route known as the *Uttarāpatha* which was in ancient times the main channel for the flow of India's overland commerce to the West.

Uttarāpatha

Pāṇini refers to articles imported (*āhṛta*) by the *Uttarāpatha* route designated as *Auttarapathika* (## V.1.77). This word also denoted those who travelled along the *Uttarāpatha* (##). According to Tarn, the Oxo Caspian trade-route from India to the West by the Oxus and the Caspian was called the northern route and is given twice by Strabo (II.73; XI.509) and once by Pliny.[5] 'Strabo, speaking of the Oxus (Amu Daria), states (XI.509) that it formed a link in an important chain along which Indian goods were carried to Europe through Caspian and the Black Sea. He cites as one of his authorities Patrocles, who was an admiral in the service of Antiochus 1, and thus makes it clear that the route was a popular one early in the third century BC.[6] Strabo also wrote that 'The Oxus is sufficiently navigable for the Indian trade to be carried across to it and to be easily brought down the river to the Hyrcanian (sea) and the places beyond as far as the Black Sea by the way of rivers'.[7] It seems highly probable that this northern route was the one which is mentioned by Pāṇini as the *Uttarāpatha*.

On the Indian side this great commercial route was connected with Pāṭaliputra and ultimately extended to the mouth of the Ganges. Fortunately the Greeks have left a detailed account of stages traversed on this road. As Rawlinson writes: 'The first thing which struck Megasthenes on entering India, was the Royal Road from the frontier to Pāṭaliputra, down which the envoy must have travelled to the capital. It was constructed in eight stages, and ran from the frontier town of Peukelaotis (Skt. Puṣkalāvati) to Taxila: from Taxila, across the Indus to the Jihlam; then to the Beas, near the spot where Alexander erected his altars. From here it went to the Sutlej: from the Sutlej to the Jamna: and from the Jamna, probably via Hastināpura, to the Ganges From the Ganges the road ran to a town called Rhodopha, and from Rhodopha to Kalinīpaxa probably Kanyakubja or Kanauj. From Kanauj it went to the mightly town of Prayāga at the junction of the Ganges and the Jamna, and from Prayāga to Pāṭaliputra. From the capital it continued its course to the mouth of the Ganges, probably at Tamluk, though Megasthenes never traversed the last stage of the road. At every mile along the road was a stone to indicate the by-roads and distances.'[8] This great highway of commerce passed through many important *janapadas* and ancient capitals mentioned by Pāṇini and Patañjali, such as Bālhīka, Kapisi, Puṣkalāvatī, Maśakavatī, Takṣaśilā, Śākala, Hastināpura, Kauśāmbī, Kāsī and Pāṭaliputra. Along this great highway passed up and down long caravans transporting a considerable volume of commercial merchandise (*bhāṇḍa*) (III. 1.20), and on it was situated Udbhāṇḍa, an emporium of transhipment on the Indus.

Articles of Trade

The list of names of saleable articles mentioned by Pāṇini in the context '*Tadasya paṇyam*' (IV.4 51) is not exhaustive; it contains only a few names, e.g, *lavaṇa* (salt, IV.4.52). perfumes like *kisara, tagara, guggulu, usira* (IV.4 53) *salalu* (an unidentified name of perfume, IV.4 54). The *lavaṇika* or salt-dealer seems to have developed later on into a separate caste which may be recognised in such forms as the *lavaniya* or *luniya*.

But in order to become fully conversant with the contents of commercial life we should explore the range of articles that were in use in everyday life as the two stand closely interrelated, the purpose of trade being to cater to the material needs of society. If we examine the *Aṣṭādhyāyī* from this point of view we are able to gather an interesting and varied list of objects that were in use. For example, we find mention of the following—Fabrics of silk *(kauṣeya,*

IV.3.42), wool and woollen stuffs (*ūrṇa* and *aurṇaka*, IV.3. 158), linen and linen goods (*uma* and *auma*, 1V.3.158), hemp (bhaṅga V.2.4); cotton (*tula*, III.1.25; *Kārpāsī*, IV.3.136) and cloth (*vastra*, II. 1.21); articles of dress (*upasamvyana*, I.1.36, *ācchādana*, IV.3.143) like *bṛhatika* (V.4 6), blankets like *paṇya-kambala* conforming to a set standard (VI.2.42; IV. 1.42), *pravara* (II.3.54) and *pāṇ. du-kambala* (IV.2.11) imported from the country of Gandhāra or Uḍḍīyāna; deer skins (*ajina*, VI.2.194): skins of tigers and leopards (*dvaipa*, *vaiyaghra*, IV.2.12) used as upholstering material for royal chariots; dye stuffs (*rāga*) like lac (*lākṣā*, IV.2.2), orpiment (*rocana*, IV.2.2), madder (*mañjiṣṭha*, VIII.3.97) and indigo (*nīli*, IV. 1.42); sacks and grain containers (*avapanas*) as *goni* (IV. 1, 42); leather-containers in big and small sizes (*kutu* and *kutupa*, V.3.89); leather goods as shoes (*Uuanah*, V.1.14), straps and thongs (*naddhri*, III.2.182, *vardhra*, IV.3.151); iron chains (*śṛnkhala*, V.2.79), spikes (*avaḥ-śūla*, V.2.76), tools and instruments like sickle (*datra*, III. 1.18), ploughshare (*kuśî*, IV. 1.42), yoke (*yuga*) axle (*akṣa*, VI. 3.104); spades (*khanitra*, III.2.184), oars (*aritra*, III.2.184), loom (*tantra*, V.2.70) and shuttle (*pravaṇi*, IV.4.160); food-stuffs like *guḍa* (IV.4.103) *phanita* (VII.2.18), milk curds, butter (*kṣira*, *dadni*, *haiyangavina*, V 2.23), vegetables (*śāka*, VI.2.128), cereals, and pulses (*dhānyas*); utensils and pottery (*amatra*, IV.2.14; *kaulālaka*, IV. 3.118) of various sizes to cook different quantities (III.2.33); intoxicating drinks like *madya* (III.I 100), *maireya* (VI.2.70), *surā* (II.4.25) prepared in distilleries (*auti*, V.2.112) and sold in booths (*sūṇḍika*, IV.3.76) and the costly *kapisāyana* imported from Kapisi in north Afghanistan (IV.2 99); gold and silver ornaments like *karṇika*, *lalāṭika* (V.3.65) and gems (*maṇi*) as *śasyaka* (V.2.68), *lohitaka* (V.4.30) and *vaidurya* (IV.3.84); metals as gold, silver copper, lead and tin; arms and weapons (*śāstra*, III.2.182) as spears (*śakti*, IV.4.59), javelins (*kasu*, V.3.90), battle-axe (*parasvidha*, IV. 4.58), bows (*dhanu*), arrows (*iṣu*, VI.2.107) and coats of mail (*varma*, III. 1.25), musical instruments like lute (*vīṇā*, III.3.65), tabon (*madduka*), cymbals (*jharjhara*, IV.4.56): and miscellaneous objects like images (*pratikṛti*, V.3.96), garlands (VI.3 65), perfumery (IV.4.53, IV.4.54), balances (*tula*, IV.4.91) weights (*māna*), measures (*parimāṇa*), coins and various conveyances like wagons (*śakaṭa*), chariots (*ratha*) and boats (*nau*, IV.4.7, etc.).

Mention should also be made of trade in cattle and animals. The *Kāśikā* illustrating Pāṇini, VI.2 13 (*Gantavya-paṇyam vaṇije*) particularly mentions merchants who dealt in cows and bulls (*govaṇija*) and horses (*aśva-vaṇija*). Pāṇini himself refers to the famous breed of bulls from the Śālva country which are even today celebrated as Nagauri bulls (VI.2 136) and also to the breed of mares from across the Indus (*para-vāḍava*, VI.2.42). There were some articles trade in which was banned to persons of higher caste. The rule III.2.93 regulates the formation of names of those engaged in unapproved trades, e.g. *soma-vikrayī*, *rasa-vikrayī*. The selling of the *soma* plant and liquids such as cow's milk is also banned in the law-books (cf. *Manu*, III.1.69; IX.86–89). The above description of articles that were in everyday use bears testimony, to the high development of economic life. To sustain the needs of a commerce bearing extensive trade relations between distant parts of the country it was necessary to maintain over-flowing stocks (cf. the denominative *rool saṁbhāṇḍayate; samacayana* or stocking, III, 1.20) in shops (*āpaṇa*, III.3.119) and warehouses (*bhāṇḍāgaras*, IV.4.70).

Exchange and Barter

Economic life in Pāṇinian society was governed both by money economy and by the system of barter. There is evidence on the one hand of a well-established currency in gold and silver with smaller coins which served as the media of exchange; there is on the other hand a reference to a system which worked by the mutual exchange of goods in kind instead of cash. It is usually seen that in rural economy barter is preferred not only as a necessity but also as a virtue for the convenience which it confers on simple rural folks.

The system of barter is referred to as *nimāna* which in fact denotes the article which serves as the *mulya* or the medium of exchange to purchase the thing intended. Barter works on this simple pattern that there is *nimāna* on the side of the purchaser and its counterpart *nimeya* with the seller. A ratio of price is determined between the cwo and mutual transfer of goods thus takes place. It is the object of Pāṇini's rules V.2.47. (*Saṁkhyāya guṇasya nimāne mayat*) to regulate the formation of the barter ratio. It is expressed by a numeral indicating that the price of a portion of one thing is equal to so many equal portions of the other. For example, when two parts of barley is the price of one part of *uadasvit*, the expression is *dvimayam udasvid yavānām*, literally "*Udasvit* is *dvimaya* or two times the value of *yava*." The comparison must be made with one portion of *nimeya* (thing to be bought), with several portions of the *nimāna*. The ratio must be X: 1, but never X: 2 or X: 3, etc., in which X denotes the *nimāna*.

Nature of Barter Transactions

The range of articles covered by barter mostly relates to simple things of ordinary use in village life, e.g. food, clothing, and animals. In one *Sūtra* Pāṇini refers to *vasana* or a piece of cloth as medium of exchange, the thing purchased in exchange for cloth being called *vasana* (V.1.27). Most probably the weavers had recourse to this means of barter. Probably *vasana* denoted a piece of cloth of standard size and weight as may be inferred by the current phrase *vasanarṇa (vasana + ṛṇa)* meaning the amount of loan incurred for the purchase of *vasana*. An analogous instance is *karnbalarṇa*, (loan for a blanket) in which the word *Kambala* as we know from Pāṇini stood for a standard blanket of 100 palas or 5 seers of wool. There is also reference to articles purchased for one *gopuccha* (*go-pucchena krītam gau-puchchhikam*, V. 1.19). Dr. Bhandarkar takes *go-puccha* to mean literally the tail of a cow as a circulating medium, and the remarks that '*go-puccha* has to be understood in the primary sense of a cow's tail, however, polluting and revolting such a custom may now appear to us.'[9] I am, however, disposed to understand *go-puccha* in the sense of a cow since the custom in olden times was to transfer the ownership of a cow by holding her tail and the grazing tax levied per head of cattle is still called *pucchi* or tail-tax in north India. There is evidence even in Vedic literature that the cow formed one of the standards of exchange and valuation.[10] The term *go-pucchika* may have been applied to an object purchased for one cow. Patañjali mentions a bigger transaction solemnized in exchange for five cows (*pañcabhir-gobhiḥ kritaḥ pañcaguḥ*, *Bhāṣya*, 1.216). The *Kāśikā* illustrates Pāṇini's word *aparimāna* by *pañchaśvā* and *daśāsvā*, *i.e.*, a female purchased for the price of five or ten horses, which must have been a transaction of substantial value (IV. 1.22). Patañjali mentions a very curious instance of the purchase of a chariot for five *kroṣtrīs* (III.273), which ordinarily means a female jackal, whatever else it may have implied in this particular context. The expressions *dvi-kambalva*, *tri-kambalva* cited on IV. 1.22 appear to be taken from life. We know from Pā . nini that *kamabalya* denoted a set measure of wool (V.1.3) equal to one hundred palas or five seers. The female objects purchased for two or three *kambalya* measures would be sheep acquired by the shepherds in exchange of wool.

There are again, three Sūtras which speak of *kaṁsa* (V. 1.25), *sūrpa* (V.1.26) and *khari* (V.1.33) in connection with purchase of commodities. Dr. Bhandarkar has rightly pointed out: 'As these are clearly measures of capacity, the only inference possible is that such commodities were bought by means of these measures and most probably with grains which were the staple food of the province.'[11] In several examples and counter-examples we find reference to other measures of weight used in bartering transactions, e.g., a thing purchased for two *añjalis* or three *añjalis* (V.4.102); for two or three *achita* or *ādhaka* measures (IV. 1.22). Besides Pāṇini's reference to articles purchased for one *sūrpa* (V.1.26) Patañjali refers to others as *dvi-sūrpa* and *tri-sūrpa* (II.346, 348). The *goṇi* measure which is mentioned by Pāṇini 1.2.50 and which was equal to two *sūrpas*, is also noticed in connection with the system of barter in such phrases as *pañchagoṇiḥ* and *daśagoṇih* (I.226). The *Kāśikā* informs us that cloth was purchased for such a price (I.2.50).

These examples show that barter prevailed not only in transactions of modest value, but also in the case of commodities of substantial amount. Probably an example of the biggest barter exchange is offered by the two words *pañca-nauḥ, daśanauḥ,* viz., a deal in exchange for five and ten boatfuls of merchandise (*Navo dvigaḥ,* V.4.99). Patañjali refers to sailings of five hundred boats—and five hundred rafts (*pañcodupaśatāni tirnāni, pañcaphalaka-śatāni tirnāni: Bhaṣya,* II.356). This is strong evidence of a flourishing riverine traffic in goods in which rich merchants referred to as *parama-vaṇija* and *uttama-vaṇija* in Pāṇini, VI.2.13 must have participated, whose strong financial position enabled them to negotiate transactions to the extent of five or ten boatfuls of commodities at a time.

Notes

1. Agrawala, 'Ancient Indian Coins as Known to Pāṇini', *JUPHS,* July 1938, vol. XI, pt. 1, pp. 74–87.
2. *Yaj. Smṛti,* II.61; also Mallinātha on *Kirāta,* XI.50.
3. *Arthasāstra,* IV.2.
4. Macdonell and Keith, *Vedic Index,* II, p. 278.
5. Tarn, *The Greeks in Bactria and India,* p. 488, appendix 14.
6. Rapson, *The Cambridge History of India,* vol. I, *Ancient India,* p. 433.
7. Tarn, op. cit., p. 489.
8. Rawlinson, *Intercourse between India and the Western World,* p. 42, also appendix I for the distances between the stages on the Royal Road, p. 64.
9. Bhandarkar, *Ancient Indian Numismatics,* pp. 169–70.
10. Macdonell and Keith, op. cit., I, pp. 196, 234.
11. Bhandarkar, op. cit., p. 170.

19

Some Aspects of India-China Maritime Trade *c.* AD 250–1200

Adhir Chakravarti

THOUGH THE *Sung-Shu* (chapter 97) (AD 204–78) vaguely alludes to maritime trade between India and China as early as the first two decades of the third century AD, definite information regarding such contact can be had only from the middle of the third century AD. The *Shui-Ching-Chu* (section 55), on the basis of Fu-Nan-Chuan of Kang Tai, states 'Travelling to the North West (from Chu-li) for more than a year, one reaches the mouth of the river of India, which is called the river Ganges. At the mouth of the river there is a kingdom called Tan-Mei which belongs to India. Its ruler sent letters to the Yellow Gate (the Chinese Court), and was appointed (by China) king of Tan-Mei.'

Tan-Mei has been taken by the author of the *Shui-Ching-Chu* as identical with To-Mo-Li-Chien i.e., Tamralipti. Now K'ang Tai came to the court of Fan-Che-Man, king of Fu-Nan some time between AD 240 and 245. There he met the ambassador from India. So it is likely that the king of Tamralipti sent an embassy to China some time after AD 245. Bengal thus took a difinite initiative in fostering India–China maritime relation, which was necessarily of a mercantile character. It must, however, be noted that 'no such embassy is registered in the annals (Pen-Chi) of the Wu in the San-Kuo-Chih.'

On his return journey Fa-Hsien (AD 399–414) embarked for Ceylon from Tamralipti. When he set sail for Canton, there were on board the merchantman two hundred Po-Lo-Man, Sanskrit Brāhmaṇa, (more properly addherents of the Brahmanical religion) from the West Coast of India, or as Legge takes, from Kulam to the Indus. It is therefore likely that people from all parts of India participated in this trade when the Gupta emperors establised their supremacy over the seas. This is corroborated from what we know of such famous Buddhist monks as Gunavarman (Kiu-Na-Pa-Mo) of Kashmir and Gunabhadra (Kiu-No-Po-To-Lo) of central India. It is interesting to note that the ship which took Guṇavarman to China was owned by an Indian named

*24th Session at Delhi, 1961.

Nandin. Guṇabhadra also first came to Ceylon and then reached Canton in AD 435.

The decline of the Imperial Guptas in India, depredation of pirates around the Ton-Kin coast and political unrest in China during the sixth century AD retarded the growth of this trade. In spite of these unfavourable human factors the trade did not die away. Thus, a south Indian king is said to have sent an embassy to China between AD 500 and 516. The Buddhist savant Paramārtha reached China by sea in AD 546. But above all Cosmas Indico-pleustes (AD 535) mentions a lively India–China maritime trade via Ceylon.

It has been assumed by Hirth and Rockhill that Hiuen-tsang was ignorant of the India–Java–China trade. But it may be pointed out that Emperor Harsa suggested to the Master of the Law that royal officers could accompany him should he like to take the southern sea-route i.e., by way of Java and Sumatra. The learned translators of *Chu-fan-Chi* mention that later in the seventh century sea-route came to be almost exclusively used; thus I tsing (AD 671–95) embarked from Kuang-Chu (Canton) for India in a Po-Sse ship. In his biography he mentions no less than 37 Chinese pilgrims who went to India by sea.

Early in the eighth century (AD 717) an Indian is said to have reached Canton but whether in a Po-sse ship is not known. Pallava Narasiṁhavarman II (Che-Li-Ma-Lo-Sen-Kia) sent an embassy to China in AD 720. Some months later, the Chinese emperor sent a return embassy. Such diplomatic activity between these two countries presupposes close trade relations. In fact the *Hwi-Chao* mentions Brāhmaṇa (West Indians) ship-owners on the river at Canton in AD 748.

After the sack of Kwang-Chu (Canton) in AD 758 by Ta-Shi (Arab) and Po-Sse merchants Canton was closed to the foreigners, and Tonkin henceforth became terminus for foreign ships. Canton was reopened in AD 792. But the Śailendra rulers of Śrīvijaya henceforth acted as the sole intermediaries between India and Chinese merchants. India–China trade came to a violent end in AD 878 by rebel Huang-Cha's sack of Canton and indiscriminate murder of foreign merchants.

Direct regular maritime contact was revived at the initiative of the Coḷas and Pālas. The Coḷas sent embassies to China in AD 1015, in 1020 and 1033 (*Sung-Shi* and *Ma-Tuan-Lin*) and in 1077 and 1106 (*Chu-Fan-Chi*). These so-called embassies' offering tribute to the Chinese Emperors, however, practically were nothing but so many mercantile delegations, which sought the favour of the Emperors for trading facilities. The *Pring-Chou-K'o-Van*, (eleventh century AD) mentions large Kia-Ling (= Kling-Kaliṅga) sea-going merchant ships and organization of such merchants. That India–China maritime trade during this period, however, was at a low ebb can be guessed from the rather humiliating status accorded to the Coḷa envoys in AD 1015 and also in AD 1106.

How far was this trade the result of Indian enterprise *vis-à-vis* the Perso-Arabs and the Chinese?

I-Tsing first, mentions the Po-Sse (= Persian) ships. Hourani has pointed out that it was not possible for the Persians to undertake such adventurous undertaking immediately after their defeat at the hands of the Arabs. Hence the beginnings of Perso-Chinese maritime activity goes back to pre-Islamic days. Even if that be so, it must, however, be accepted that the Indians retained control over the Eastern Oceanic trade till the middle of the seventh century AD. The earliest Arab narratives concerning the China trade are by Suleiman (AD 851) and Ibn Wahab. But Suleiman noted that 'the goods of China are rare (in Persia and Mesopotamia)'. From Buzurg's story of 'Abharah, however, it appears that Arab mercantile activities in the China sea began somewhat later. Then in the time of al-Mas'udi Arab enterprises in China proper ceased. Thus the state of Indian initiative during *c.* AD 750–1000 cannot be definitely ascertained. But if any thing can be argued from the unusual efflorescence of Indian culture in Java, Sumatra, Cambodia and Champa during the period, it may be stated that at least indirect maritime contact between India and China continued.

The extent of Indian initiative in the years following AD 1000 may be known from the activities of such mercantile corporations like the Manigraman Cettis (Takua-Pa Inscription, Malay Peninsula) and Nanadesa–Tisaiyayirattu–Ainnurruvur (Loboe Toewa Inscription, Sumatra, AD 1088). Indeed, the daring enterprises of such mercantile organisations have been brought to relief by the Baligami inscription (Mysore). Shall we be far wrong to think that such organisations carried on trade directly with China, particularly after Java's secession from Śrīvijaya and Sung rulers of China offering special privileges to foreign merchants?

The theory that the Indians fared badly in maritime competition with the Arabs has no basis in fact. Hourani has, of late, conclusively shown that the Arabs did not come to develop any speciality on their own in the art of boat-building. On the other hand, he points out that before the days of Ibn-Battuta, the Arabs and Persians even used 'to go and build their ships on the spot. The Maldives and Laccadives were the scene of a remarkable shipbuilding activity ....' Indians therefore maintained their supremacy, usually naval and sometimes even political, over the Bay of Bengal till the collapse of the Colas and decline of Śrīvijaya in the thirteenth century AD.

Beazley holds the view that the Chinese used the mariner's compass in making voyages from Canton to Malabar as early as the first century AD. But it may be recalled that neither Fa-Hsien nor I-Tsing makes any mention of Chinese navigation to India. The *Tang-Kuo-Shi Pu* by Li-Chan (AD 713 to 825) mentions foreign (Fan) traders at Canton. They were registered in the office of the Inspector of Maritime Trade. Hourani has shown that the alleged Chinese participation in the Western trade before Islam does not stand scrutiny. He takes such expression as Sufun min al-Sin of al-Tabari, Sufun Siniyah or Markab Sini to mean Moslem ships on the China run. The Chinese prisoners at the battle of Talas river, however, returned home in Chinese Junks in AD 762. Hirth and Rockhili believe that these may have been built in China, but it seems highly improbable that they were owned or navigated by the Chinese'. Their view, however, is somewhat contradictory. Early in twelfth century AD the Chinese traders frequented India as far as Quilon. (Ling-Wai-Tai-Ta. 11.13 of Chou-Ku-Fei). The decline of the Coḷas and of Śrīvijaya undoubtedly helped them but their supremacy over the Bay of Bengal in the following centuries was primarily due to their superior boat-building technique and invention of the mariner's compass.

20

The Role of the Arab Traders in Western India During Early Medieval Period

V.K. Jain

THE OCEANIC trade in the East, before the seventh century, was being shared by the Persians, Indians, Indonesians and Ceylonese.[1] But with the rise of Islam we find the Persians being replaced by the Arabs who slowly and gradually spread their economic fangs to the farthest East and studded the whole sea route to China via western India, Ceylon and South-East Asia, with their resident trading settlements.[2] The comparative silence of the indigenous texts makes the available data too meagre to define exactly the role these Arab traders played in the economic history of western India. However, some idea can be obtained from the accounts of the Arab geographers and the Chinese authors and also from the Arabic inscriptions of the thirteenth century found in western India. They show that Arab traders and shippers were stationed there in large numbers and that they carried on their commercial activities freely and peacefully. They also indirectly demonstrate that the initiative in foreign trade and shipping had slipped out of the hands of the Indians to those of the Arabs. As a result the west Indian traders were confined to the internal or coastal trade, and they tended to act more as middlemen between the people of the hinterland and the Arabs than as foreign traders.

To understand the role of the Arab traders in western India, two facts have to be borne in mind: (a) increase in the use of the sea route, and (b) decline in direct trade contact between the Far East and the Middle East during our period.

*39th session at Hyderabad, 1978.

**The term 'Arabs' denotes all those Muslims of Arabia, Iraq and Persia who came to western India much before its full-fledged Muslim occupation in AD 1297.

***By 'Western India' we mean the region over which the Cāḷukya kings during the heyday of their glory ruled, i.e. Marwar in the north to Konkan in the south and western Malwa in the east to Cutch and Saurashtra in the west, cf. A.K. Majumdar, *Cāḷukyas of Gujarat*, pp. 82, 119, 208.

From the last half of the eighth century, the land route through Central Asia was cut off by the struggles of both the Chinese and Muslims with the tribes of Central Asia, and was reopened only by the Mongol in the thirteenth and fourteenth centuries. The decline of land route led to a corresponding increase in traffic by sea which was encouraged by the Abbasids.[3]

The preference for the sea route during twelfth century is mentioned by Ibn Madjid, the Arab navigator of Vasco da Gama.[4] The Chinese sources also demonstrate how the Central Asian route was being replaced by the sea route[5] via Indonesia. The itineraries of Marco Polo, too, confirm this fact. It is known that Marco Polo (thirteenth century) on his way back adopted the sea route from China to Persian Gulf because it was not only shorter but also free from the rigours of the overland route.[6]

It shows that during the period under study the sea route, though perilous, was considered better than the land route which took longer and was tougher. Consequently we see the rise of international commerce in the areas of the Persian Gulf, western India, southern India, South East Asia and South China which lay on the coasts. In this trade, the traders of all the concerned regions participated but the Arabs who had established their trading settlements all over the East became the most important and dominant group.

Regarding the decline in direct contact between the Far East and the Middle East, it may be noted that the Arabic sources of the eleventh and twelfth centuries add remarkably little to our information on the East or the Eastern trade. The later sources are in fact more or less copied from the earlier texts of Sulaiman, Ibn Khurdadbih, Abu Zaid, Al-Mas'udi, etc., of the ninth and tenth centuries. It is tempting to believe that the long distance Arab trade slowly declined in our period. It is possible that some Arabs might have sailed from the Persian Gulf to South China, but it is doubtful whether there was much of direct intercourse by sea between the Far East and the Middle East.[7] According to the Arabic literature of the period the important Arabian port, Kish, had contacts only with India and East Africa, and its wealth came from there.[8]

As a result of the decline in direct trade contact, the west Indian coast got prominence in the eyes of the Arab traders, and their settlements in Gujarat emerged as chief intermediaries of trade between the Middle East and the Far East. Initially, these trading Centres were semi-permanent settlements for roving merchant population. Many individuals stayed in them only for seasons to change or for collecting cargoes. But the increasing commercial activities of the Arab traders and the swelling up of their number due to the inclusion of local converts[9] soon made them powerful enough to elicit personal and commercial rights from the local kings; and these settlements, became the chief centres where they could conveniently and congenially stay for a longer period. The decline in direct contact also changed the character of the trading activities of the Arabs from exclusive foreign trade to local and regional trade. It led to their steady penetration into the hinterland of India.

The first Arab raid[10] of western India came only a few years after the death of the Prophet when in AD 636 the governor of Bahrein sent naval expeditions against Thana and Broach, but they met with no success. The conquest of Sind by the Arabs in AD 712, however, altered the picture. Their expeditions against western India were henceforth directed from the base near Gujarat and were therefore more effective. Though their military and political advance in land was checked by the powerful Rajput Kings of the period,[11] they continued to make periodical raids on west Indian coast, the most important and successful of which was against the Saurāṣṭra port and town of Barada or Balaba, identified with Vala or Valabhi, in the later half of the eighth century. It marks the beginning of the ascendancy of their commercial dominance in westen India.[12] It exhibited the superior naval power of the Arabs with whom the Indians found difficult to compete. It scared away the Indian traders to the interior where they developed new centres of trade.[13] The sudden silence of indigenous sources after the eighth century on the Indian foreign traders may be taken to mean that now Indians took more interest in internal than in foreign trade.

The Arab attack on Valabhi also compelled the Indians to look for an alternative port safer than Vala and Broach which being on the sea coast were more susceptible to foreign attacks. This led to the rise of Cambay inside the Gulf. We feel that the generally accepted view of A.K. Majumdar[14] and others that Cambay was developed by the Pratihāras as a rival to the port of Broach is not convincing.

By the tenth century, the Arabs were settled in large numbers in the coastal areas of Cutch, Saurastra and Gujarat and were carrying on the profession of trade and commerce. In Cutch, Sindan was the earliest acquisition of the Arabs. Al Biladuri tells us that Fazl took Sindan in Cutch and built a Jama mosque over there in the ninth century.[15] He also informs us that Muhammad, son of Fazl, proceeded from Sindan with sixty vessels against the Meds of Dwarka, who were pirates and a great menace to the, traders, and defeated them.[16] However, later the Indians made themselves the masters of Sindan but they spared the mosque where the Muslims were allowed to pray on Fridays.[17] It shows that though the political authority had slipped out of the hands of the Arabs, they remained there as traders and enjoyed religious freedom. Their number must have been too large to make any reprisal against them possible.[18]

Slowly and gradually the Arabs started penetrating inside the country for the collection of local goods. As Ibn Hawkal informs us, there were Jama mosques not only at Cutch, Sindan, Saimur and Cambay but also at Famhala (Anahilvada). All these were strong and great cities where Muhammadan precepts were openly observed.[19] The references to mosques show that the Muslims were stationed there in large numbers. A1 Idrisi (twelfth century) includes Khabirum (Kapadvanj) and Asawal (Ahmedabad) in the list of the towns where the Muslims had reached. This shows the deeper penetration of the Muslims in Gujarat.

The inscriptional reference to earlier settlers in western India are not available, but those belonging to the thirteenth century confirm the accounts of the early Arab writers and recount the past history of these Arab traders for several centuries. The inscriptions ranging from AD 1218 to 1291 have been found[20] in the coastal towns of Cambay and Prabhas Pattan and also in the inland towns of Junagadh and Anhilavada Pattan.

A Cambay epitaph (AD 1249) refers to one Sharafu'd Din Abu Sharaf who as it seems from the inscription 'drowned by drowning'.[21] If so, he must have died presumably in the course of one of the frequent trade voyages to foreign countries. Another epitaph (AD 1291) refers to Haji Ibrahim, who was one of the wealthy merchants of Cambay. He is mentioned in the text as the 'chief of merchants and prince of shipmaster'. According to Desai, he seems to have been trading in betel-nuts.[22] Since betel-nut is grown mainly in the coastal regions of Konkan and Malabar or in north Bengal and some portions of Assam[23] it is certain that the Haji brought the commodity in his ships to Cambay from somewhere outside and later transported it to the West.

The most important and informative record of the period is the bilingual inscription from Somanatha.[24] It is dated in three different eras-AH 662/VS 1320/Valabhi Sam. 945, i.e., AD 1264.[25] It throws considerable light on the social divisions and communal organizations of the Muslims of the period. It records the endowment of a mosque by a wealthy shipowner, Nuru'd-Din Firuz, son of Abu, Ibrahim of Hurmujadesa. The inscription also mentions that incomes were to be administered and the place of worship maintained jointly by the following congregations: of the *nakuyaorika*, or owners and commanders of ships and sailors, of the *ghamchikas* or oilmen belonging to the town together with their *khatib* or leader of the prayer, of the Muslim *chunakaras* or lime workers, masons, etc. In other words, it was to be maintained by the various Muslim communities of sailors, shipowners, the clergy and the artisans, which must have been living there in fairly large numbers. It further says that any surplus which remained was to be sent to Mecca and Medina.

Inscriptions also confirm that the Arab traders and shippers held commanding positions at the important ports and marts of western India. A reference in the *Prabundhacintāmaṇi* indicates that an Arab trader Saida (*Sayyad*) had become so poweful as to venture a naval fight with Vastupala, the governor of Cambay.[26] The Arab hold on the Saurastra coast can be inferred from the fact that before the Calukya king Siddharaja constructed a new military road from Wadhwan to Junagadh, a place which was connected with various parts on the coast, the traders and travellers generally followed the coast line. But later this military road became the regular trade route and the coast line was gradually neglected.[27] It may be suggested that the construction of a new road was aimed at maintaining internal communication with the ports, as the coastal route was under the control of the Arabs.

The solitary reference in the Somanātha inscription (AD 1264) that the '. . . balance (of the amount set forth for meeting the expenses or the mosque) will be sent to Mecca . . .'[28] shows that it was probably a normal practice for the Arab traders to send their earnings to their countries. If it is so, India was being depleted of its wealth by the Arab traders. However, in the absence of more definite references, it is difficult to measure the volume of this drain or to determine the form in which it took place.[29]

It may be asked as to why the west Indians who had the will, skill and enterprise in foreign trade allowed their military, religious and commercial rivals to settle in western India. We contend that the decline in the Indian techniques of ship construction and navigation *vis-a-vis* those of the Arabs and Chinese[30] forced the Indians to follow a peaceful policy towards the foreigners.

Marco Polo describes the ships of Manzi or South China as larger than those of India.[31] In the matter of speed, too, the Indian ships lagged behind.[32] Besides, though there is evidence that the Indians built ships on a large scale and equipped them with trading and piratical expeditions, there is no reference to any Indian monarch of the Hindu period, with the possible exception of the Coḷa kings, who seemed to have appreciated 'the value of sea power as an aid to conquest and expansion.'[33] In other words, Indian traders did not appear to have done much by way of providing for the safety of their ships, and it is no wonder that whereas references to the Arab,[34] and Chinese[35] ships being manned with soldiers are forthcoming. We have not much to suggest this for the Indian counterparts in western India. The result was that they failed to compete with the mounting pressure of the Arabs who had already proved their navigational and striking skill by conquering Sind and storming Valabhi in the eighth century.

It is pointed out that one of the factors for the decline in Indian shipping might have been the taboo against sea voyages[36] in the literature. We, however, believe that religious restrictions must have been a frail barrier to the desire of profit accruing out of sea trade and that the religious prejudice was the expression of the decay of Indian maritime activity due to other practical reasons.

The decline in Indian navigation resulted in the loss of Indian control on foreign trade. It is confirmed by the Contemporary Chinese text of Chau Ju Kua, which in the list of countries exporting large merchandise to China enumerates in order Arabia (Ta-Shih), Java (Sh'o-po) and Palembang (San-fotsi) but does not mention India. It is, however, not unlikely that India along with many others belonged to the next rank referred to by Chau Ju Kua.[37]

There is no doubt that the traders from western India continued to make voyages to foreign countries,[38] but the number and the details of their travels are so scanty that we are forced to accept that they played only a second fiddle to the Arabs in foreign trade. Many contemporary foreign authors[39] such as Benjamin of Tudela (AD 1170), Marco Polo, etc., refer to Indian merchants taking their goods to China in the East and Aden and Kish in the West, but they do not identify these merchants by their religion. We tend to believe that while some of them were Hindus, the majority of them were Muslims who, during our period, were settled in large numbers on the west Indian coast and traded in Indian goods.

With the decline in the hold of the Indians on foreign trade, the kings of western India tried to regulate sea trade in such a manner as they could earn revenue in the form of customs, tolls, etc., on the goods traded in by the foreigners and therefore tended to encourage them to settle in their realms.[40] The *Mānasollāsa*[41] recommends that the king should charge 1/10 of the cargo as duty from the ships which arrived at the ports and provide protection to shipping.

With the passage of time the Arabs strengthened their economic hold on the ports of Gujarat, and the local kings were forced to come to an understanding with them. It seems the Arabs paid a regular tax or toll on the goods they traded in and got, in return, personal and communal protection. Though our sources do not refer to any give-and-take arrangement, in the contemporary West such commercial pacts were quite well known between the Christians and the Muslims.[42]

Driven away from foreign trade, the Indian merchants were now confined to the coastal and internal trade. Since, there is no reference to indicate that the Arabs controlled the internal markets as well, the Indians continued to be predominant there. In fact, the Arabs, except in certain ports in western India where they lived with the local Muslims with full rights and privileges, had no intimate contact with the interior of the country and being unaware of local customs and dialects had to depend upon local merchants who acted as their 'agents' in procuring goods from the hinterland. They were also dependent on the Indian traders for disposing of their cargoes. This led to the rise of a 'mercantile bourgeoise' which amassed enormous wealth on the basis of middleman-profit, the type of profit for which Gujarat being 'gateway of India' was most suitable.[43] Their wealth is reflected in the accounts of *Koṭī- śvaras* or millionairs of Gujarat whose mansions had huge banners and ringing bells[44] and also in the construction of large temples during this period.

Regarding the *modus operandi* of the Indian traders, A1 Idrisi points out that when the ships landed at the port of Daybul (Sind), the merchants purchased the goods 'wholesale' and sold them only after the ships left[45] only after creating artificial scarcity. What is true of Daybul must have been true of western Indian merchants too.[46]

This sort of mercantile structure in which bulk purchases were made required a considerable amount of capital investment which, as it seems, was arranged by the bankers who had found banking a very profitable business. It is noteworthy that the economic strength of Vastupāla, the minister of a Vāghela king and an important merchant prince of the period, emanated from the 'banking houses which he had at various commercially important centres of Gujarat. The Girnar inscriptions (AD 1222)[47] repeatedly mention that Vastupāla was carrying on banking transactions with the cities of Gujarat of which Dhavalakka (Dholka) was the chief, in the year, Samvat (12)76."

The trade based on the concept of middleman-profit was beneficial to the state, big merchants, and the big bankers.[48] It is doubtful whether any profit accrued to the local peasants, artisans or small merchants who continued to produce heavier surplus for those who expropriated it.[49] The merchant princes felt happy in collecting the goods at the minimum cost and selling them at the highest price. It is something unlike what happened in the West where, if we agree with Henri Pirenne,[50] the development of commerce after the rise of the Arabs led to increased local production and the consequent disintegration of feudalism.

Notes

1. For details, see Wang Gungwu, 'The Nanhai Trade, a Study of the Early History of Chinese Trade in the South China Sea', *JMBRAS*, vol. XXXI, no. 182, pt. II, 1958, pp. 2ff; also V.A. Velgus, 'Some Problems of the History of Navigation in the Indian and Pacific Oceans', *The Countries and Peoples of the East*, ed., Olderogge, Maretin, Valskaya tr., Gavrilov and Kostyiik, pp. 45–90.
2. For Arab settlements in South East Asia and Far East see, G.R. Tibetts, 'Early Muslim Traders in South East Asia', *JMBRAS*, vol. XXX, pt. I, 1957, pp. 28–9, 36–41.
3. Earlier the Umaiyads with their capital at Damascus had no occasion to make any great use of the luxurious trade of the East. Whatever contact they had with the East was of a military nature and it was conducted overland. 'They did little to foster trade in the Gulf so that during the first hundred years pf the Arab Empire the Persians still dominated the shipping population of the Gulf', ibid., p. 9.
4. cf. T.A. Shumovsky. 'Two Chapters from the fifteenth century Encyclopedia of Arabic Maritime Geography', *The Countries and Peoples of the East*, pp. 94–5.
5. F. Hirth and W.W. Rockhill, *Chauju-kua*, pp. 201–2.
6. E. Samhaber, *Merchants Make History*, Eng. tr. by E. Osers, p. 113.
7. Tibbetts, op. cit., p. 33.
8. H.H. Wilson, *The Persian Gulf*, pp. 96–100; Kazwini (thirteenth century) also tells us that the prosperity of Kish was because of the costly Indian goods shipped to that

place; S.S. Nadvi, *Arab Aur Bharat Ke Sambandh*, Hindi tr. by R.C. Verma. p. 46. It may be noted that with the rise of the Fatimids by AD 1000, the Red Sea became important for international commerce, but the sources of our period generally speak of contact of western India with the ports of Persian Gulf, viz. Kish and Hormuz, only.

9. During the eleventh and twelfth centuries, a number of missionaries belonging to Bohia. Khoja and Sunni communities came to Gujarat and claimed many new converts, cf, S.C. Misra, *Muslim Communities in Gujarat*, pp. 8–14.
10. Elliot and Dowson. *The History of India as Told by Its Own Historians*, vol. I, pp. 115–16. 415–61. It seems that these were no more than plundering raids as they were conducted without the permission of the Caliph' Umar (AD 634–43), ibid. It is possible that these expeditions were aimed at securing a foothold in western India for safeguarding the interests of the Arab ships plying between Ceylon and the Persian Gulf.
11. *Bombay Gazetteer*, vol. I (i), p. 109.
12. It may be noted that the attack on Valabhi roughly corresponds with the destruction of Canton by the Arabs and the Persians in AD 758, see Hadi Hasan, *History of Persian Navigation*, p. 99.
13. The Jaina traditions tell us that after the Arab attack of Valabhi, the Jaina merchants made their was to Siva Pattan (Somanātha), Srīmālapura Panchasur and other cities. See A K. Forbes, *Rasmala—Hindu Annals of Western India*, p. 13.
14. A.K. Majumdar, op. cit., p. 265.
15. Elliot and Dowson, vol. I, p. 129.
16. Ibid.
17. V.A. Janaki, *Gujarat as the Arabs Knew it*, p. 58.
18. Ibn Hawkal (tenth century) tells us that in Cutch Sindan the Muslims were greatly respected, *Bombay Gazetteer*, vol. V, p. 250.
19. *Bombay Gazetteer*, vol. I, p. 521: Ellist and Dowson, vol. I, pp. 34–8.
20. Z.A. Desai, 'Arabic Inscriptions of the Rajput Period fiom Gujarat', *Epigraphia Indica, Arabic and Persian Supplement*, pp. 1–24; also see Z.A. Desai, 'Muslims in the Thirteenth Century Gujarat as Known from Arabic Inscriptions', *JOJB*, vol. X, 1960, pp. 253–54.
21. Z.A. Desai, *Epigraphia Indica, Arabic and Persian Supplement*, pp. 9ff.
22. Ibid., pp. 22ff.
23. George Watt, *The Commercial Products of India*, pp. 83–95.
24. For Sanskrit portion, see Hultzsch, *IA*, vol. XI, 1882, pp. 24–45; D.C. Sircar, *EI*, vol. XXXIV, pp. 141–50. For Arabic portion see, Z.A. Desai, op. cit., pp. 10–15.
25. Reference to the Valabhi era, not otherwise mentioned in the other inscriptions of the period may be indicative of the fact that Muslims were staying in the area since the time of the Maitrakas whose capital Valabhi they are known to have destroyed, see *supra*. It may be noted that a Persian manuscript translated by James Tod also refers to the existence of Muslim oilmen in Somanātha. See James Tod, *Travels in Western India*, p. 345ff.
26. The *Prabandhacintāmaṇi*, tr. M.A. Tawney, Calcutta, p. 162.

27. M.R. Majumdar, *The Cultural History of Gujarat,* p. 63.
28. Desai, op. cit., nos. 21 and 22, p. 15.
29. Ibn Battuta informs us that, 'it is the custom of the inhabitants of India, not to interfere with the property of the dead even when they leave thousands behind them. The money remains in the hands of the chief of the Muslim *(Kabir-ul-muslmin)* until it is taken possession of by one who has a legal right to it.' In Jurfattana in the Malabar region, he claims to have met a scholar from Baghdad who was 'preparing to leave' for his native place along with the wealth which his deceased brother, a rich trader had earned in India. Mahdi Hussain tr., *The Rehla of Ibn Battuta,* p. 186. He also refers to one Shaikhzada of Isfahan, who was 'uncommonly rich' and who 'continually sent money to his native land', ibid., p. 173.
30. A.L. Basham, 'Notes on Seafaring in Ancient India', *Arts and Letters,* vol. XXIII, N.S., 1949, p. 69.
31. H. Yule, *The Book of Marco Polo,* II, p. 391n.
32. Lallanji Gopal, *The Economic Life of Northern India,* AD 700–1200, p. 126.
33. Basham, 'Notes . . .' op. cit., p. 64.
34. The Arab ships on which Ibn Battuta left Gandhar (south of Broach) for South had 'fifty arrowmen and fifty Abyssinian warriors.' Mahdi Hussain, op. cit., p. 176.
35. Defremery and Sanguinetti ed., *Voyages d'lbn Batoutah,* vol. III, pp. 88–91.
36. A.L. Basham, op. cit. p. 60ff L. Gopal's view that the rise of the Vaishya traders, contributed towards the decline of Indian navigation does not seem to be convincing. Ibid., p. 126.
37. Chau Ju Kua, op. cit., p. 23.
38. *Jagaducharita* refers to ihe merchant Jagadu who traded with Persia in his own ships—see, A.K. Majumdar, op. cit., p. 267; Abu Zaid (tenth century) informs us that the Indian merchants visited Saraf, G. Ferrand, *Voyase du Merchant Arabe Sulaiman,* p. 138, quoted in L. Gopal op. cit., p. 142: Muh, ufi, refers to a merchant of Naharwala (Anhilavada) who had flourishing trade with Ghazni, Elliot and Dowson, vol. II, pp. 200–1.
39. K.A. Nilakanta Sastri, *Foreign Notices of South India,* p. 134; H. Yule, op. cit., vol. II, p. 107; vol. II, p. 231.
40. *The Prabandhacintdmani,* pp. 19–20.
41. *Mānasollāsa,* ed. G.K. Shrigondeka, vol. I, vv, 374–76, p. 62.
42. We know that the Venteians offered 10% tax on all their turn over to the Sultan of Trebizond (NE Turkey) in return for permission to buy and sell goods without let or hindrance throughout his empire. They also paid a tax of 6% to the Sultan of Aleppo (NW Syria) in return for permission to the Venetian merchants to equip their own quarters where they could enjoy their own jurisdiction in civil as well as in criminal cases. The Genoese and other Christian states are also known to have entered into similar commercial pacts with the contemporary Muslim kings, for details see Samhaber, op. cit., p. 106 ff.
43. Gujarat was connected with the whole of India by ancient trade routes, for details on routes see, M.R. Majumdar op. cit., pp. 63ff. It may be noted that even later when the Europeans controlled the foreign trade, the economic strength of the

Banias was based on the hold they had on internal trade, see Surendra Gopal. 'Merchants in Western India in the sixteenth–seventeenth centuries'. *Indian Society: Historical Probings (in memory of D.D. Kosambi)*, ed. R.S. Sharma, p. 236ff.

44. *Moharājaparajaya*, cd. M. Chaturvijaya Intro, p. x.
45. Maqbul Ahmad, *India* . . ., no. 6, p. 41.
46. In the *Prabandhacintāmaṇi*, p. 105, we read of a merchant who invests his capital in purchasing sacks of *mahjistha* (Indian madder) imported from outside. Talking about Kolam (Quilon) Ibn Battuta says that the 'merchants of the place are so rich that they purchase the whole cargo of the ships and sell it after having stored it in their godowns', S.S. Nadvi, op. cit., p. 242.
47. James Burgess, *Lists of the Archaeological Remains in Bombay Presidency*, p. 283ff.
48. Generally big merchants and big bankers were the same people.
49. For feudalisation of merchants and artisans see, R.S. Sharma, *Indian Feudalism* (*c.* AD 300–1200), pp. 235ff, 238ff.
50. Henrij Pirenne, *Economic and Social History of Medieval Europe*, p. 30ff.

21

Trade in the Growth of Towns: A Case Study of Karnataka, c. AD 600–1200

Om Prakash Prasad

THE ROLE of commercial activity in the development of towns can be understood on the basis of the history of particular towns between the fifth century and the thirteenth century. Several towns which, on the basis of inscriptional data, appear to have been either administrative centres or places of religious interest between the fifth and the tenth century suddenly indicate a marked degree of commercial activity centred round them from the eleventh-twelfth centuries. Some examples are Sravana Belgola, Lokkigundi, Arsikere and Mangalore.

Sravana Belgola was an important religious centre from very early times. In the records[1] of the fifth-eleventh centuries, of which there is a large number, the information furnished relates generally to the religious activities of the Jain monks and their disciples. The religious significance of the place is very well attested by the term Sravana Belgola itself. The term means Belgola of the Sravana or white pond of the monks.[2] The place is repeatedly characterised as a holy place of pilgrimage (*tīrtha*)[3] and as *dakṣina Kāśī* or *Kāśī* (Banaras) of the southern country. In some inscriptions[4] the place is described as Gommaṭapura. The name was probably applied to this place following the erection of the colossal statue of lord Gommaṭa or Gommaṭeśvara. The image of Gommaṭa was installed in the last quarter of the tenth century by Cāvuṇḍarāya, a high minister of a western Cāḷukya king. It seems that after the erection of the colossus the place attained greater importance and attracted people, including merchants, from all directions. The ever increasing size of the congregations at the place appears to have encouraged the traders to use Sravana Belgola as a profitable centre of commercial exchange. This might explain the fact that in inscriptions, datable from the twelfth century onwards, interesting details concerning the mercantile activities of traders at this place are frequently met

*41st Session at Bombay, 1980.

with. Such details are not reported in any of the numerous inscriptions of an earlier period which have come from the place.

The growing mercantile importance of the settlement can be seen from the presence of several groups of traders who not only carried on their trading activities from this place but even shared the responsibility of proper administration of religious and economic affairs of the town and its surroundings. In a record[5] of the twelfth century reference is made to the *nānādesîs* the *ma. nigāras* and the *śeṭṭis* of Sravana Belgola. It is reported that these communities of merchants carried on their trading activities with a large number of sea ports. The mention of *nānādesîs* is significant. The term refers to a group of merchants who travelled far and wide in connection with their commerce. Reference is also made to wealthy jewel merchants (*māṇikya nagaraṅgal)* of this town who are stated to have managed the endowment relating to the daily anointment of the Gommaṭesvara image with milk.[6] In another interesting record[7] mention is made of rows of shops selling numerous articles. Yet another inscription shows that the town was fast developing as a market for goods produced in the neighbourhood and also those which were brought from distant places. In an inscription[8] of 1181 it is stated that foodgrains, coconuts, arecanuts, betel leaves, pepper, turmeric and cotton were brought to the city markets from the surrounding countryside. The record also refers to 20 shops in front of Parśvanātha *basadi* which were asked to make contributions for the purpose of maintaining certain Jain monastic establishments of the town.

The transformation of the settlement from a place of religious interest into a prosperous mercantile town is in consonance with the fact that increased commercial activity from the eleventh century onwards transformed many old administrative and religious centres into mercantile towns besides encouraging the foundation of new market towns in areas which were commercially viable.

Similar development can also be noticed in respect of Lokkiguṇḍi or Lokkundi, which lay in the Gadag taluk of Dharwar district along the great road which passed from Kovālalapura to Aihole through Gadag and Ron. The place was also connected with the Honnavar road which connected the coastal parts of Karnataka with the plateau region of the state. As such, Lokkiguṇḍi commanded sufficient communicational facilities in order to develop as a trading mart. The town appears to have been founded in the eleventh century, or to have developed from a rural settlement as a result of increasing commercial activity from the close of the tenth century and the beginning of the eleventh.

It is not possible to trace the existence of Lokkiguṇḍi as a town before the beginning of the eleventh century on the basis of inscriptional records. The inscriptions of the eleventh–thirteenth centuries appear to bring the settlement into limelight. In the eleventh century itself, the town is noticed first as a settlement of merchants[9] and later as a capital[10] and a mint town.[11] Some idea of the activities of the merchants of Lokkiguṇḍi is provided by the epigraphic records. First, the donations recorded in favour of the local religious establishments were all made by the mercantile community of the place,[12] an indication of the fact that the chief support for the religious establishments came from the traders. Second, the merchants of Lokkiguṇḍi are stated to have been organized into separate guilds such as the guild of clothier[13] and the guild of jawar merchants.[14] The importance of Lokkiguṇḍi as a market place can be seen from references to the organized bazaars of the town, presence of several merchant guilds and the variety of goods brought into the town for the purpose of sale. An inscription[15] of the thirteenth century refers to sandalwood, camphor, pearls, rubies and the various garments which were to be found in the markets of Lokkiguṇḍi.

It may be argued that while commercial interests transformed the settlement into a prosperous urban centre in the initial stages of its development, the attention paid to it by the royal administration helped the prosperity of the city at a later stage. In the last decade of the eleventh century Lokkiguṇḍi became a capital town[16] and at about the same time it developed as a centre of minting activities.[17] The mints of Lokkiguṇḍi figure prominently in inscriptions of the late eleventh–twelfth centuries. The coins manufactured by the mints at Lokkiguṇḍi were named after the place itself, for example, *lokkigadyāṇa*[18] *hosalokkigadyāṇa,*[19] *lokkiyaccinagadyāṇa*[20] *lokkisrahegadyāṇa,*[21] *lokkxpoṇ,*[22] *lokkiniṣka,*[23] *lokkipriyasrahigadyāṇa*[24] *and lokkiyavisa.*[25] The foundation of the mint at Lokkiguṇḍi seems to have been necessitated by the special exchange requirements of the region which followed increased commercial activity of a much more organised nature. It would be seen that other towns where mints were founded about this time were also situated in the same north-western region of Karnataka as Lokkiguṇḍi.

Minting of coins on a large scale, which presupposes large scale commercial activity, seems to have been a determining factor in the foundation and development of new towns about the eleventh and twelfth centuries. Mention has already been made of Lokkiguṇḍi which owed its development as an urban centre to commercial and minting activities. As other examples of settlements which illustrate this process of urbanization we may refer to Sudi,[26] Kurgod,[27] Hiriya Gobbur,[28] Balligave,[29] Tumbuia,[30] Kottitone,[31] Malligeynahalli,[32] etc. It is significant to note that in the inscriptions of the eleventh–twelfth centuries, these settlements figure as important towns, or more properly as mint-towns, and that no evidence is forthcoming to show that any of these settlements was a town before this date.

Sudi, which lies in the Ron taluk of the Dharwar district, was favourably located along the road which passed from Kudatini to Aihole through Kurgod, Koppal, Ron and Kisuvolala, all of which were important towns about this time. The influence of mercantile communities in towns can be seen from the fact that the government often entrusted the administration of trading marts and market towns into the hands of merchants. Sudi, the headquarters of the Kisukad-70 province, was one such market town. One inscription[33] specifically mentions that the corporation of six *gāvuṇḍas* and eight *seṭṭis* of the town of Sudi received from the king a constitution on the basis of which the town was to be administered.

Referring to the minting activities in the town of Sudi, inscriptions[34] state that Uttavoja, the goldsmith had the monopoly of supplying coins of a particular standard which the local community of goldsmith manufactured there under his supervision and control. The coins struck here were marked by a specific emblem denoting the locality. The details pertaining to the gift reveal that Uttavoja was the royal mint master who was incharge of the die (*kammatadani*), containing the royal seal (*uṇḍige*).[35] A record[36] of 1103 refers to several other minting centres besides the one controlled by Uttavoja.

The distribution of mint towns in the north-western districts of Karnataka can be meaningfully related to the numismatic needs of the different commercial sectors in this broad area. The mints were all founded in the twelfth century and, on an average, each of the six districts of this region came to have a minting centre. Thus the district of Bellary had one mint town at Kurgod, the district of Dharwar two at Lokkiguṇḍi and Sudi, the district of Raichur one at Hiriya Gobbur, the district of Belgaum one at Belgaum itself and the district of Shimoga one at Balligave. Since minting activity was largely a private enterprise undertaken by the merchant guilds and assisted by the petty feudal principalities, it may be stated that the manufacturing capacity of a mint was limited in terms of both technical capacity and supply of the necessary quantity of metal. Each of the mints appears to have served a commercial zone not extending beyond a radial distance of 100 kilometres on an average. However, the coins must have been manufactured by the different mints on the basis of a commonly acceptable exchange ratio in terms of weight and the denomination.

The role of commerce in the development of towns can be further illustrated by reference to two important towns in the southern region of Karnataka, Arsikere in the Hassan district and Banavar in the Chikmagalur. Arsikere was favourably situated on the great trade route between Alur and Banavar. From Banavar the road turns to the west to reach Mangalore beyond the ghats, passing, on its way, through the towns of Dorasamudra and Belur. Evidently the town had a direct connection with the coastal trade and also with the internal trade between important towns and between towns and the countryside.[37] The settlement of Arsikere had a modest beginning as petty administrative headquarters.[38] But the commercial potentiality of the region around Arsikere became conducive to its growth as a major market town of the twelfth century. Of the several luxuries, which appear to have been produced in marketable quantities, inscriptions[39] refer to sandalwood, silk, and camphor, besides arecanuts. There are copious references to the cultivation, harvesting and processing of arecanuts in the inscriptional records of the period.[40] In one inscription[41] mention is made of the *Koylasis* who harvested arecanuts and also of the *mottakaras* or the wholesale dealers who prepared arecanuts for the market. The importance of the place as a large trading mart is suggested by the mention of godowns made of palmyra wood for storing goods.[42] In an inscription[43] of the twelfth century Arsikere is described as the southern Aihole or the Aihole of the southern country, with its prosperous merchants equated with Kubera or the god of wealth.[44] A record[45] of 1188 shows that the merchants of Arsikere were big importers of foreign items such as horse, elephants, and pearls which travelled to the shores of Karnataka in large ships. The horses and elephants were evidently requisitioned by the feudal chiefs of the period to fight their engagements and also to use these as regal paraphernalia.

Banavar, another town of this period, lay on the main road between Arsikere and Mangalore, and was in close proximity to both Arsikere and Dorasamudra. The importance of Banavar, which figures in the inscriptions of twelfth century and onwards, consisted in the fact that it served as an entrepot of southern Karnataka. The town supplied most of the goods required by the Hoysaḷa rulers and the citizens of the Hoysaḷa capital of Dorasamudra.[46] Large number of foreign merchants had taken up their residence at this place along with native traders. Of the items imported by the merchants of Banavar, the inscriptions[47] make pointed reference to horses, elephants and pearls.

The foregoing examples give sufficient indication of the fact that revival of large scale commercial activity at both the local levels and over long distances did contribute to urbanization. The illustrative evidence is not, however, exhausted by the above examples. Some of the inscriptions belonging to the eleventh–thirteenth centuries seem to emphasize that town was a commercial necessity. While this is evident from the sudden increase in the number of towns, particularly the commercial towns, there are several examples of towns being founded by merchants of merchant guilds with the assistance of the king or the ruling chief. In some cases the king is seen to be inducing groups of merchants to settle down at a particular place by offering them trade concessions and tax remissions; in other cases, merchants themselves took the initiative to establish or develop a town and in return for such work were rewarded by the king or the ruling chief. This is in addition to the fact that in a large number of cases, particularly in respect of mercantile towns, the merchants' guilds or even individual merchants are found to be sharing a large part of the municipal responsibility.

The founding of the towns appears to have been encouraged by the fact that a *pattanasvāmī* who took the initiative in constructing a town, received, as reward, *inam*, or tax concessions which constituted an important source of his personal income. According to an inscription,[48] four *pattanaśeṭṭs* of Taiakad were given numerous tax concessions as a reward for the work they had done to develop a town. We also learn that when a new town known as Upendrapattana in the Madduru taluk of Mysore district was built, its *paitanasvāmī* was granted rent-free houses.[49] A record[50] refers to the village of Kolaturu in Pulinādu which was converted into a town named Pallavādityanagara. This village was first settled by merchants and when it slowly developed into a market town, its management was enstrusted to the most important group of traders, the bangle merchants (*baligara*).

References

1. *EI*, vol. IV, no. 2. p. 28; *EC*, vol. II, Sravana Belgola, pp. 31, 67, 333–4, 355–6, 481–2.
2. *EC*, vol. II, p. 352.
3. Ibid., pp. 333, 344–5, 355–6.
4. Ibid., pp. 333, 345.
5. Ibid., pp. 244–5, 247.
6. Ibid.
7. Ibid.
8. Ibid.
9. *EI*. vol. XV, no. 24, p. 362.
10. Ibid., vol. VI, no. 10, p. 93.
11. *SII*,. vol. XV, no. 61.
12. *KI*, vol. II, no. 10, p. 33.
13. *EI*, vol. XII, no. 3, pp. 25–7; vol. XV, no. 24, p. 361.
14. *KI*, vol. II, no. 10, p. 33.
15. *EI*, vol. XII, no. 3, pp. 25–6; vol. XV, no. 24, p. 361.
16. *EI*, vol. VI, no. 10, p. 93.
17. Ibid., vol. XV, no. 24, p. 362.
18. *SII*, vol. XX, no. 320.
19. Ibid., vol. XV, no. 22.
20. Ibid., *ARSIE*, no. 233.
21. *ARSIE*, no. 430.
22. *SII*, vol. IX (i), no. 164.
23. *PKRDS*, 1941–46, p. 19.
24. *SII*, vol. XV, no. 160.
25. Ibid.
26. *SII*, vol. XI (ii), no. 153, p. 192.
27. *EI*, vol. XIV, no. 19-A, p. 273.
28. *HAS*, vol. XVIII.
29. *EC*, vol. VII (i); *SK*, 133.
30. *SII*, vol. IX (i), no. 295, p. 318.
31. Ibid., no. 164.
32. *EC*, vol. V (ii), *BI*, 188.

33. *EI,* vol. XV, no. 6, pp. 76–7, 80.
34. *SII,* vol. IX (ii), no. 153; *BKI,* vol. I (ii), no. 153.
35. *BKI,* vol. I (ii), no. 153.
36. *HAS,* vol. XVIII, no. 8.
37. *EC,* vol. V, *AK,* 78.
38. *ASM,* 1934, p. 112.
39. *MAR,* 1930, no. I, pp. 107–8, 112; *KI,* vol. IV, p. 123; *EC,* vol. V, *AK,* 22, 77–8.
40. Ibid.
41. *EC,* vol. V, *AK,* 78.
42. Ibid., 77.
43. *KI,* vol. IV, p. 123.
44. EC, vol. V, *AK,* 77.
45. Ibid., 22.
46. *EC,* vol. V, *AK,* 22.
47. Ibid.
48. *MAR,* 1920, p. 35.
49. EC, vol. IV. *YI,* 39.
50. *ARE,* no. 242.

22

Trade Guilds Under the Cāḷukyas of Kalyāṇi

G.S. Dikshit

Their Part in the Economic Life of the Country

From very early times down to our own times, guilds have played a very important part in the promotion of trade in our country. Just as the village panchayats preserved self-government in the villages, the guilds preserved self-government in trade. Their long life and vitality are amazing. On account of the paucity of records it is very difficult to write a continuous history of the guilds in India. A comparative account of ancient and modern guilds we have in Hopkins' *India Old and New*. About their achievement he says, 'If we review their history we must, I think, see in them an important factor in the development of mercantile interests at a time when such a combination as they represented was indispensable to the advancement of the middle classes in their struggle for recognition at the hands both of despotic kings and of an organised priesthood that was bent on suppressing the elevation of the third estate. With the growth of the guilds the new axiom of later law was evolved, whereby the king was advised not to oppress the guilds and not to tax too heavily. So commerce in the modern sense became possible." But the commerce which the guilds promoted was not confined only to India. Fragmentary references enable us to assume that their part in foreign trade and colonisation especially of South-East Asia was not inconsiderable. The activities of the south Indian guilds are referred to in the inscriptions of Ceylon, Burma and Sumatra.[1]

It is proposed to illustrate the work of the guilds by taking the example of a federation of guilds which flourished in the Deccan and south India in medieval times, roughly from the tenth to the thirteenth centuries by studying inscriptions mostly of the Cāḷukyas of Kalyāṇi and also of their neighbours and contemporaries namely the Hoysaḷas.

*14th Session at Jaipur, 1951.

Their Federal Organisation

This federation, the most important component of which consisted of the *Nānādaśis* (a very significant name for merchants who visited many countries) was made up of all the traders in a place, such as the grain merchants, gold merchants, cloth dealers and oil merchants. The merchants dealing in various articles had their own organisation, but they combined with the other merchants of the place.[2] We also find merchants dealing in one article combining occasionally with similar merchants in other neighbouring places[3] and we also find meeting of all the merchants or their representatives in a district or a region. The different kinds of meetings had different names and probably they had their own particular procedure of work when they met.[4]

Their International Organisation

In a particular place local merchants dealing in one commodity sometimes had their own organisation as distinct from outside merchants dealing in the same commodity.[5] The *Nānādeśis* and the *mummuri-daṇḍas* were divided on a linguistic basis also. Thus *Nānādeśis* were divided into Cola, Malaya and Kannada. The latter had an officer who was the leader of 4000 Kannada *mummuridaṇḍas*.[6]

The relation between caste and guild has been best explained by a contemporary writer namely Vijñāneśvara. He defines *Śreṇiyah* as guilds of persons earning their livelihood by the same kind of labour though belonging to different castes or the same caste. The best example for this definition is that of the Banajigas or *Nānādeśis*. In the beginning they were Jain and later on they became converts to Viraśaivism, and the Malayāḷa *Nānādeśis*, who had their stronghold in Arasikere in central Karnataka claim to be ornaments of *Vaiśyakula*. In the same place we find reference to some great merchants of Brahmin descent;[7] whether they were Jain, Vaiśya, Brahmin or Vīraśaiva, all of them claim to support the *Vīra Baṇanju Dharma*.

Their Strongholds

Their strongholds were in northern and central Karnataka. Here they concentrated their activities in capitals of either kingdoms or provinces or in religious centres like Sravaṇa-Belgōla, Belgamve, Belūr, Arasikere and Uchchangi.

Their Functions

Their most important function was to carry on trade. The way in which they carried on their trade is described in many inscriptions. One (Sk, 118) of them describes them as a class of wandering merchants visiting all countries, *grāmas, nagaras, kheḍas, pāṭṭanas* and *droṇamukhas* with valuable articles in their bags. They used asses, buffaloes and carts for transporting goods. They sold wholesale or by hawking about with articles on their shoulders. The chief articles in which they traded were precious stones, spices, perfumes, drugs, elephants and horses and grains.

Their headquarters were at Ayyavoḷe or Aihole near Bādāmi; they established branches in different parts of the Deccan and south India. They established fairs in towns and villages and appointed officers to be in their charge.

They took part in local administration, by administering certain towns. They were consulted by the central authorities in matters of local administration such as levying of taxes. They were well-known for philanthropic activities—such as the construction of tanks, temples, and making provision for worship in temples. They were also entrusted with the task of supervising the charities of others. They received deposits and paid interest on them for the ear-marked beneficent purpose.

Their Officers

They had two important officers. One was known as *Vaḍḍa Vyavahāri* or senior merchant. He was the head of the merchants in a place. The second was known as *Paṭṭanasvāmī*. The first corresponded to *Sārthavāha* of the Gupta inscriptions and the second corresponded to Nagara-Śreṣṭhin of the same times. The senior merchant is usually referred to as the head of the *Nānādesîs* and as their benefactor.[8] He led the merchants in making grants to temples (25 of 1939–40). His rank in society was high. In inscriptions he is mentioned soon after the provincial governor.[9] He was of course wealthy. One of them is described as the lord of all wealth.[10] He also had a big establishment. Another is described as master over 72 officials.[11] Some of them were noted for their bravery.[12] One of them is described as a mine of courage and a source of bravery.[13] He was also very efficient in business. One Dāmodara Seṭṭi was an expert in the examination of goods and animals. Like the senior merchant, the *Paṭṭanasvāmī* was also present on important occasions, with the government officers and the elite of the town. He was most probably a municipal officer. In Vjjayaragara the various suburbs had one *paṭṭanasvāmī*. In our period Belagamve had two or three *Paṭṭanasvāmins*, probably to look after the different suburbs. In Vijayanagara times *Paṭṭanasvāmins* were also appointed wherever a new fair was established. It was his business to manage the fair. And for this purpose he was given grants of land It is very likely that he performed a similar function in our period. The relation between the senior merchants and the *Paṭṭanasvāmī* is not clear. Probably the former was the head of the guild and the latter represented the guild in town administration.

Other officers below the rank of the two mentioned above are an officer known as the governor of the ware-houses[14] and another was in charge of the passport department.[15] Some other officers are mentioned, but their exact duties are not specified: they are *Maṇigāra, Nād-heggaḍe,*[16] *Nāḍ-Svāmi*[17] and *Nā ḍ-Prabhu.*[18]

Strength of the Bond Among the Guildsmen

A few instances will illustrate the closeness of the bond among the guildsmen and their devotion to their faith. According to one inscription[19] all the property of the guildsmen dying without sons was to be used for the festivals and sacred rites of their patron god.

Another strictly forbids disunity among the merchants as follows: 'If without the consent of the merchants, one or two leaders enter into the house of the *ācārya* (the head of Gummattapura or the famous Śravana-BeIgola) they are traitors to the creed.'

A third inscription says, 'if any merchant denies or conceals his income (from the guild) his race shall be childless. He shall be a traitor to God, King and Creed.'[20]

The State and the Guild

It was their devotion to 'God, King and Creed' which was the cause of their phenomenal success. Wherever they went, they cooperated with the ruling dynasties, in the task of administration. As soon as Tailapa of the later Cāḷukya dynasty came to power he had to fix local cesses. 'At the request of the fifty Mahājahas and the five hundred (merchants) the king confirmed the toll contribution of betel leaves formerly fixed by Kannaradeva' of the Rāshtrakūṭā dynasty.[21] The relations of the five hundred (another name for the *Banajigas* or *Nānādesîs*) with the Hoysaḷas and the Coḷas were equally cordial. The *Mitākṣarā* of Vijñāneśvara[22] enjoins on the king the important duty of preserving their peculiar rules of conduct.[23] Thus unity among the guildsmen and harmonious relations between the state and the guilds were responsible for their long life and prosperity.

Notes

1. Majumdar, Corporate Life in Ancient India, p. 90: Majumdar, Survarnadipa, II, pt. I, p. 188.
2. *EC*, VII, *SK*, p. 118.
3. *EC*, II, p. 334.

4. *South India Inscriptions* (*SII*), IX, part I, p. 391; *EC*, XI, Davangue, p. 59.
5. *EC*, VII, p. 118.
6. *SII*, IX, pt. I, p. 297; *EC*, XI, Davangue, p. 3.
7. *EC*, V, Arsikere, p. 22.
8. *EC*, VII, p. 118.
9. *SII*, IX pt. I, no. 353; *EC*, V, p. 82.
10. *EC*, VII, p. 242.
11. Ibid., p. 247.
12. Ibid.
13. Ibid., V, p. 108.
14. Ibid.
15. Ibid., XI, p. 124.
16. Ibid., II, p. 159.
17. Ibid., XI, p. 134.
18. Ibid., VII, p. 94.
19. Ibid., VII, p. 242.
20. Ibid., VII, p. 119.
21. Ibid., II, p. 336.
22. *SII*, IX, pt. I, insc. 76.
23. II, p. 192.

23

Merchant Guilds in Medieval Āndhra

R. Narasimha Rao

THIS PAPER is an attempt to picture the organizational and functional aspects of the various corporate bodies which played a very important role in medieval Andhra with the aid of all available inscriptional evidence.

Numerous merchant organisations flourished in medieval Āndhra and played a prominent role in the economic life of the period. Prominent among these were the Teliki-1000, the Nakaramu, the Pekkanḍru and the Deśī. The Teliki or oil-millers, as a corporate body existed from the early Sātavāhana period. It was a closely knit orgainzation, with members spread all over the Āndhra country, controlling and regulating the socio-economic activities of its members. The Nakaramu was an organization of traders in five metals. Like the Telikis the Nakaras were also organized on a countrywide basis with separate units corresponding to the various territorial divisions of the time. Again, like the Telikis, this guild had wide jurisdiction over its members. The Pekkandru was a federal organisation with local and territorial units and enjoyed extensive power in regulating the activities of its members. Representing almost all the *varṇas* in the trading community, this guild had its own flag. The Deśī, conforming to the general pattern of corporate bodies of the period, was also organised on a federal basis and wide powers of controlling the activities of its members. The members of this guild traded in all kinds of articles and commodities. Many of these organisations had *praśastis* of their own containing a number of honorific titles attesting their warlike qualities and *śāstric* knowledge.

The Telikis

From the early centuries of the Christian era the Telikis, i.e. oil-millers, seem to be organised into a separate corporate body. Records[1] of the Sātavāhana period mention the Tilapistakas as one among several guilds that existed in

*17th Session at Ahmedabad, 1954.

their dominion. We hear of them next in the Tek plates[2] of Rājarāja Coḍa Ganga, which record the grant of certain social privileges to this community and describe them as devoted to the Cāḷukyan family as having accompanied Vijayāditya, the Lord of Ayodhyā, to the south, as having protected the Cāḷukyan kings with their lives, and as divided into 1000 families such as Velumanūḷḷu, Pattipāllu, Nariyūḷḷu, Kumudāḷḷu, Ponandḷu, Śrāvakulu, U ndrūḷḷu, Ammagonḍaḷu. The obvious inference is that the institution continued to flourish throughout the intervening period of about eight centuries.

Many records[3] of this guild contain a *praśasti* which supplies interesting details about it. In there Vakkaṇa, the Teliki-vevuru or the Teliki-1000, as they were commonly called, are described as *Yama-dharma niyama-parāyaṇulu* (devoted to the observance of *Yama, dharma,* and *Niyama), Brahma-sambhava-Paulastya-kula-kramāgata-Manuvaṁśodbhavulu* (born in the race of Manu who was of the lineage of Paulastya, an offspring of Brahmā), *Sakala-śāstra-viśāradulu)* well versed in all the *śāstras), Kanakāpurī-Ayodhyāpurī-Gojapur-ādhināyakulu* (lords of the cities of Kanakāpurī, Ayodhyāpurī, and Gajapurī), *Ayodhyāpuravareśvara-bhṛtyulu* (the servants of the Lords of Ayodhya), *Indrakīlanagaśrī-Kṛṣṇaveṇyānadītīra-śrī-Vijayavaṭīpur-ādhinayakulu* (lords of the city of Vijayavāṭa, situated on the banks of the river Kṛṣna near the Indrakīla mountain), *Sakalaiśvarya-sadhānvayulu* (enjoyers of all kinds of wealth and happiness), *Kapilamahāmunivara-prasāda-labdha-Cāḷukyarāajya-mūḷasthambhāyamānulu*[4] (supporting pillars of the kingdom of the Cāḷukyas by the grace of great sage Kapila), *Satya-śaucācāra-virā jitulu* (devoted to truth, purity and good conduct), *Gurudcvapād-ārādhakulu* (worshippers of the feet of their gurus), *Biiagavatī-labdha-varaprasādulu* (receivers of the grace of Goddess Bhagavatī), *Kapilamaṭha-pratiṣṭhiiulu*[5] (establised in the Kapilamaṭha), *Paula-ṣṭhi-Bhagavati-sthāna-pratiṣṭhitulu* (established in the strongholds of Paulasṭhī and Bhagavatī), *Paulasthayasahasra-śākhānvaya-gotrulu* (the *gotrins* of the 1000 branches of families which sprang from Paulastya), and *Bezavàḍa-Malliśvara-śrīpāda-padmārādhakulu* (worshippers of the holy feet of God Mallīśvara of Bezawad).

From the above *praśasti* it appears that the Telikis came to the south as the camp-followers of the progenitor of the Cāḷukyan race and continued to be staunch supporters of the Cāḷukyas in their Struggle for the acquisition and consolidation of power in the south, that Goddess Bhagavatī was the tutelary deity of the community, that though by profession oil-millers they were equally good at arms and *śāstric* knowledge.

This guild figures as Teliki-1000. The meaning and implication of the figure 1000 are not known. While *the praśasti* found in many records describes the community as *Paulastya-sahasra-śākhānvaya-gotrulu* (the *gotrins* of the 1000 branches of families which sprang from Paulastya) the Teki plates referred to above also mention the Teliki as divided into 1000 families obviously branches of the Paulastya *gotra*. The Teki plates also mention many *gotras* which must be taken to have been included among these 1000 *śākhā-gotras* or branches. To these may be added the Velandunūdla[6] and Enaddumusunudla[7] *gotras* mentioned in other records of this community.

We do not know anything definite as to the headquarters and other centres of this corporation. There are, however, certain expressions in some of the records which help us to draw certain conclusions in this regard. This community is described as *akhiladeśāla-Teliki-vevuru*[8] (Teliki 1000 of all the countries). A record from Bezawada,[9] dated in s. 1475, mentions an agreement made by members of this community of Teliki 1000 from Kondavidu, Kondapalli, Rajamahendravaram and other countries. Obviously the *akhila-deśālu* mentioned above included the towns mentioned in the Bezawaḍa record. Some records[10] exclusively describe these Telikis as *Bezawāḍa-śāsanulu* which literally means 'rulers of Bezawada'. It was customary in the middle ages for many people who lived in a particular town or excercised any authority or influence therein to describe themselves in the above manner as *śāsanulu*. From this it may be inferred that the Teliki 1000 had some special relation with Bezawada. From the fact that in spite of their being mentioned as hailing from several other places like Kondavidu, Kondapalli, Rajamahendravaram, etc., and from the fact that the expression *śāsanulu* is mentioned only in the case of Bezawada, it may be reasonably inferred that their principal seat was located at Bezawada. If so, it seems that in several important centres like Kondavidu and Rajamahendravaram they had branch organisations.

Some interesting details are available from inscriptions regarding the corporate life of the members of this community. Reference[11] has already been made to certain social privileges granted to this community by prince Rājarāja Coḍa Gaṅga of the Cāḷukya-Coḷa dynasty. A record from Bezawada,[12] also referred to above, gives details regarding a contract made by members of this community in relation to certain marriage customs. One record from Srikakulam[13] states that an oil-mill was exempted from the payment of a duty named *ari* by the Teliki 1000 for setting up a lamp in the local temple. These instances indicate how the corporate body excercised several powers over individual members of the community. The expression *samaya-drohulu* (traitors to the *samaya*) occurring in another record implies that the corporation possibly exercised some penal powers like excommunication over offenders of its decisions or agreements.

Thus the Teliki 1000 seems to be a closely-knit organisation with members spread all over Andhradesa and with the powers of controlling and regulating the life and customs of its members on both the social and economic sides.

Nagaramu

The Nagaramu seems to be another important merchant guild that existed in medieval Andhra. Some interesting details are available from inscriptions about this organisation.

The expressions Nakaramu and Nagaramu appear in several records and may be taken to be the general name of this organisation. There is also the expression Nakaras[14] appearing in one of the records of the period, relating to one particular place and its obvious implication is a member of the Nakaramu. An inscription from Tripurantakam[15] in the Kurnool district, dated ins. 1172, describes the Nagaramu as worshippers of Nagareśvara. This suggests that the name of the body was derived from the name of its tutelary deity.

The nature of the work done by this organisation is somewhat dubious. One inscription from Mattewada[16] belonging to the reign of the Kākatīya king Gaṇapatideva, describes them as traders in five metals. Another undated record from Srikakulam[17] in the Kistna district, mentions the Pañcalohādhipatulu (masters of the five metals). This give the impression that these were either workers or traders in five metals. Since other information shows that this was primarily a trading corporation, the term mentioned above must be taken to mean that this body only traded in the five metals. The Mattewada record also states that the Nakaramu gifted 2 *vis* of sandal on every cart load (to a temple). This implies that they carried on trade in sandal and other goods, for, otherwise they could not reasonably gift taxes on these commodities. It may therefore be concluded that the Nakarmu was a body of general merchants trading particularly in five metals.

Inscriptions[18] mentioning the Nakaramu are available from several parts of Āndhradeśa. This indicates that this was a fairly widespread organisation which played a prominent part in the economic life of the country.

Several inscriptions[19] of this period contain the expression Nakarapuvāḍa as belonging to particular towns. The obvious inference is that in each of these towns there was a *vāḍa* or suburb in which the Nakaramu had its place of bussiness or its members resided. Evidently, this was the exclusive business area where all transactions relating to trade in metals and other articles were carried on under the authority and supervision of the Nakaramu.

Many varieties of the Nakaramu are known from the epigraphical records. There are expressions like Anumakoṇḍa-Nakaramu,[20] Ciramiṭṭa Nakaramu,[21] Karakaṇṭhapura-Nakaramu,[22] meaning the Nakarams of well known towns like Anumakoṇḍa, Ciramiṭṭa and Karakaṇṭhapura. These are all guilds located in particular towns. An inscription[23] from Triparantakam, dated in s. 1172, mentions a Pottapināṭi-Nakaramu Pottapināḍu was a wellknown territorial division. On the analogy of Anumakoṇḍa-Nakaramu, etc., it may be inferred that there was a Nakaram for a *nāḍu*, besides the Nakarams of individual towns. Evidently, the Nakaras like the Telikis were organised on a countrywide basis, and had separate units corresponding to the various territorial divisions of the time. There are two more expressions, Nānādeśī-Nakaramu[24] and *aśeṣa*-Nakaramu.[25] The first of these indicates that the Nakaras were Nānādesī, meaning thereby that they belonged to different localities. Perhaps members belonging to various guilds, located at different places, present at a particular place went under this name. Similarly, the word *aśeṣa* means all and without exception. The combined expression *aśeṣa*-Nakaramu may be taken to mean a combination of all Nakarams. It is possible that at Warangal, where this inscription is found, there was both a local guild and a territorial guild as well and that both kinds of guilds transacted the business referred to in the record. From these instances it appears as though there were local, territorial, and general organisations of the Nakaras.

An inscription from Ghantasala,[26] in the Kistna district, mentions that 102 of the Nakaramu (*Nakaramu-nūṭa-ibbaṇḍru*) should protect a gift made to the local temple. This implies that there were 102 members in the local Nakaramu. No other instances are available regarding the numerical strength of a Nakaramu.

An inscription from Srikakulam[27] states that the Nakaramu gifted the *Bogaram-pannu* and all other taxes to the local temple, while another record from Karakanthpuram[28] refers to the gift of a portion of the toll revenue by the local Nakaras to the temple. From these instances it may be inferred that this organisation enjoyed the right of gifting to temples certain taxes payable by its members. Then there is the expression *śuṅkaparivarjitulu*[29] occurring in connection with the Nakaram. This means exemption from the payment of *śuṅkamu*. A tax named *śuṅkamu* of various kinds is known from inscriptions. Since the Nakaramu is a body of traders, the *śuṅkamu* mentioned above may be taken to be the *śuṅkamu* levied on the shops (*angadi-śuṅkamu*) or on articles sold *(ammakuḍa-śuṅkamu)*.

The inscription from Srikakulam,[30] referred to earlier, mentions the titles *Ekāṅga-vīrulu, Prauḍha-vīrulu, Kadana-pracaṇḍulu* with references to the Nakaramu. All these seem to be honorific appelations attesting the war-like qualities of the Nakaras.

The Pekkaṇḍru

Several inscriptions from Āndhradeśa mention peculiar organisations whose names end with the expression Pekkaṇḍru. An undated inscription from Bezawada,[31] in the Kistna district, mentions a business settlement effected before the Suravaram Pekkaṇḍru. Another record from Yenamadala[32] in the Guntur district, mentions the gift of *magama* by the Yenamadala-sthalamu-Pekkaṇḍru. A third inscription from Nellore district,[33] a fourth from Tangesh in the Guntur district, and a fifth from Tripurantakam[34] in the Kistna district, mention gifts made by the Nānādeśa-Pekkanḍru. One record from Tripurantakam,[35] two from Yenamadala[36] and one from Tangeda[37] mention gifts made by the Ubbayanānādesī-Pekkaṇḍru. In all these instances the term Pekkanḍru is a common suffix. A series of organisations like Deśi or Svadeśi, Paradeśi, Nanādeśi and Ubhayanānādeśi also figure in other records as such.[38] The suffix Pekkaṇḍru distinguishes the former from the latter. Again most of the records[39] that mention the Pekkaṇḍru contain titles which those that mention the second series do not mention. Further, two records from Yenamadala[40] belonging more or less to the same time, mention the Ubhayanānādeśi and the Ubhayanānādeśi-Pekkaṇḍru. It may be reasonably concluded that all these records refer to two distinct and different groups of organisations, one in whose names 'Pekkaṇḍru' figure? as a common factor and the other in whose names 'Deśi' occurs as a common factor. Hence the Deśi and the Pekkaṇḍru seem to have been two different kinds of organisations.

There seem to be four varieties in the Pekkaṇḍru. The Suravaram-Pekkaṇdru was obviously an organisation confined exclusively to one single village, Suravaram in the present instance. *Sthala* as a territorial division, occurs in many inscriptions from Āndhradeśa.[41] Yenamadala-sthala mentioned above[42] must have been a division of this type. Yenamadala-sthalamu-pekkaṇḍru, therefore, denotes the Pekkaṇḍru that pertained to a *sthala* or a territorial Pekkaṇḍru. One of the Tripurantakam inscriptions,[43] referred to above, states that the Nānādeśa-pekkaṇḍru assembled at Tripurantakam for transacting a *samaya-kārya* or business. *Samaya* means an organisation, technically a guild. Nānādeśi means those coming from different regions. Obviously, this *samaya* or guild had under its jurisdiction an area wider than a *sthala,* mentioned above as in the case of Yenamadala-sthalam-pekkaṇḍru. Then there is the fourth name Ubhaya-nānādeśi pekkaṇḍru. Ubhaya means both. Ubhayanānādeśī-pekkaṇḍru may be reasonably taken to mean an institution belonging to different regions both indigenous and foreign. This interpretation is justified by the mention in one inscription[44] from Tangeda of this organisation making a gift together with the eighteen *samayas* of Tangeda-sthala. This shows that the Ubhaya-nānādeśī-pekkaṇḍru was outside of and distinct from and therefore possibly higher than the *sthalam* organisation.

The following gradations in this general organisation going by the name Pekkaṇḍru seem to have existed—(1) village-Pekkaṇḍru; (2) Sthalam- Pekkaṇḍru; (3) Nānādeśa (probably Sima) Pekkaṇḍru; (3) Ubhayanānādeśi (probably *nāḍu* or several *nāḍus)* Pekkaṇḍru.

One of the inscriptions from Yenamadala, referred to above, mentions the Pekkaṇḍru as having jurisdiction over such a wide territory as Pākanāḍu, Veṅgī, and Anumakoṇḍa-*sthala* of which the Yenamadala-sthalam-pekkaṇḍru was obviously a branch. Thus the Pekkaṇḍru seems to be a federal organisation with local and territorial units.

Some of the records[45] mentioning the Pekkaṇḍru contained certain titles pertaining to it. Among these the following deserve *mention,—Brahma-kṣatriya-vaiśya-cāturvarṇaśram-dharma-pratipāli-tulu Pañcaśata-vīraśāsana-labdnāneka-guṇaganālaṁkṛtulu; Virabalamjya-dharma-pratipālitulu; Viśuddha-garuḍa-dhvaja-virājitulu; Ahicchtrā-nirghātulu.* The first of these titles indicates that the members were from the three main social divisions. But the mention in the Tripurantakam inscription 50 of several Reḍḍis and Seṭṭis in this connection shows that the fourth *varṇa* was also represented in this organisation. Another title shows that the organisation had some connection with Ahicchatrā in the north. Yet another title shows that it had the Garuḍa or eagle banner. One of the remaining titles implies that they were governed by 10 rules pertaining to Vīras or heroes, while the other shows that they professed the Vīrabalanjya *dharma*. A record from Alampuram[46] contains the alternative title of *Vīrabhadra-rājya-dharma-pratipāli-tulu*. These two titles, almost similar, may be taken to imply that the Vīrabalanjya *dharma* is the same as Vīrabhadra *dharma* in which case it follows that the members of this organisation were primarily followers of the Vīrabhadra cult although they also honoured Brahmā, Viṣṇu and Śiva.

The Suravaram record, referred to above, mentions a decision arrived at by the Pekkaṇḍru of Suravaram in a transaction between a certain Mollagunta Kuniśeṭṭi who borrowed 1200 ṭaṅkas from Kumara Tenungurāya and a certain Pinakunu Mācābattuḍu who stood surety for the borrower. The borrower having failed to redeem the debt, the Pekkaṇḍru decided that he should give a promisory note to the surety for the principal amount and, in lieu of the interest, surrender to the surety merit that accrued to him on account of the several good deeds such as the performance of thread-marriages and marriages to Brahmins, the construction of tanks, etc. It may be inferred from this that the *samaya* performed some judicial functions also besides the usual *samaya-kāryas* for the transaction of which meetings were usually held in a temple.[47]

The Desī

Many inscriptions from Āndhradeśa mention an organisation of merchants known by several names containing a common factor.

There is reference to the Deśī or Svadeśī, Paradeśī, Nānādeśī, and Ubhaya-Nānādeśī. These names imply local, neighbourly, both local and neighbourly, and these together with outside groups. Deśī, common to all groups, may be taken to be the general name of the organisation. These very names indicate that the Ubhayanānādesī was, as in the case of Pekkaṇḍru, the larger unit to which the other three were affiliated at lower levels.

A record from Warangal, belonging to the reign of the Kākatīya king Pratāparudradeva, registers gifts by the four 'Deśī' organisations mentioned above and besides by the Gandhavāru, Taggaramuvāru (traders in tin), Mūseravāru, and Ākūla-kuragāyala-beharulu (traders in betel-leaves and vegetables). Some of these groups of merchants gave gifts of taxes on commodities on which the Deśi organisations also gifted taxes. This implies that these organisations had some connection or other with these groups. Probably, these groups were affiliated, perhaps loosely, to the four standard Deśī organisations.

The articles in which members of this guild traded were camphor, civet, musk, lead, copper, tin, ivory, sandal, cotton, yellow-silk, dāsūripaṭṭu, paṭṭu-māli (silk-thread or spun silk), coral, pearl, rudrākṣa (seeds of Elaeocarpus ganitrus), gāṭūpusa-red-paint, queues, turmeric, nūlamalaga (yarn), ura (?), red-jaju (red chalk or colour made of lac), goru-padāla-malaga, indigo, oil, arecanuts, betel-leaves, sesamum-seeds, ginger, coconuts, tamarind-ūrugāyalu, vegetables, fruits, green-gram, paddy, honey, mustard seed, black-pepper, nūvula penta, uppupenta, etc.

Like the other merchant guilds of the period, the Deśi seem to have enjoyed certain powers of taxation. Generally duties were imposed on the goods sold by its members for the benefit of some temple.

Notes

1. *Lüder's List,* no. 1137.
2. *EI,* VI, 334–47.
3. *SII,* IV, 699, 774, 766, *SII,* VI, 149, 152.
4. This differs from '*Bhagavati-vara-prasāda-labdha-rājyānāṃ-Cālukyānām*' found in Cālukyan inscriptions.
5. This was obviously a celebrated Śaiva *maṭha* but its identity is not known.
6. *SII,* I, 152.
7. *SII,* VI, 149.
8. *SII,* IV, 774, 796, 797.
9. *SII,* IV, 797.
10. *SII,* X, 221, 554; *SII,* VI, 152.
11. Teki plates.
12. *SII,* IV, 797.
13. *SII,* V, 136.
14. *SII,* IX, 294.
15. *SII,* X, 429.
16. *CTI,* no. 11.
17. *SII,* IV, 972.
18. *CTI,* nos. 7, 10, 11.
19. Ibid., V, 1046, 1114, 1142.
20. *CTI,* no. 7.
21. Ibid., no. 10.
22. *SII,* IX, 294.

23. Ibid., IX, 429.
24. Ibid.
25. Ibid., VII, 734.
26. Ibid., X, 115.
27. Ibid., IV, 972.
28. Ibid., IX, 294.
29. Ibid., IV. 972.
30. Ibid.
31. Ibid., IV, 784.
32. Ibid., IV, 935.
33. *NDI,* no. 78.
34. *SII,* X, 565.
35. Ibid. 473.
36. Ibid., 480.
37. Ibid., IV, 939; X, 381.
38. Ibid., X, 495.
39. Ibid., VII, 734.
40. Ibid., X, 473.
41. Ibid., IV, 939.
42. Ibid., 935.
43. Ibid., X, 473.
44. Ibid., 495.
45. Ibid., 473.
46. Ibid.
47. Ibid., VII. 734.

24

Rate of Interest During Early Medieval India

O.P. Srivastava

In recent years scholars have also paid some attention to the problem of usury and banking system in early India.[1] However, the problem of rate of interest and its implication needs further investigation. The present essay attempts to trace the varied rates of interest from the fifth–fourth century BC to the eleventh and twelfth centuries AD, as gleaned from the literary texts and epigraphs, and to correlate the same with the changing economic conditions including the state of money economy.

References to rate of interest are found from the fifth-fourth century BC onwards. *The Baudhayāna Dharmasūtra*[2] which is the earliest work prescribes 10 per cent annual interest. Gautama,[3] whose work was composed later, states the legal rate of interest as 5 *māṣakas* per month for 20 *paṇas*. According to Manu,[4] 16 *māṣakas* are equal to 1 *paṇa* and thus according to this ratio the rate comes to 18.75 per cent yearly. If the ratio, as calculated by Haradatta,[5] a commentator of Gautama who flourished in the twelfth century and Lakṣmīdhara,[6] a lawgiver of the same century, viz., *1 paṇa* = 20 *māṣakas,* is accepted, then the rate of interest works out to exactly 15 per cent per annum. In this context the rule of Manu seems to be more applicable to the ancient period, and Haradattta a late commentator of Gautama might have modified the ratio in order to adjust the rate of interest to the common rate of 15 per cent per annum, prescribed in the Smṛtis. The interest rate at 15 per cent per annum finds mention not only in the Smṛtis of Manu,[7] Yājña-valkya,[8] Nārada,[9] and Vaśiṣtha[10] but also in the *Arthasāstra* of Kauṭilya[11] In view of this it seems that the verse of Gautama containing the above-mentioned rule may have been inserted in his law book sometime in the Gupta and post-Gupta times.[12] The fact of laying down the rules regarding the percentage of interest appears to have been started in the wake of money economy as well as the growing tendency towards money lending. This is further confirmed by the currency system of ancient period.[13] Taking more than 15 per cent yearly interest has

*43rd Session at Kurukshetra, 1982.

been regarded as a sinful act in the early *Dharamasāstra* works.[14] However, Manu at one place takes a lenient view of it by allowing the creditors to take 24 per cent yearly interest, keeping in view the duties of righteous person.[15] Expressing a similar view Nārada[16] prescribes the same rate of interest. But the order of his reckoning is different from that of Manu. Manu, first, sanctions the legal rate at 15 per cent[17] per annum, then allows the creditors to charge 24 per cent per year...[18] in certain cases, and lastly formulates the rule to this effect according to *varṇa* order.[19] Contrary to this, Nārada enumerates the ordinances of Manu given under the second and third categories in the reverse order.[20] Yājñavalkya who was posterior to Manu and anteior to Nārada lays down no rule in this regard. The significance of the verse of the *Nāradasmṛti,* which lays down the interest at the rate of 24 per cent per annum, may be clearly judged from the comments of Asahāya, who flourished in the first half of the eighth century AD. He tells us that from an honest man the interest may be realized at the rate of 24 per cent per annum irrespective of his *varṇa.*[21] Thus in the light of the verse of the *Manusmṛti*[22] enjoining the same rate of interest seems to have been an interpolation which may have been made sometime after the date of the composition of the *Nāradasmṛti.* Even if we take it as genuine we can safely say that it was neither the legal rate of interest nor the generally accepted. However, Manu has allowed it. Thus it may be inferred that the rate fluctuated from 15 per cent per annum to 24 per cent in the time of Manu and onwards. Vyāsa's law book, regarded as a post-Gupta text,[23] states for the first time that the monthly rate of interest was one-eightieth of the principal, i.e. 15 per cent per annum when a pledge was made against a loan. In the case of surety and in secure loans, according to him one-sixtieth (20% yearly) and 2 per cent per month (24% per year) respectively were charged.[24]

On the whole, during the first phase of early medieval period, i.e. between AD 600 and 1000, the rates of interest were increased. The legal text of this period show that the normative rate of interest is shifted from 15 per cent per annum to 24 per cent.[25] This trend may be noticed for first time in the commentary of Viśvarūpa on the *Yājñvalkyasmṛti,* composed in the early ninth century in the Malwa region. According to him, 15 per cent yearly interest was the commonly accepted normal rate.[26] However, it was to be realized only from the Brāhmaṇas. The other there *varṇas* were required to pay a quarter of the one-eightieth per month more, i.e., 20 per cent per annum.[27] The way in which he generalises the rule tends to indicate that the fact of raising annual interest rate from 15 per cent per annum to 20 per cent per annum had become fairly noticeable by the time of Viśvarūpa. Hārīta, who may be assigned between AD 600 and 900 lays down that in case 25 Purāṇas fetch an interest of 8 *paṇas* which comes to 24 per cent per annum, it should be deemed as legal rate of interest.[28] He adds that according to this rate the principal would be doubled at the end of four years and two months.[29] According to him, the ratio is 1 Purā.

na 1:16 *paṇas.*[30] Vṛddha-Hārīta, who belongs to the same period, prescribes double of the normal interest prescribed in the early law book, i.e., 30 per cent per annum, in case no pledge has been offered to secure the debt.[31] Asahāya[32] (8th century) commenting on a verse of Nārada speaks of Brāhmaṇa Śrīdhara, who had lent his hard earned money at the rate of 24 per cent yearly interest to earn the sustenance (*vartanartham*) for his family. It clearly shows that the creditor had lent his money under straitened circumstances and he, therefore, was bound to accept the minimum rate of interest, i.e., 24 percent per annum. Medhātithi,[33] who flourished in the ninth century and whose commentary on Manu has generally been taken to reflect the changing social and economic order from Antiquity to the Middle Age, has also sanctioned 24 per cent per annum as minimum rate of interest. This was really a departure from the *Manusmṛti,*[34] In this context it may further be noted that though he belonged to Kashmir, the relevant verses denoting the change can by no means be taken to reflect the conditions prevalent in that region only. Commenting on one of the verses of Manu, he states that 24 per cent per annum should be charged as interest. According to him the clause 'Considering the practice of the virtuous man *(satāṁdharma)* is merely declamatory (*arthavāda).*[35] That 24 per cent per annum was the normal rate of interest during the first phase of the early medieval period, is further confirmed by Alberuni,[36] who visited India in the first half of the eleventh century and whose work reveals some earlier traditions also. He states, 'Usury or taking percentage is forbidden . . . only to the Śūdras it is allowed to take percentage, as long as his profit is not more than one-fiftieth of the capital (i.e., he is not to take more than two per cent). In this regard R S. Sharma[37] rightly maintains that the picture drawn by Alberuni seems not only the idealistic one but also projects Islamic ideas. He further adds that in view of the sanction given to the Vaiśyas to take interest, by almost all the law books of ancient and medieval period, it appears untenable that only the Śūdras were allowed to take percentage.[38] Keeping in view the rulers laid down by the law givers of the early centuries of the early medieval age, it may be said in this respect that 2 per cent per mensem or 24 per cent per annum as is stated in Alberuni's account, denotes possibly the normal rate prevalent in his time.

Thus, the foregoing analysis would reveal that during the first half of the early medieval period the normal rate of interest was raised from 15 to 24 per cent per annum and also acquired a prevalence.

We again witness a change during the eleventh and twelfth centuries which may be taken to represent the second phase of early medieval period. The law givers of the period prescribe 15 per cent per annum as the normal rate of interest. Haradatta[39] and Lakṣmīdhara,[40] mentioned above, favoured 15 per cent per annum as the normal rate of interest.

So did Caṇdeśvara,[41] a native of Mithila, who flourised in the thirteenth century. Vijñāneśvara[42] (eleventh century) and Kulluka[43] (twelfth century), the well known commentators of Yājñavalkya and Manu respectively, reiterate the older interest rate of 15 percent per annum sanctioned in Yājñavalkya. Thus they repeat and maintain the tradition of early law-givers[44] and are seen to have reverted to the older rate of normal interest against the normal rate of 25 cent per annum during the first phase of the early medieval period. This clearly shows a tendency towards decrease in the normal interest rate during the second phase of the early medieval period.

Consideration of *varṇa* in connection with the payment of interest which for the first time is found in the *Vasîṣtha Dharmasūtra*[45] and is followed by the lawgivers[46] of the early centuries of the Christian era, prescribes that 24, 36, 48 and 60 per cent per annum should be charged respectively from the Brāhma nas, Kṣatriyas, Vaiśyas and the Śūdras. Yājñavalkya enjoins that the *varṇa* order is applicable to these cases where no security has been offered.[47] Medhātithi[48] (ninth century), commenting on the relevant verse of Manu, states that the above rates are allowable as alternatives to those creditors who are in distress and cannot maintain their family at 15 per cent yearly interest, or in case of those who have only a small capital, or in case of the debtor being a dishonest person. In no case was it to exceed 60 per cent per annum.[49] However, at another place Medhātithi considers the term '*Kusīda-pathamahustam*' (taking up the usurious way of lending) simply as declamtory (*arthavāda*).[50] In view of this it may be said that, sometimes, the interest may have been realized at more than the rates sanctioned according to *varṇa* order. This shows a departure from the rule of Manu. Kulluka,[51] differs from the rules of Medhātithi and Govindarāja (tenth century) relating to the interest rates according to *varṇa* order and allows the creditor to take 24, 36, 48 and 60 per cent per annum as interest on unsecured loans but not as alternatives in distresses.[52] He has also quoted a verse from the *Yājñavalkyasmṛti* (II.3.7) in his support, denoting exactly the same import. He again says that people of this time, however, give the different rules with their own conscience.[53] This shows that Kulluka has simply tried to befit the rule of the early smrtis and thus he overlooks the prevalent practices of his period, which were different from his prescription. It also tends to reveal the feudal tendencies of the age wherein the rates of interest vary from region to region and person to person.[54]

The secular texts of the early medieval period also have some significant bearing on the increased and decreased rates of interest. The *Gaṇitāsāra-saṅgraha* of Mahāvīracārya, a treatise on mathematics, composed in AD 850 in Karnataka region, throws some significant light on the actual practice regarding the rates of interest, in respect of secular loans. This work supplies us with interest rates varying from 1¾ per cent to 3⅓ per cent per month (or from 21 per cent to 160 per cent per annum).[55] Those between 36 per cent and 60 per cent per annum are comparatively more in number and they appear to have been commonly accepted rates of interest. It may be noted that only one mathematical problem in, the book refers to the interest rate of 2 per cent per month or 24 per cent per annum, which was the normal rate of interest sanctioned in the *Hārītasmṛti*[56] and the commentaries of Medhātithi[57] and Asahaya[58] on Manu and Nārada respectively. The interest rates around 6 per cent per month has been mentioned as many as ten times in this work.[59] This may indicate that the normal rate of interest was not usually followed in practice.

In actual practice the second phase of the early medieval period also witnessed some deviations from the normal rate of interest in regard to loans given for secular purposes. However, these were lower than the interest rates of the preceding centuries. In the *Bijagaṇita*[60] of Bhāskarācārya, which was composed in southern India in the twelfth century, the rates of interest vary from 1 to 10 per cent per month (from 12 to 120 per cent per annum). According to the *Lilāvati*[61] the text on mathematics by the same author, the rates of interest ranged from 36 per cent per annum to 50 per cent per annum. Those between 24 to 50 per cent per annum are predominant and seem to have been the commonly prevalant rates of interest. These rates correspond to those sanctioned in the law books of this period with a view to the *varṇa* order.[62] Some specimen documents, collected in the *Lekhapaddhati* (thirteenth century) which was compiled somewhere in the region lying between Gujarat and Rajasthan, have some significant bearing on the rate of interest. Some of these refer to an interest of 2 per cent per mensem, i.e. 24 pre cent per annum.[63] But these rates of interest which were in actual practice during the eleventh and twelfth centuries were lower than those prevalent during the first phase of the early medieval period.

The rules given above are mostly applicable to ordinary loans in normal times. The loans given for trade fetched higher interest. On commercial loans the rates of interest i.e., 120 and 240 per cent per annum, mentioned in the *Arthasâstra,*[64] are found in the *Yājñavalkyasmṛti*[65] also. However, Manu[66] who flourished earlier than Yajñavalkya, left the rates of commercial loans to be fixed by experts according to place and time. These very rates continued to be prescribed by the law-givers of the early medieval period.

Prior to going into the details of the problem on the basis of inscriptional evidence it would be relevant to draw attention to the fact that money lending developed with its two main prerequisites, the practice of giving loans, in cash and kind, for secular purposes, and making investments or endowments of property on perpetual interest for religious purpose. The former involves moral retrogression on account of human weakness of avarice and selfishness. With a view to minimising these immoral longings lawgivers of every age might have arrived at a certain percentage which would be known as the normal rate of interest. The latter one did not suffer from moral stigma, and it seems that, on account of its religious nature the rates of interest on religious endowments were generally lower than what had been sanctioned by the lawgivers of the early medieval period and also than those which we find in the secular texts like *Gaṇitasārasaṁgraha*[67] (850) and the *Bīja-gaṇita*.[68] The lower rates of interest appear to have been due to religious consideration. Temples also lent money on lower interest and also charged higher interest if the debtors agreed to pay the same.

The epigraphic pieces of evidence also reveal that the rate of interest witnessed a gradual increase from the antiquity to the madieval age.[69] The extent epigraphs of the early centuries of the Christian era supply us with three different rates—12 per cent,[70] 9 per cent,[71] and 6 per cent[72] per annum on religious endowments. It shows that even the highest rate, i.e. 12 per cent per annum which was in vogue during this period, was lower than the normal rate (15 per cent per annum) of interest prescribed in the ancient law books. Inscriptional evidence does not throw any light on the rate of interest from the third to the eighth century. There are a number of inscriptions[73] of south India belonging to the ninth and the tenth centuries which mention the rates of interest on religious endowments to the temples ranging from 15 to 17 per cent per annum. A careful study of the numerous inscriptions[74] of south India also reveals that during the eleventh and twelfth centuries the usual rate of interest was from 15 per cent to per cent per annum.

The loans taken for secular purposes, such as cousumption, meeting the demand of ruling aristocracy and for paying the government dues, would have certainly been lent on higher rate, of interest. Some inscriptions[75] of the same region belonging to the ninth and tenth centuries refer to such loans given to some village assemblies and settlements on which interest rates varied from 25 to 40 per cent per annum.[76] These rates of interest were much more than the normal rates prescribed in the legal texts of this age during the eleventh and twelfth centuries The loans taken by debtors for provision or providing sustenance to their family fetched interest between 25 and 37½ per cent per annum Some inscriptions from Rajasthan supply us with two categories of rates of interest. Those[77] from Jalore city give 10 and 12 per cent per annum (which were below normal rate sanctioned in the law books of this age) and those[78] from Bhinmal, mention the interest rates from 30 to 33½ per cent per annum. These rates were not only higher than the normative rate found in the law books but also more than the rates that were in vogue in other regions. According to D. Sharma[79] the political crisis on account of continued Muslim invasion might have been the probable reason behind it, because during the period vs 1306 and vs 1325, which yielded the lower interest rates. Cācigadeva was firmly seated on the throne and his reign was free from such trouble.[80] However, an alternative probability may also be suggested. Since the inscriptions bearing the higher interest rates are dedicated to the Brāhmaṇa deities and the epigraphs registering the lower rates of interest are offered to the Jain *tīrthaṅkaras,* this difference may, therefore, be understandable to some extent in relation to the prevalent sectarian rivalary in this particular area.[81] The higher rates of interest appear to have been an exceptional situation which may have been created in a state of gross insecurity from Muslim invasion also.[82]

The foregoing survey would, thus, reveal the general tendency towards an increase in the rate of interest during the first phase of the early medieval period. The normal rate was raised from 15 per cent per annum to 24 per cent per annum between AD 600 and 1000.[83] But it was reduced in the succeeding two centuries.[84] It is interesting to note that the epigraphic evidence also reveals similar trend.[85] In respect of religious endowments the rate of interest ranges from 9 per cent to 12 per cent per annum during the first four centuries of the Christian era. But by the end of the ninth century and beginning of the tenth it is so raised so as to range from 15 per cent to 17 per cent per annum. During the eleventh and twelfth centuries it was brought down to 15 and 12.5 per cent per annum. Besides, the specified time for maximum accumulation of interest on loans in cash was reduced from 6 years and 8 months[86] to 4 years and 2 months[87] during the period from the sixth to ninth century. The dishonest debtors of post-Gupta times were also compelled to pay a fine which was twice[88] the fine stipulated in the early law books,[89] Devanabhaṭṭa[90] (thirteenth century) did not stipulate any fine but only laid down that such a debtor was to be compelled to pay the principal plus interest. The first phase of the early medieval period obviously coincides with the languishing state of economy characterized by the paucity of coins,[91] growing insecurity on account of political disturbances[92] and robbery,[93] poverty to the common people on account of repeated famines and floods[94] and the oppressive features of taxation[95] as the arbitrary exactions[96] by the *sāmantas* and rapacious, officials, who could not afford to pledge something against the loans taken by them. These phenomena appear to have been the main reasons for the increasing rates of interest. Besides, during this phase the normal rate of interest was not palatable to the consciousness of all people. It meant the exploitation of the miseries of the poor to a considerable extent. During this period people made little use of loans for productive purposes and the loans were taken chiefly for consumption, meeting the demand of lesser lords, and some times for religious purposes.[97] In such a state of affairs the rate of interest was also used as an instrument of domination against the poor and the lower peasantry.[98] Apart from these the theory of the supply and demand was one of the determinants. Bṛhaspati,[99] whose work is taken to reflect the conditions of the Gupta and, to some extent a later age, for the first time allows the creditor to bargain with debtors according to their need and risk. In this respect he further adds that a special bargain may be made in the time of distress between the creditors and debtors.[100] In such, cases the breach of normative prescriptions was possible and the interest rates could go beyond the normal one. Such a dictum is not found in the earlier law books. This rule of Brhaspati, therefore, may be taken to throw light on the increasing tendency towards rate of interest which may have matured during the first phase of the early medieval period, and, thus, it was raised to a maximum during this phase.

The rates of interest were, generally, reduced to a considerable extent in the second phase of the early medieval period on account of redeveloping money economy and urban life,[101] Needless to say, the act of reissuing of gold coins after a gap of five centuries[102] following the fall of the Gupta empire as well as other bullion currencies[103] and circulation of hoarded money on account of Mahmud Ghazanavi's invasion[104] the comparative security and the comparative prosperity on account of redeveloping traffic and industries[105] might have lessened the scarcity of money. Insecurity, and poverty may also have been reduced to a considerable extent. Thus, this phenomenon may have brought down the rate of interest during this phase and may have partly been connected with the revival of trade and commerce.

Notes

1. A.N. Bose, *Social and Rural Economy of Northern India,* [vol. II, pp. 101–7; S.K. Maity, *Economic Life in the Gupta Period* (c. AD 300–550), pp. 229–40; L. Gopal, *Economic Life of Northern India, c.* AD 700–1200 (*ELNI*), ch. VIII; R.S. Sharma, 'Usury in Early Medieval India', *Comparative Studies in Society and History,* vol. VIII, no. 2, 1965. This article is reproduced in his book *Light on Early Indian Society and Economy (LEISC),* ch. XI; M.A. Buch, *Economic Life in Ancient India,* vol. II, p. 80; A. Appadorai, *Economic Conditions in Southern India* (1000–1500 AD), vol. I, pp. 112–32; ibid., vol. II (Appendix V), pp. 786ff; R.C. Mukerji, *Foundations of Indian Economics,* pp. 265–79; P.V. Kane, *History of Dharamasastra,* vol. III, pp. 411–61; Dipakaranjan Das, *Economic History of the Deccan,* pp. 271–7; Irfan Habib, 'Usury in Medieval India', *Comparative Studies in Society and History,* vol. VI, pp. 400ff. Some of the regional and dynastic studies also devote a few pages on money-lending. For example; D. Sharma, *Early Chauhan, Dynasties,* p. 336 f., ibid., *Rajasthan Through the Ages,* vol. I, pp. 505–7; A.K. Majumdar, *Chaulukyas of Gujarat,* pp, 274–83; A.S. Altekar, *Rashtrakutas and their Times,* pp. 371–75; K.A.N. Sastri, *The Coḷas,* pp. 599ff.
2. *Kasi Sanskrit Text Series,* no. 104, 1.10.22.
3. XII.29, the line reads '*Kusīdāvṛdhirdharmya-vimśatiḥ-pañcamāsika-prati-māsam.*
4. VIII, 134–36.
5. On *Gautama,* XII.29.
6. *Kṛtyakalpataru (vyavahārākāṇḍa),* ed. by K.V.R. Aiyanger, (G.O.S. no. CXIX), p. 279. The line runs '*māsovimsatibhāgastu, paṇya parikirtitaḥ.*
7. VIII. 140.
8. II. 37.

9. *Nāradasmṛti,* I.99.
10. II.51.
11. III.11.
12. R.S. Sharma has rightly observed that some of the passages in the *Gautama Dharmd-sutra,* which have some significant bearing on social and economic matters pertaining to early medieval period, appear to have been interpolated in this law book sometime in the Gupta and post-Gupta times; idem, *LEISE,* p. 119, n. 20; *Sudras in Ancient India,* pp. 83 84.
13. In the time of Kauṭilya and during the Kuṣāna period there are ample evidences to different types of coins which would show that there was an established currency system between the fourth century be and the third century AD.
14. *Manu.,* VIII.140; *Nāradasmṛrti,* 1.99, *Vasîṣṭḥa,* II.51.
15. *Manu.,* VIII.141.
16. *Narad,* II.101.
17. *Manu.,* VIII.140.
18. Ibid., VIII.141.
19. Ibid, VIII.142.
20. *Nāradasmṛtī,* I.100 (cf. third category of Manu) and I.101 (describes the second point of Manu).
21. Asahāya On *Nārada* I.101 vide Laxmanshastri Joshi ed., *Dharmakośa,* vol. I, pt. II, pp. 692–93.
22. VIII. 141
23. R.S. Sharma has assigned the *Vyāsaṃṛti* between AD 600 and 900 (*LEISE,* p. 121). But according to P.V. Kane the *Vyāsasṛti* would have been compiled sometime in the fourth–fifth century AD (*HDS,* no. 5, pt. II, pp. 529–35). In the light of above arguments the significant references, to money-lending found in this lawbook may be placed between AD 500 and 700. However, some of its passage related to social and economic matters may be assigned to some later dates.
24. *Kṛtyakalpataru* XIII, p. 279; P.V. Kane, *History of Dharmasastra (HDS),* vol. III, p. 421; R.C. Majumdar, ed., *The Classical Age,* p. 602.
25. R.S. Sharma has traced a tendency of gradual increase throughout the centuries of early medieval period, *LEISE,* p. 121.
26. Kane, *HDS,* vol. I. pt. II. pp. 553–65.
27. On *Yājñavalkya,* cited in *Kṛtyakalpataru,* XII, p. 279, fn. 3. The verse reads '*Yādyapiviseśeṣṇāsatibhāgo bhihitaḥ tathāpi brāhmaṇasyaivāyam Anyeśāṃ tu pādavṛddhāya vṛddhikalpananm*'
28. Quoted in the *Kṛtyakalpatru* (XII) of Lakṣmīdhara. The passage runs *Purāṇapañca-viṁśatyām māse-aṣtapaṇavṛdhih',* p. 280.
29. Ibid., p. 280; the line reads '*evaṁ saḍviṁaśaiścaturbhir-varṣaiḥ dvih-pa yagatam saṁtiṣṭhate eṣa-dharmavṛddhiḥ.*'
30. Loc. cit. p. 280, '*Purānāḥ ṣoḍaśa paṇāh*'.
31. *HDS,* III, pp. 420–21 cited in *LEISE,* p. 121.
32. On *Nārada,* quoted in *Dharmakośa,* vol. I, pt. II, pp. 692–3.
33. On *Manu,* VIII.141.
34. Cf. *Manusmṛti,* VIII. 141.
35. On *Manu.,* 141.

36. E. Sachau ed. and trans, *Alberuni's India*, vol. II, p. 150.
37. *LEISE*, p. 120.
38. Loc. cit.
39. On *Gautama*, XII.29.
40. *Kṛtyakalpataru*, XII, p. 279.
41. *Gṛhastharainākara* of Caṅḍeśvara, ed. by Mm. Kamalakṛṣṇa Smṛtitīrtha BI, no. 249, p. 446.
42. On *Yājñ*, II.37.
43. On *Manu*, VIII. 142.
44. Ibid., VIII.142.
45. II.48.
46. *Manu*, VIII, 142; *Yājn*., II.87; *Viṣṇu*., VI.2; *Nārada*., I.100.
47. *Yājñ*, II.37.
48. *Manu*., VIII.142.
49. Ibid., 152.
50. On *Manu*. VIII.152.
51. Ibid., 142.
52. Medhātiṭhi and Govindarāja On *Manu*, VIII.142.
53. Kulluka On Manu, VIII.142. The verse reads, '*vedantodaita-mahaso-munervyākhyānmadriyekadviruddhamsvabudhya-ca-nibaddhamadhunatanaiḥ*, II. 37.
54. Such a tendency was prevalent even in European countries during the medieval ages. For the purposes of comparison see K. Marx, *Capital*, vol. III, p. 597. He states, 'In the Middle Ages no country had a general rate of interest.... There were large divergences both in interest rates and the conception of usury'.
55. *Gaṇitasārasāṁgraha* of Mahāvīrācārya, ed. by L.C. Jain, *Jain Granthamālā*, no. 127, VI, 15–79, pp. 94–107.
56. Quoted in *Kṛtyakalpataru*, XII, p. 280.
57. On *Manu*, VIII. 141.
58. On *Manu*., I.101.
59. *Gaṇitasārasaṁgraha*, pp. 94–107.
60. Bijagaṇita *of Bhāskarācārya*, ed. by Achyutananda Jha, pp. 232–48.
61. *Līlāvatī of* Bhaskarācārya, ed. and trans, in Hindi by Lasanalala Jha *Vidyabhavana Sanskrit Granthamala*, no. 62, pp. 117–25.
62. Kulluka, On *Manu*., VIII. 142; Vijñāneśvara, On *Yājñ*, II.37.
63. *Lekhapaddhati*, ed. C.D. Dalai and G.K. Shrigondekar, pp. 19, 21, 33, 38 and 55.
64. III. 11.
65. II.38.
66. VIII.157.
67. vv, 15–78.
68. pp. 232–48.
69. Even in Europe during the Middle Ages the rates of interest were much higher in individual cases. It was because of the limited circulation of money and the compelling need to make the most of payments in cash. See Marx, op. cit., p. 597.
70. *EI* vol. VIII, pp. 82–83ff; *Lüder's List*, no. 1133.

71. Loc. cit.
72. *Archaeological Survey of Western India,* vol. V, no. 15, p. 80.
73. *IA,* XIII, pp. 133–36; see Altekar, op. cit., pp. 371–2; *Inscriptions from Madras Presidency,* Chingelpur no. 1048, ibid., Arcot no. 636; *SII,* III, part 3, no. 236–7; ibid., nos. 103, 105 and 728.
74. *ARSIE,* 218 of 1921, *ARIE,* 1922, pt. II para 14; *SII,* II, pt. 6, nos. 6, 24, 26–27, 37; *ARSIE,* 176, of 1915; *ARIE,* 1916, pt. II, para 12 (it gives 15 per cent per annum): *SII,* II, nos. 9, 11, 13–19; 257 of 1612; *ARIE,* 1913, pt. II para 12 (15 per cent per annum).
75. *SII,* III, 165; ibid., III, pt. 3, 239 (1/4 *Puttakam* was charged on I *lakkāśu* for one month and *lakhāśu* was equal to 7 *puttakaṃ.* Thus it works out 40 per cent per annum; *EI,* XII, p. 273.
76. *EC,* IX; Channapattana, 129; *SII,* III, 56; 243 of 1921; *EI,* XII, p. 273; *SII,* III, X; Bowring et. al., 32; ibid., Davangere, 48; ibid., II, p. 247; ibid., vol. V, Arsikere, 174, 421, of 1921; *Ep. Car.,* XI, Davangere, 33; ibid., X, Mula begol, 45.
77. *Jain Inscriptions,* II, no. 363; D. Sharma, op. cit., p. 507, fn. 3; idem, *ECD,* p. 337, fn. 29.
78. *Bombay Gazetteer,* vol. I, pt. I, no. 7, p. 474; *EI,* XI, p. 56ff; D. Sharma, op. cit., p. 507, fn. 1 and 2; idem *ECD,* p. 337, fn. 27–28.
79. Op. cit., pp. 506-07; idem, *ECD,* p. 331.
80. Loc. cit.
81. The *Kathākośa prakaraṇa* of Jineśvara Sūri (story no. 32), which throws some significant light on the conditions of Gujarat and Rajasthan of the eleventh–twelfth century, states that Jainas were against the granting of extra immunities of any kind to the Br"ahmaṇas on account of their birth alone (D. Sharma, op cit., p. 445). On the other hand, Jainas were not only getting more facilities as compared to those of the Brāhmaṇas but they also enjoyed the patronage from Rajputs and other royal families of Rajasthan between the ninth and the twelfth centuries and onwards. Though the *Ādi Purāṇa* of Jinsena (tenth century), which reflects the condition of the Karnataka, we may have some ideas aLout the bitterness and opposition of the Jainas against the immunities that were granted to the Brāhma. nas (ibid., 42, vv.187–92).
82. Marx has also expressed a similar view. According to him, the rate of interest reaches its peak during crises, when money is borrowed at any cost to meet payments (idem, op. cit., p. 361).
83. cf. *LEISE,* p. 143.
84. *See supra.*
85. *See supra.*
86. *Brhaspati,* X.22,, quoted in the *Kṛtyakalpataru,* XII, p. 279; *SBE,* XXXIII.11 3, p. 320.
87. *Harītasmṛti, quoted in Krtyakalpataru,* XII, p. 280.
88. *Yamasmrti quoted in Krtyakalapataru,* XII, p. 331
89. *Manu,* VIII. 139; *Yājñ.,* II. 42.
90. *Smrticandrikā* of Devanabhatta (Vyavahārakāṇḍa), p. 167, ed. and trans. by J.R. Gharpure, p. 312.

91. R.S. Sharma, *Indian Feudalism*, pp. 87–8, 151-2; B.D. Chattopadhya, *Coins and Currency System in South India*, ch. VII, pp. 116, 118; V. Prakash, *Coinage of South India*, ch. III; ibid, pp. 52, 77, 93; A.S. Altekar, *Rashtrakutas and Their Times*, p. 364; *Rhythm of History*, pp. 59–60. For the absence of seals and guilds, see K K Thaplyal, *Studies in Ancient Indian Seals*, O.P. Srivastava, 'Śulka in Ancient and Early Medieval India', *Journal of G.N. Jha Sanskrit Vidyapeetha*, vol. XXXVII, pp. 158–60, Yadava, Presidential address.
92. Medhātithi on *Manu*. VIII.156; VII.120; *ELNI*, pp. 102–3, 254–5; B.N.S. Yadava. *SCNI*, Allahabad, 1973.
93. Yadava, op.cit., pp. 271–2; *ELNI*, pp. 101–2. For details see O.P. Srivastava, op. cit., pp. 142–44.
94. Some pieces of literary evidence of the early medieval period give a vivid account of famine and flood. *Visnu Purāṇa*, 6.1.34–36; *Brhannāradiya Purāṇa*, 38 86f. See R.C. Majumdar ed., *A Comprehensive History of India*. vol. III, pt. II, p. 985; *Rājataraṅgini*, vv. 270–78; VIII, 1206; *Agni Purāṇa*, 263, 19–21; *Kathākośa, tr.* C H. Tawney, p 161; *ELNI*, pp. 246f.
95. O.P. Srivastava,'Oppressive Features of Commercial Taxation During the Early Medieval India, in *Prāchya Pratibhā*. Commercial Taxation was comparatively more excessive during the first phase of early medieval period than that of the succeeding one, cf. B N.S. Yadava, *SCNI*, pp. 298ff, *IHR*, vol. V, nos. 1–2, pp. 49–51.
96. Yadava, *SCNI*, p. 297ff; O.P. Srivastava, 'Oppressive Features. . . .' *Prāchya Pratbihā*.
97. See *supra*.
98. For details about money-lending as the source of the emergence of debt bondage and peasants' subjection during the first phase of early medieval India, see B.N.S Yadava,'The Accounts of the Kali Age and the Social Transaction from'Antiquity to the Medieval Ages', *IHR*, vol. V, no. 1–2, pp. 41–2, 45,' idem., 'Presidential Address''Section I, *IHC*, Bombay, 1980, vol. 41, pp. 30–9; R.S. Sharma,' Usury in Early Medieval India', *Comparative Studies in Society and History*, vol III, no. 1, pp. 60, 65, *ELNI*, p. 246.
99. *Brhaspatismṛti*. XI.9.10, vide *SBE*, ed. by F. Max Müller and trans, by J. Jolly, vol.XXXIII, p. 321.
100. Ibid., I 1.0.
101. See *SCNI*, p. 275ff; the growth of cities and towns during the second phase of early medieval India may be associated with revival of trade. See B. Stein, *Peasant Slate and Society in Medieval South India*, pp. 250–1; K.R. Hall, *Trade and Statecraft in the Age of the Coḷas*, pp. 162f.
102. Kalacuri king Gaṅgeyadeva (1019–40) issued gold coins, for the first time, after a gap of about five centuries, Cunningham, *Coins of Medieval India, from the Seventh Century Down to the Muhammadan Conquests*, p. 34.
103. See, *ELNI*, ch. IX; B.D. Chattopadhyaya, op. cit , ch. VIII; L. Gopal, *Early Medieval Coin Types of Northern India*, all chapters, *SCNI*, pp. 282–3; R.S. Sharma, *Indian Feudalism*, p. 255ff. In South India, too, similar conditions prtvailed (see Chattopadhyaya, op. cit.; V. Prakash, op. cit., chs. IV, V and V.

104. Cunningham, op. cit., p. 66; O.P. Srivastava, 'Sulka in Ancient and Early Medieval India', op. cit., pp. 156–7.
105. For the growth of industries, see *SCNI*, p. 262ff. *ELNI*; pp. 238–9; K.A:N. Sastri. *The Coḷas*, p. 592ff; R.C. Majumdar ed., *The Struggle for Empire*, pp. 516–21 see *supra* fns. 100, 101 and 102 (All references described under above footnotes are related to the growth of trade and traffic).

25

Minting in Medieval Karnataka

P.B. Desai

NUMISMATIC EXPLORATIONS have revealed the prevalence of various coins and coin-specimens of the dynasties that ruled in Karnataka prior to the advent of Vijayanagar. But meagre is the information available concerning the technical aspects of minting operations.

For instance, it is not clear how far minting was a state monopoly or whether the private agencies also had their hand in these transactions during this early period. In the event of the latter alternative, it is not known in what manner the state was able to exercise its control over this specialised industry. And again, our knowledge of the localities where the minting establishments functioned is scanty.

However, in the course of my epigraphic studies I have come across some incidental passages which throw welcome light on these and other interesting problems. I propose to discuss them here.

By far the largest number of allusions to the minting transactions are found in the inscriptions of Lakkundi, a fairly big village in Gadag Taluka of Dharwar district. These allusions comprise technical terms and phrases which, as gathered from the context, were related to various aspects of manufacture and circulation of coins. The epigraphs in question, which are as many as six, belong to the later half of the twelfth century and fall during the reign period of the last two monarchs of the later C"aḷukya dynasty, *viz.*, Taila III and Somesvara IC. The inscriptions were copied in the nothern parts of the present Mysore State (present day Karnataka) during the field season of 1926–27 by the office of the Government Epigraphist for India and noticed under the collections of the Bombay–Karnataka area in the Madras Epigraphical Report for the year. The numerical figures cited as reference in the following discussion, indicate the particular numbers of the epigraphs as registered in the same Epigraphical Report.

An important fact disclosed at the outset in our study is that minting was not a state monopoly, but that it was licensed to private sectors. The industry, however, was controlled by the State through its own officials according to

*23rd Session at Aligarh, 1960.

regulations. One such officer mentioned in an epigraph (no. 48) was Pergaḍe Keśava, Suprintendent of minting transactions (*accina keniya adhikari*).

The factory where coins were manufactured was called by the general term *kamata* (no. 62, etc.), evidently derived from the Sanskrit word *karman*. This was distinguished from *akkasala* (Sanskrit *akṣāsalā*) which denoted a workshop equipped with minting apparatus (nos. 48 and 62). These workshops, it appears, were founded by the state and leased out to contractors who undertook to manufacture coins on specific terms.

The contractors are referred to as *kenikara* (Sanskrit *kreṇī*[1] from the root *kri*) in inscriptions (nos. 48, 60, etc.). The coins were Struck on dies which were framed like nails or pins *accina mole*, no. 67). *Anikaras* were a class of craftsmen associated with this industry (nos. 61, 62 and 70). The task assigned to them seems to be one of the testing the genuine quality of the metal used for minting and maintaining the good, round shape of the standardized coins (*ani* = roundness and excellency).

The inscriptions also speak of a class of dealers engaged in the purchase of coins in lumps from the factories and releasing them for circulation.[2] They are called *pottha-grahaka* which literally means 'collectors of coin bags', (nos. 60, 62). In the context of contracting we meet the phrase *patra-hastar-agu* (*i.e.* signing the document, which goes to show that the contracts were settled by committing them to writing (nos. 61, 63).

It is gathered that three kinds of coins were manufactured in the factories. One was gold *gadyāṇa* or *honnu* of a particular standard. Another was globule of gold called *chinna vatta* (Sanskrit *vrtta*), (no. 48). The third was a silver coin. This is indicated by the expression 'manufacturers of silver coins' (*belliya kammatadavaru*), occurring in an epigraph (no. 67).

It is thus seen that Lakkundi was a renowned centre of numismatic operations, where coins of various types were manufactured on a large scale. There resided in this place a considerable number of contractors, dealers and mechanics as well as state officials who were all associated with this industry. These businessmen formed themselves into an independent corporate body or guild. In religious matters, on account of their different persuasions, they followed the traditional faith of their choice, erecting shrines for the, worship of their deities. An epigraph (no. 67) mentions two such religious institutions, *viz.*, Kammaṭeśvara (i.e., the god of minting) and Kammaṭa Jinālaya (i.e., the shrine of the Jina of the minters).

Coins manufactured at Lakkundi were in circulation over an extensive area and we find them mentioned in inscriptions of other places.[3] For instance, *Lokki gadyāṇa* and *Lokki poṇ* figure in epigraphs hailing from Alur in Mundargi Petha and Kudatini in Bellary district. The word Lokki in the above expressions evidently stands for Lokkiguṇḍi which was the early name of modern Lakkundi.

Another centre noted for its minting activities was Hiriya Gobbur in Raichur district. This is disclosed by an inscription of the place dated AD 1109 in the reign of the later Cāḷukya king Vikramāditya VI. The epigraph introduces three categories of persons associated with the manufacture of coins. They were the state officials in charge of the mint-factories *(kammaṭada adhikāri),* the mint masters *(kammaṭakara)* and moderators who maintained the uniform standards of coins (*savakattukara).*[4]

Sudi in Ron Taluka, Dharwar district, was another town where coins were minted. This seems to have been the native place of the goldsmith Uttavoja who had the privilege of catering to the royal household of the Cāḷukya monarch Vikramāditya VI. This Uttavoja, it appears, held the monopoly of supplying coins of a particular standard and the local community of goldsmiths manufactured them under his supervision and control. The coins struck here were marked by a specific emblem denoting the locality. Here again figures the guild deity Kammaṭeśvara. The epigraph furnishing the above information comes from Sudi[5] and is dated AD 1103.

Two more mint-centres were functioning in the period of the eleventh and the twelfth century. One was Kudatini in Bellary district and the other Peddatumbalam formerly in the same district, but now in Kurnool district. The former place which is situated in the orbit of the famous shrine of Kārttikeya near Sandur, also contained a temple dedicated to the deity. An inscription of this village (i.e., Kudatini).[6] dated AD 1098, names two goldsmiths who manufactured gold coins bearing the figure of a peacock (*navil-achchina poṇ*). This was evidently devised to commemorate the god Kārttikeya who had the peacock as his vehicle. The goldsmiths of Tumbola (i.e. Peddatumbalam), as an inscription from Bapuram[7] states, were versed in casting pins which served as dies for striking coins (*kammaṭada-achchina moleya akkasātigalu*).

Notes

1. The Kannada word *geni* more commonly used in the transactions of the north and south Kanara districts is evidently a later form of *keni* derived from Sanskrit *kreṇī.*
2. *Bombay Karnātaka Inscriptions,* vol. I, pt. II, no. 136.
3. *South Indian Inscriptions,* vol. LX, pt. I, no. 164.
4. I have edited this inscription and discussed this topic in my *A Corpus of Inscriptions in the Kannada Districts of Hyderabad State,* pp. 30–1, 51–2.
5. *Bombay Karnataka Inscription* vol. I, pt. II, no. 153. I differ from the learned editor of the volume in interpreting certain passages of the epigraph; contra, Introduction, p. vi.
6. *South Indian Inscriptions,* vol. IX, pt. I, no. 164.
7. Ibid., no. 295.

PART 6

Patterns of Setbacks and Tensions in Early Indian Economy

26

Socio-Economic Tensions in Bhojakaṭa Rājya of Vākāṭaka Kingdom in the Time of Pravarasena II

Raghavendra Vajpeyi

THE CHAMMAK land grant inscription (hereafter, Chammak grant/inscription) of Pravarasena II of the main branch of the Vākāṭaka is unique in more than one sense. It is the first land grant which puts the donor and the donee both under obligation to honour terms of grant. It makes the otherwise perpetual grant liable to be confiscated if and when the grantees (or their successors), decide to violate the terms of grant. Apart from throwing welcome light on political aspect of grant of land made for religious purpose, the Chammak grant offers unassialable evidence on existence of an atmosphere of socio-economic tension and political unrest in the Vidarbha region of Maharashtra in the fifth century.

According to the Chammak grant, Pravarasena II had, in the eighteenth year of his reign, granted to one thousand Brāhmaṇas, belonging to various *gotra* and *caraṇa* groups, eight thousand *nivartanas* of land in the village Carmāṅka, situated on the bank of the Madhunadī in the Bojakaṭa Rājya[1] (the present-day village Chammak in the Amaravati district of Vidarbha. Bhojakaṭa is identified with Bhatkuli—a village about eight miles from Amaravati).[2] Scholars are of the opinion that Pravarasena II had put the grantee under a negative obligation.[3] But the original text of the condition-portion offers unimpeachable evidence which proves that the Vākāṭaka ruler had charged the grantee Brāhmaṇas with the duty of waging war against killers of Brāhmaṇas, robbers, adulterers and traitors to the king. He had also warned the grantee that their fief would be confiscated if and when they would indulge in prohibited activities or else would offer moral support to people indulging in them.[4] That is, the grantee were put under a positive as well as a negative obligation.

*45th Session at Annamalinagar, 1984.

J.F. Fleet,[5] D.C. Sircar[6] and V.V. Mirashi[7]—all are in agreement that the original text of the condition-portion reads thus:

Line-39. . . *Śsā (śā) sana*
Line-40. sthitiś=c= eyaṁ brāhmaṇair = iśvaraiś=c= ānupālanīyā tad=yathā rajñaṁ sa—
Line-41. ptāṅge rājye addroha-pravṛntā (ttā) nāṁ brahmaghna-caura-paradarika-rājā-
Line-42. pathyakāri-prabhṛti (ti) nāṁ saṅgrāma-kurvvatāṁ anya-grameṣv = an-a
Line-43. par (ā) ddhānāṁ ā-candr-āditya-kālīyaḥ ato=nyathā kurv-vatām = anumodatām vā
Line-44. rājñaḥ bhū (bhū) micchedaṁ kurvvataḥ a-steyam-iti.

Translation: 'And this condition of the charter should be maintained by the Brāhmaṇas and by (future) lords; namely (the enjoyment of this grant is to belong to the Brāhmaṇas) till the moon and the sun endure, provided that they commit no treason against the kingdom, consisting of seven constituent parts, of (successive) kings; (provided) that they *keep on waging war against* killers of Brāhmaṇas, thieves, adulterers, traitors to king; and that they do not raid other villages. But if they act otherwise or assent (to those acts) the king will commit no theft in taking the land away.

Thus, the condition-portion is quite informative. It hints that Pravarasena II took enough precaution of ensuring that the unusually large number of grantees—the said one thousand Brāhmaṇas—belonged to various *gotra* and *caraṇa* groups. That is, the grantees could not have common *gotra* and *caraṇa* affinity and that their meeting ground was to remain the royal favour and the obligation attached with it.

The condition-portion suggests the following things:

(a) That the village Carmāṅka of the Bhojakaṭa Rājya had become the epicentre of anti-village and anti-state activities in the eighteenth regnal year of Pravarasena II— the year of the issue of the Chammak grant;
(b) That instead of remaining a sporadic or individual criminal activity, the happenings in areas around Chammak had assumed the position of organised crime and of something like class struggle. Apart from other caste groups, Br"ahmaṇas were taking part in killings of Brāhmaṇas, and in robberies, adultery and village raids. Pravarasena II was somewhat convinced that, unless warned that their fief would be confiscated in the event they decided to change their loyalty and stand, even Brāhmaṇas of the Chammak grant could decide to participate in anti-village community and anti-state activities or else could offer moral support to people indulging in those acts. Obviously, targets or victims of the class struggle were the rural poor who were being exploited and humiliated by their resourceful and influential counterparts, i.e., the landed aristocracy;

(c) That, despite being well-versed in ritualistic religion and sacred texts, the grantee Brāhmaṇas of the Chammak grant were the men of this world. They were proficient in the knowledge of intricacies of politics and administration. They had agreed to act as loyal agents in the Chammak area armed with royal authority to wage war against, agents of class struggle; and

(d) That, though the land granted to the Brāhmaṇas amounted to eight *nivartanas* per head and was not in any way an economically viable proposition, it was the royal patronage and accompanying resources and authority which had made the grantee powerful. The secret of the royal patronage was enshrined in their willingness to curb the struggle which had engulfed the Bhojakaṭa Rājya in an acute class war.

However, Fleet was unable to reconcile with the fact that a donor could place the grantee under obligation to wage war against killers of Brāhmaṇas, etc. He was somewhat convinced that the engraver had carelessly omitted to engrave the letter *a* before *brahmaghna* (line-41) and *saṇgr"ama* (line-42) which, in his considered opinion, should have been engraved as *a-brahmaghna* and *a-saṅgrāma*, respectively.[8] Thus, he not only interpolated the letter *a* where he had found it missing but also changed the entire structure of the condition portion. Now, according to him, the condition-portion meant—'And this condition of the charter should be maintained by the Brāhmaṇas and by (future) lords; namely (the enjoyment of this grant is to belong to the Brāhmaṇas) for the same time with the moon and the sun, provided that they commit no treason against kingdom, consisting of seven constituent parts, of (successive) kings; that they are not slayers of Brāhmaṇas, and are not thieves, adulterers, poisoners of kings, etc.; that they do not wage war; (and) that they do no wrong to other villages. But, if they act otherwise, or assent (to such acts) the king will commit no theft in taking the land away."[9]

Fleet's text of the condition-portion and its translation inspired D.D. Kosambi to observe: 'The conditions are not unusual only their specific statement. The village had already been occupied by the brāhmaṇs, who would henceforth cultivate it without taxes: But clearly they have no right over previous occupants—obviously non-cultivating pastoralists—who are carefully protected. The village was to remain peaceful, never to take to arms, nor encroach against other villages. Such disarmed villages were the norms of settlement, the brahmin grants were used only for seeding.'[10]

One wonders how a discerning scholar like Kosambi could fall in the trap created by Fleet's misplaced confidence and faith in infallibility of his decision to convert *brahmaghna* (line-41) and *saṅgrāma* (line-42) of the engraver into *a-brahmaghna* and *a-saṅgrāma,* particularly when Sircar had challenged Fleet's text and had opted for the original text much before the publication of Kosambi's book.[11] The same is true of Mirashi whose *Corpus of Vākāṭaka Inscriptions* was published in 1963.[12] We are compelled to agree with Sircar because of two things. First, that a careful study, of the condition–portion shows that the engraver has left no space for making any addition of any letter, much less for the addition of the letter *a*. Second, even if we, for the sake of convenience, agree to accept Fleet's interpolation as correct, the text will lose its present form. The *anusvāra* of the word *pravṛnta(tta)naṁ* which precedes the word *brahmaghna*, because of the interpolation of the letter *a* as prefix before the latter, will automatically become *ma*. The same will be the case of *anusvāra* of *prabhṛti(ti)nāṁ* which precedes the word *saṅgrāma*, the moment the letter *a* is prefixed to *saṅgrāma*. That is, instead of remaining a group of words, the entire portion following *rājye* (line 40) and preceding *va* (line-43) will become unusually long and unwieldy compound.

Further, Fleet, Kosambi and others have not cared to ask as to how grantee Brāhmaṇas could indulge in anti-village community and anti-state activities if they were really religious and peace-loving people? Unless Brāhmaṇas, particularly grantee Brāhmaṇas were known to have taken part in anti-village community and anti-state activities, why and how Pravarasena II was apprehensive of their future criminal activities? Village raids and acts of treason were the activities which required weapons and organisation. Unless the grantee possessed both, how could they resist or hope to overcome organised and collective armed resistance? And, if the 'Chammak grant was issued primarily for a religious purpose, why was it made in favour of such a large number of Brāhmaṇas who got less than one-third of the average minimum of twenty-five *nivartanas* of land which grantees of Pravarasena II's other grants received?[13]

A careful study of Pravarasena II's land grant inscriptions issued between his regnal years 18 and 23 will suggest that the Vākāṭaka kingdom was engulfed in a serious crisis during that period. The Jamb grant of his second regnal year and all grants issued till the Siwahi grant of his 18th regnal year maintain that Pravarasena II had claimed to have established the *kṛta-yuga* (the golden age) because of the grace of Śambhu (Śiva).[14] But the grants issued after the Siwani grant and before the Wadgaon grant of his 25th regnal year[15] do not make that claim. On the contrary, the grants issued between his regnal years 19 and 23 make reference to three categories of feudatories: those who had accepted the Vakataka overlordship because of the fear of invasion, those against whom, steps were taken and those who were actually defeated and warn them of the consequences of their deliberate attempts to undermine the grants made by their Vākāṭaka overlord.[16]

Second, Pravarasena II originally retained his *senāpati* for at least a period of seven years.[17] His inscriptions suggest that *senāpati* was a very important officer and was next to the king in authority. Under his supervision grants were normally drafted, executed and maintained.[18] But after the execution of the Chammak grant things started changing. The office of *senāpati* drew special attention of the rule and those who occupied that office were frequently changed. Thus, Citravarma, who remained the *senāpati* from Pravarasena II's regnal year 11 to 18[19] was replaced by Bappadeva with the issue of the Siwani grant of the 18th year,[20] who, in turn, was replaced by Namidāsa in 23rd year.[21] However, Bappadeva again became *senapati* in 25th year of Pravarasena II's rule.[22]

Thus, Pravarasena II's decision to grant eight thousand *nivartanas* of land in Chammak to one thousand Brāhmaṇas of various *gotra* and *caraṇa* groups becomes meaningful. Since no one could justify killing of Brāhmaṇas, robbery, adultery, village raids or efforts to destroy any constituent element of kingdom and attempts to rise in revolt against the reigning king, Pravarasena II instructed the grantees of the Chammak grant to keep on waging relentless war against the people indulging in anti-village community and anti-state activities. Since the Vākāṭaka ruler had made the grant in the feudatory area of Śartughnaraja's son Koṇḍarāja, he ordered the latter to make a notification. This hypothesis is supported by two things namely, that the occasion of the issue of the Chammak grant was the only occasion when the name of the father of the notifying authority was recorded in any land grant of Pravarasena II and, second, that there seems to have been some connection between removal of the *senāpati* Citravarmā after the issue of the Chammak grant and presence of Koṇḍarāja at Pattan as the officer who executed the Pattan grant of Pravarasena II's 27th regnal year.[23]

There is a fair possibility that Satrughnarāja was originally independent ruler of the Bhojakata Rajya[24] who had agreed to become a feudatory of the Vākāṭaka kingdom because of his inability to withstand Vākāṭaka onslaught on his Bhojakaṭa kingdom. His son Koṇḍarāja was, however, not happy with his inferior status of a feudatory of the Vākāṭaka kingdom. In order to regain independence, Koṇdarāja tried to take advantage of the unwritten law which governed the relations of feudatories with their overlord. That is, though the feudatory surrendered his sovereign rights on his own territory in favour of the overlord and paid feudal dues and obeyed the commands of his overlord, the latter was not supposed to interfere in the internal matters of feudatory fief. Any armed interference in a feudatory area could arouse the sentiments of other feudatories as well as a rallying point in favour of the feudatory in question. Koṇḍarāja took advantage of that convention and converted his fief into a centre of anti-Vākāṭaka activities and insurgency, by blessing the forces of destabilisation. With Koṇḍarāja's blessings, the landed aristocracy waged class war against its weaker cousins involving killing of Brāhmaṇas, robbery adultery, raids on neighbouring villages as well as attempts to destroy the Vākāṭaka kingdom. Such attempts involved economic resources, organisation and weapons which could withstand organised resistance from the people attacked and also from the army units deployed by the coercive authority of the state. Gains of such anti-social and anti-state activities were so lucrative that the so-called religious people like Brāhmaṇas did not have conscience problems while attacking their poor and less resourceful brothers. Pravarasena II had apprehension that, unless put under definite obligations, even grantee Brāhma. nas could, at some later date, decide to take part in anti-village community and anti-state activities.

Though the overall picture was quite distressing, it had one redeeming feature. The overlord enjoyed the prerogative of making of grants of land for religious purposes even in feudatory territories. Thus, Pravarasena II decided to curb the insurgency in the Bhojakaṭa Rājya by making grant of land in favour of Brāhmaṇas—the seemingly religious Brāhmaṇas—who had agreed to fight and curb violence, etc., taking place in the Chammak area. What was more peculiar about the Chammak grant was the fact that Pravarasena II asked Koṇḍarāja to make the notification which armed the grantee with the duty and right to wage war against Koṇḍarāja's own men whom he could not openly own.

We do not know whether Pravarasena II had created a situation in which some family rival of Koṇḍarāja had staked his claim for the position of the feudatory chief of the Bhojakaṭa Rājya. So also, we do not know how the Vākāṭaka ruler had convinced Koṇḍarāja to give up his feudatory position and to enter the imperial service—the position in which he had executed the Pattan grant.

Thus, the Chammak grant throws welcome light on the factors which had contributed to the transformation of ancient economy and polity into feudal system in the Vākāṭaka kingdom in the fifth century. It clearly shows that emergence of powerful feudatories and Brāhmaṇa fief holders as intermediaries between the state and the peasantry had given rise to the new class of landed aristocracy which had tremendous resources wherewith it could create socio-economic tensions in the rural areas. Such islands of power, by their very existence in the vicinity of tax paying peasantry, could create an atmosphere of dissatisfaction and heart burning among those who paid heavily for the protection and facilities for which their privileged neighbours had to pay nothing. By virtue of being resourceful and well-organised, fief lords could harass their dependent peasantry and could, with equal ease, harass the neighbouring free-peasantry.

Finally, what needs to be underlined is the fact that, at least in the case of the Vākāṭaka kingdom, beginnings of feudalism were offered favourable climate for growth, etc., by the unwillingness of the state to own and shoulder its administrative responsibility. Existence of feudatory territories and large scale grants of land to the Brāhmaṇas accelerated the pace of fragmentation of land and state power.[25] The result of such a convenience-oriented attitude was creation of situations of socio-economic tensions, struggle and and political unrest which attacked the very roots of the Vākāṭaka kingdom.

Notes

1. J. F. Fleet, ed , *Corpus Inscriptionum Indicarum,* III; D.C. Sircar ed., *Select Inscriptions,* I; V.V. Mirashi, ed., *Corpus Inscriptionum Indicarum,* V, lines 17–20.
2. The Village Chamuck of the *Indian Atlas,* sheet no. 54, Lat. 21°12′ N. and Long, 77°31′ E. It is about four miles south-west of the erstwhile Ilichpur of the Ilichpur district of East Berar—the present-day Amaravati district of Vidarbha region of Maharashtra.
3. R.S. Sharma, *Aspects of Political Ideas and Institutions in Ancient India,* p. 204.
4. Lines, 41–4.
5. Fleet, op. cit., p. 239.
6. Sircar, op. cit., pp. 447–8.
7. Mirashi, op. cit., p. 25.
8. Fleet, op. cit., p. 239.
9. Ibid., p. 242.
10. D.D. Kosambi, *An Introduction to the Study of Indian History,* p. 297.
11. Sircar had rejected Fleet's reading as early as in 1942, see *Select Inscriptions,* pp. 423–24.
12. Mirashi decides to prefix *a* before *brahmaghna* (line 4) but rejects Fleet's-*a-saṅgrāma* (line-42) reading in favour of his own *a-kurvvatam* reading. By offering an additional *anusvara* after *saṅgrāma,* he makes the text read as *saṅgrāma akurvvatam* (line-42), see. Mirashi, op. cit., 25.
13. Pravarasena II's Dudia grant of 23rd regnal year mentions that 25 *nivartanas* of land was granted to one individual (Mirashi, [op. cit., p. 45 line 15). The same grant refers to grant of 60 *nivartanas of* land to another individual. His Jamb grant of second regnal (Mirashi, op. cit., p. 12, line 20). Belora grant of 11th year (ibid., p. 19, lines 13–14), Siwani grant of 18th year (ibid., p. 30, lines 21–23) and Tirodi grant of 23rd year (ibid., p. 50, lines 17–18), all assert that entire village was granted to one individual in each case.
14. Jamb grant (ibid., p. 12, lines 15–16), Belora grant (ibid., 19, lire 12) Chammak grant (ibid., p. 24, lines 16) and Siwani grant (ibid., p. 30, line 16) all of them assert that Pravarasena II had established the *kṛta-yuga.*
15. The Indore, Dudia and Tirodi grants of Pravarasena II's 23rd regnal year do not make any mention of the *Kṛta-yuga.*
16. Riddhpur plates of Prabhāvatigupta of Pravarasena II's 19th year (ibid., p. 36, line 26), Indore plates (ibid., p. 41, lines 29–30), Dudia plates (ibid., p. 46, lines 25–26) and Tirodi plates (ibid., p. 51 lines, 27–28) all repeat the Riddhpur warning to the feudatories saying this *(saṅkalp-ābhiyoga-parākkram-oparjitān-varttāmānān ājñapayamaḥ).*
17. The Belora plates of 11th year (ibid., p. 20, line 36) and the Chammak plates of 18th year (ibid., p. 25, line 59) tell us that Citravarmma was *senāpati.*
18. Ibid.
19. Ibid.
20. Ibid., p. 31, line.
21. Ibid., p. 46, lines 28–9.
22. Ibid., p. 56, line 41.

23. Ibid., p. 61, line 45.
    However, Pattan Plates of 27th year (p. 61, line 4) saw him replaced by Kātyāyana who, in his turn, was replaced by Madhappa of the Pandhuroa plates of 29th year (p. 6k, line 54).
24. Sircar is not sure whether territorial division *rājya* under the Vākāṭaka rule was still being ruled by a local ruler. According to him, 'If Bhojakaṭa rājya was under the local ruler Śatrughnarāja or Kaṇdarāja *Senapati* Citravarman was a High Commissioner or the Viceroy of the region included in that area', (*Select Inscriptions*, p. 445 n. 1).
25. *Aspects of Political Ideas and Institutions in Ancient India*, pp. 202–5.

27

Famines and Relief Measures Under the Imperial Coḷas, AD 850–1279

A. Mohan Ram

THE STATE of famine is a common phenomenon in agricultural countries, more particularly those depending mainly on the monsoon. The Tamil country is no exception to this. Instances of famines of varying magnitude causing considerable wrecking and crippling, at times, the very economy of the country are recorded in the Coḷa epigraphs.

The aim of this article is to focus on the socio-economic aspect of 'Famines and Relief Measures under the Imperial Coḷas, AD 850–1279.'

II

Causes of Famines

The famines were usually caused by the unfortunate circumstances of nature. The failure of monsoon, unprecedented floods and also the ravages of war seemed to be the factors that led to severe famines in the Coḷa period, as they were ever.

(1) *The Failure of Monsoon*: That failure of monsoon, generally caused the outbreak of famine is attested by a number of epigraphs.

An inscription of Rājendra I from Tirukkarugavur (Thanjavur district., AD 1019)[1] refers to the failure of the crops probably caused by the failure of monsoon.

The most outstanding instance of a somewhat widespread distress is known from two Alangudi (Thanjavur district.) records. The first record[2] states that in the reign of Vijayarajendradeva (eleventh century AD)[3] the village Alangudi had been afflicted with a famine caused by the failure of rain. Another

*45th session at Annamalainagar, 1984.

record[4] mentions that in AD 1121 a severe drought was anticipated owing to the failure of monsoon resulting in the rivers *Jananathapperaru* and *Parantakapperaru* being dried.

In the year AD 1160, a severe drought had occurred at Panjai[5] and Tirukkadaiyur[6] in the *Avani* and *Purattasai* (August, September and October) months, resulting in consequent failure of the crops. This drought was caused by the failure of monsoon.

Inscriptions of Kulottunga II (AD 1178–1218) also refer to cases of famines caused by drought. The inscription of AD 1201 from Tiruppamcuram (Thanjavur district)[7] and of AD 1202 from Tiruvannamalai (North Arcot district[8] mention the famine of a serious character probably caused by drought, along with wide-spread scarcity of food grains. The Ayyampettai record (Thanjavur district)[9] of AD 1208 registers a state of much confusion and trouble in realising the produce from the lands owing to drought. Besides, the Tirukkachchur records (Chingleput district)[10] state the failure of crops at Tirukkachchur caused by drought in AD 1188 and AD 1215 respectively.

An inscription of Rājarāja III from Tirumangalakkudi (Thanjavur district.)[11] also refers to a famine caused by the failure of rain in AD 1239.

(2) *Unprecedented Floods:* Apart from the failure of monsoon, another obvious cause of famine was unprecedented floods. References to floods in the Kaveri which laid waste a number of temple lands are many.[12]

The Srirangam records of Kulottuṅga I[13] and Vikramacoḷa[14] are very helpful in knowing the floods that occurred in the Kaveri delta region. They mention that the land was uncultivable for the past 50 years, 100 years and number of years on account of sand silt thrown up by the over flooding of Kaveri.

R. Nagaswamy has pointed out that if it is taken that the years 50 and 100 recorded nearly accurate, it would indicate that over-flooding of Kaveri has occurred at least twice in hundred years, causing considerable damage to the fields and crops. That means that the Kaveri had flooded disastrously in the reign of Rājendra I and earlier in the reign of Uttamacoḷa.[15]

Floods in the Palar river is revealed by the inscriptions of Tirumalpuram (AD I004)[16] and Puduppadi (AD 1071)[17] in the North Arcot district.

Vikrama's time also witnessed famines caused by inundations. An epigraph from Tiruvottur (North Arcot district.)[18] refers to a big flood which destroyed both the village and the crops there in the year AD 1125.

The Somangalam (Chingleput district) record of Kulottunga III[19] refers to heavy rains and consequent breach of the tank bund in AD 1190 and AD 1191 probably resulting in a famine.

III

(3) *The Ravages of War:* As has already been pointed out, it would be manifestly inapporopriate to ascribe famines solely to droughts and floods. More frequently they were brought about by the ravages of war also.[20]

Though the Coḷa inscriptions are emphatically silent about the ravages of war on Coḷa territories and their aftermath during the late thirteenth century AD, it may not be wrong to surmise that the war ravages would have led to serious consequences including famines. Though there is paucity of epigraphic evidence indicating the occurrence of famines in this period, the description given in the Pāṇḍya *praśasti*[21] about the war ravages on the Coḷa region leads us to conclude that there would have been severe famine.

IV
Symptoms of Famines

Failure of crops, due to lack or excess of rain was the first symptom of famines. This is explicit from the inscriptions of Tirukkarugavur (AD 1019)[22], Tiruvottur (AD 1125),[23] Punjai (AD 1160),[24] Tirukkadaiyur (AD 1160)[25] and Ṭirukkachchar (AD 1188 and 1215).[26]

Epigraphic records also reveal the failure of crops resulting in the scarcity of food and rise in the prices of food-grains. The Tirppamburam inscription of Kulottuṅga III (AD 1201)[27] not only mentions a famine of a serious character but also wide-spread scarcity of food grains and a high rise in the price of food grains. It is stated that paddy was sold at 3 *nali* for 1 *kāśu*. This would mean 1-1/5 measures of rise per *kāśu.*[28] Similarly, in Tiruvannamalai, rice was sold at 1/4th of a measure per *kāśu* owing to a famine and scarcity of rice during the reign of the same ruler in AD 1202.[29]

If the *kāśu* was the same coin in both instance, the famine must have prevailed over a somewhat, wider area and have become very much acute in the late year of the scarcity than the first.[30]

Occasionally the effect of famine was seen in the desertion of villages and in the migration of the people to the neighbouring villages.

The village of Tirupper (Koviladi, Thanjavur district) became deserted owing to the advent of famine in AD 1129.[31] Besides, the Arakandanallur record (South Arcot district)[32] states that as a consequence of a famine, which occurred in the thirteenth regnal year of Vikramacoḷa (AD 1131), several families began to move out of their village with intent to settle down elsewhere.

The contemporary records from the adjacent area indicate that such migrations were often temporary and the people returned to their original houses after a certain period of time. Such temporary internal migration led to unauthorised occupation of land, property and to consequent disputes, and the state government or the local government had to interfere to set them right.[33]

Such an instance is recorded in the inscription from Nandaluru, Rajampet taluk, Cuddapah district, dated AD 1259.[34] It records that a chieftain Mukkanti Kaduvetti established and gave the village Perungandur to 52 Brāhmaṇas in AD 808. The donees were in enjoyment of their shares for a long time when some Velumas from Inumbrolu escaping from the *Mari-Jvaram* (small-pox) of their place, settled in fields near them, agreeing to pay rents to Br"ahmaṇas for their lands. During a famine that followed the Brāhmaṇas left their places had when they returned they found their entire possessions occupied by the newcomers who had in the meantime named their new settlement as Koduiu, and refused to give the rent due to the Brāhmaṇa landlords. The latter then made a representation to the chief Manumasiddhi a feudatory under Rājendracoḷa III. The chief, after due enquiry with witnesses, decided the case in favour of the dispossessed Brāhmaṇas, to whom he renewed the grant of the village Koduru.

In any case the usual result was that lands lay uncultivated for some considerable period, the scarcity lasted for one or two years, the effects being felt also in the decline of state revenues.

Sometimes, acute famine conditions enforced individuals to sell their personal liberty for want of food and thus reduced them to a state of slavery. An inscription of Kulottuṅga III (dated AD 1201) from Tiruppamburam[35] illustrates this point. It states that owing to famine condition and the high price of food-grains, a *vellalan* of the village sold himself and his two daughters as slaves (*adimai*) to the temple of Tiruppamburam Udaiyar for a sum of 110 *kāśus*, in order to escape death by starvation.

V

No Remission of Land Tax even in Distressed Condition

Remission of land tax was unknown even when the crops were destroyed by natural disasters. This fact is obtained from the inscriptions.

The Tiruvottur records (North Arcot district)[36] mention that when a big flood destroyed both the village and the crops, the villagers were unable to pay the taxes. As a result they had to sell some of their wet lands to settle the tax arrears of the year AD 1125. But this did not solve their problem, for they had to sell once again some of their dry lands for the same purpose in the next year (i.e., AD 1126).[37]

The Tiruvadi record[38] of the same reign (AD 1125) states that the *Mahāsabhā* had to sell some of the common land on account of difficulty experienced in the payment of the land tax (*lademai-t-tattu*).

The Tirukkachchur records[39] refer to the failure of crops and the consequent troubles in connection with the payment of taxes in the 10th (AD 1188) and 37th (AD 1215) years of Kulottuṅga III. The residents finding it difficult to pay the taxes, borrowed a loan from a nobleman in the neighbourhood.

Though it is widely believed that the rulers were forced to remit land taxes during the natural calamities, the epigraphic records pertaining to the Coḷa period do not reveal the remission of land taxes. This is an important point worth mentioning.

VI

Famine Policy

The inscriptions reveal no information on the action taken by the government as famine relief. But it would not be safe to conclude that the state did nothing in such situations. As pointed out by K.A. Nilakanta Sastri, it should not be forgotten that the inscriptions are the records of a narrow range of transactions and are by no means the moral and material progress reports of the times.[40] Hence it is difficult to prove the existence of any 'famine policy' which guided the government. Isolated instances of the role the state played in relieving famine distress can only be gleaned from some inscriptions.

In the Coḷa period a tax or levy called *Pañcavara* was collected. According to Sastri, *Pañcavara* was a kind of tax or levy to provide against famine (*panjam*). The duties assigned to the *Pañcavara vāriyam* (committee) were connected with the assessment and collection of this levy.[41]

If, the *Pañcavara vāriyam* was considered to be introduced to fight against famines, the accurate land survey under Rājarāja I and his successors, the abolition of tools (*saṅgam*) under Kulottuṅga I, the irrigation works under the Coḷa rulers should also be taken as similar positive steps to relieve the people from the distress during the famines, etc.[42]

VII

Relief Measures

Available evidence points to the fact that the village assemblies, the temples and the private individuals were very anxious to afford relief measures to the suffering people during the times of famine.

(1) *Relief offered by the village assemblies:* The village assemblies frequently strove to fight against famines. The Alangudi record[43] of about AD 1054, for instance, states how in a certain village affected by famine, the assembly itself, expecting no succour from the king, moved in the mailer of providing relief for the people. When the village was affected by famine. The villagers had no funds to purchase paddy on their own for consumption and for seeds and other necessities for cultivation. Owing to this circumstance, the village assembly secured a loan of 1011 *kalañjus* of gold and 464 *palams* of silver consisting of temple jewels and vessels in order to maintain the people and buy seeds and manure for resuming cultivation. In lieu of this, the members of the village assembly mortgaged 8¾ *velis* of the common land of the village in favour of god.

Another record of the same place[44] states that in AD 1121 when a severe drought was anticipated owing to the failure of water in the rivers *Jananāthap peraru* and *Parāntakap-peraru,* funds had to be found for starting certain artificial methods of irrigation. On that occasion, the assembly of Jananātha *caturvedimaṅgalam* gave certain jewels belonging to the temple of Paśupatīśvaram Udaiyar of the village in exchange for certain communal land.

The Erumbur record (Chidambaram, AD 1153)[45] mentions a similar case where, in a period of famine (bad time) and scarcity of grains, a loan was arranged for from the temple treasury by the village assembly to tide over the distress. The rate of interest on this loan (60 *kāśus)* was fixed at 2 *tuni* and *kuruni* of paddy per *kāśu.*

Another case of self-help is reported in the reign of Kulottuṅga III. The inscription of Kulottuṅga III from Tirukkachchur[46] points out that in the 37th year of reign of the king *(i.e.* AD 1215) the crops failed and troubles arose in connection with the payment of taxes. For this the members of the assembly borrowed a loan (15 *kāśus)* from an individual. As interest, they give him a piece of common land belonging to the village, also agreeing to pay the taxes to the government on that land.

(2) *Relief offered by the temples:* The temples also took an active part in relieving distress of the people during famines by various means. It is known that during the period of distress individuals and the village assemblies borrowed money and food-grains from the temple treasury.

The Tiruppamburam record[47] states that when the time was very bad and paddy was sold at 3 *nali* per *kāśu,* a *vallalan* borrowed 110 *kāśus* from the temple treasury in AD 1201.

Owing to famine and scarcity of grains, the assembly of Alangudi Village[48] and Erumbur village[49] secured a loan from the local temple treasury in AD 1054 and AD 1153 respectively.

Besides the economic aid, the temples also offered asylum for the victims. For instance, the inscription of Rājarāja III from Pallicendal (South Arcot district)[50] state that Nemināth who was in charge of *Gaṇḍārādittap-perum palli* declared a portion of the village called Jambai alias Vīrarājendrapuram as an asylum for the distressed, by an order.

(3) *Munificence of private individuals:* Charitable individuals also offered help in cases of accidental famines. It is known from the Tiruvannamalai record (North Arcot district)[51] that there was a famine in the village of Tiruvannamalai and rice was selling at 1/4th of a measure per *kāśu*. Two persons started relief works in the form of constructing an embankment to the river and also a fresh tank with a sluice at the village, paying the labourers in gold, paddy or other form as they desired, out of their private funds in AD 1202.

VIII

Thus it can be safely concluded that during the Coḷa period, the role of the government in relieving the famine disaster is not appreciable. As far as the epigraphic records are concerned, no organised relief measure was undertaken by any ruler at any time. Circumstantial evidences may be stretched to say that the government might have undertaken some methods to relieve the victims. However, this needs further probing. On any account the spontaneous help offered by the village assemblies, the temples and the genera public are worth mentioning.

Notes

1. *ARE*, no. 404 of 1961–62.
2. *SII*, vol. III, p. 191; *ARE*, no. 5 of 1899; pt. II, para 53.
3. K.A. Nilakanta Sastri, *The Coḷas*, p. 562.
4. *ARE*, no. 521 of 1920–21, pt. II, para 35.
5. *ARE*, no. 191 of 1925.
6. Ibid., no. 258 of 1925.
7. Ibid., no. 86 of 1911; pt. II, para 29.
8. Ibid., no. 560 of 1902.
9. Ibid , no. 114 of 1927–28.
10. Ibid., nos. 274, 279 of 1909; and 1910, pt. II, para 29.
11. Ibid , no. 225 of 1927; pt. II, para 30.
12. Ibid., no. 64 of 1892; 375 of 1903; 158 of 1937–38; 125 o f 1938–39; 108, 112–13, 118–19, 121, 130–31 of 1947–48; 8, 10, 38 of 1948–49; 308 of 1965–66.
13. Ibid., nos. 125 of 1938–39; 108, 112–13, 118–19, 121, 130–31 of 1947–48; 8, 10 of 1948–49.
14. Ibid., no. 38 of 1948–49.
15. R. Nagaswamy, 'Srirangam Temple under Kulottunga I' *Studies in Ancient Law and Society*, pp. 70–1.

16. *ARE*, no. 322 of 1906.
17. Ibid., no. 428 of 1905.
18. *SII*, vol VII. no. 96; *ARE*, 1900, pt. II, para 24.
19. Ibid , no. 393; *ARE*, no. 183 of 1901; *EI*, vol VII, p. 6.
20. P.N. Ramaswami. 'Early History of Indian Famines' *IA*, LII, August 1923, p. 193.
21. *IPS*, no. 290; K.V. Raman, *Pandiyar Varalaru* (Tamil), p. 106.
22. *ARE*, no. 404 of 1961–62.
23. *SII*, vol. VII, no. 96; *ARE*, no. 87 of 1900.
24. *ARE*. no. 191 of 1925.
25. Ibid., no. 258 of 1925.
26. Ibid., nos. 274, 279 of 1909; and 1910, pt. II, para 29.
27. Ibid., no. 86 of 1911.
28. K.A. Nilakanta Sastri, op. cit., p. 400.
29. *ARE* no. 560 of 1902.
30. K.A. Nilakanta Sastri, op. cit.
31. *Sir*, vol. VII, no. 496, *ARE*, no. 276 of 1901.
32. *ARE*, no. 151 of 1934-35; pt. II. para 14, p. 60.
33. A. Appadurai, *Economic Conditions in Southern India*, AD 1000–1500, vol. II, p. 750.
34. *SII*, vol. XXIII, no. 580.
35. *ARE*, no. 86 of 1911. pt. II, para 29, p. 74.
36. *SII*, vol. VII, no. 96; *ARE*, no. 87 of 1900; pt. II, para 24.
37. Ibid., no. 97; *ARE*, no. 88 of 1900; pt. II, para 24.
38. *SII*, vol. VIII, no. 303; *ARE*, no. 30 of 1903.
39. *ARE*, nos. 274 of 279 of 1909; and 1910, pt. II, para 29.
40. K.A. Nilakanta Sastri, op. cit.. p. 399.
41. Ibid., *Studies of Chola History and Administration*, pp. 142–3.
42. M. Balasubrahmanian, *Colarkalin Araciyal Kalacara Varalaru* (Tamil), pt. II, p. 245.
43. *ARE*, no. 5 of 1899; pt. II, para 53.
44. Ibid., no. 521 of 1920; and 1921, pt. II, para 35.
45. Ibid., no. 397 of 1913; and 1914, pt. II, para 14.
46. Ibid., no. 279 of 1909; and 1910, pt. II, para 29.
47. Ibid., no. 86 of 1911; pt. II, para 29, p. 74.
48. Ibid., 1899, pt. II, para 53.
49. Ibid., no. 397 of 1913; and 1914, pt. II, para 14.
50. Ibid., no. 448 of 1937–38.
51. Ibid., no. 560 of 1902; V. Venkayya, 'Irrigation in Southern India in Ancient Times', *ARASI, 1903–04*, p. 211.

28

Socio-Economic Implications of the Concept of Mahāpātaka in the Feudal Society of South India

M.G.S. Narayanan

IN THE period of the later Cera kings of Makotai of Mahodayapura (Kodungallur) who presided over the destinies of Kerala from *c.* AD 800 to 1124, we come across a number of Early Malayalam inscriptions dealing with the decisions of village councillors (*Uralar*) belonging to the Aryan Brahman settlements of this region.[1] Some of these resolutions contain imprecatory passages threatening those among the *Uralar* who violated the agreements, or disturbed the agreements, with dire consequences. The passages are often couched in the language of a curse.[2] They seek to invoke horror in the minds of readers by suggesting a strange awareness of what may be called 'Oedipus Complex' in terms of Freudian psychology. This paper contains the author's attempt to crack their bizarre code and analyse the socio-economic implications of the apparently unrealistic message inscribed on copper and stone.

The Valappalli copperplate of the 12th year of Rajaśekhara (c. AD 820) lays down that any one of the council who obstructs the daily sacrifice (*bali*) in the temple shall have to pay the sovereign (Peruman Atikal) and amount of one hundred *dīnāra* as fine. As if this is not enough, the council has caused the following words to be added:

> 'Those will also be (deemed as) persons
> who cohabit with their own mother.'[3]

A few years later a stone inscription of the 11th year of Sthānu Ravi Kulaśekhara (AD 855) from Irinjalakkuda states:

> The *Uralan* who violated this agreement shall be guilty of matricide. Those who support them also shall suffer from the evil consequences.[4]

*37th Session at Calicut, 1976.

From the context it is clear that the aim is to frighten and dissuade would be offenders by all possible means. There are parallel statements in many records outside Kerala too. Sometimes the offenders are stated in Alupa records of Karanataka (seventh cent, AD) to have incurred great sins.[5] Interpreting these, Dr. B A. Saletore says that such imprecations at the end of the grants 'show the communal sense of the people' and that the 'fear of incurring punishment in the next world brought home to the people a sense of loyalty and respect for royal orders and public endowments.'[6] This would suggest that the effectiveness of the imprecations and threats depended, as far as these and similar passages are concerned, entirely on the people's faith in the other world, i.e., *paraloka*. It is partly true but there seems to be a greater immediate threat implied in the apparently religious or moral strictures.

Prof. K.A. Nilakanta Sastri has brought similar instances to light in the Tamil country where offenders are often described as cow-killers on the banks of the Ganges or enemies of Lord Śiva.[7] Several scholars have dismissed such statements as merely indicating the strong sentiments of the authors which prompted them to invoke the power of the curse. The idea seems to be that in an age of faith people were expected to fear the odium of the curse.[8]

The five great sins according to Manu and Yājñavalkya were the following:

(i) Killing of a brahmin, (ii) drinking liquors, (iii) stealing gold, (iv) committing incest with the wife of the *guru* or with one's own mother, and (v) associating with anyone guilty of these crimes. There are some instances where inscriptions like the Sasanakota plates and Dadda's grant threaten violators of the endowment stating that they shall be equated with those who committed the five great sins.[9] The injunctions contained in Dharmasūtras of Baudhāyana and Āpastamba, who are largely followed by the brahmins in south India, have introduced a classification of sins distinguishing between (a) *Pataniya*, major sins causing loss of caste, (b) *Upapātaka*, minor sins causing no loss of caste, and (c) *Aśucikara*, sins causing impurity.[10]

Information found in epigraphic records would show that offenders who violated the given agreements came to be treated as being guilty of some of the *Mahāpātakas* (great sins) for which there is no *prāyaścitta* (atonement intended for purification) according to Hindu scriptures. In other words the violation of certain socio-economic regulations was considered, by an extension of the concept of *Mahāpātaka*, to be tantamount to the great sins which attracted the clauses concerning the highest punishment i.e. the loss of caste. Thus, the equation really implies a specific addition to the list which in effect adds another political dimension to the moral code, adjusting it to the needs of changing limes.

There were serious consequences for Brahmins in losing caste in the context of the feudal set-up with oligarchic Brahmin corporations which owned Devasvam or God's property collectively and Brahmasvam or Brahmin property individually on behalf of their families which were founder-members of the chartered rural settlements of Kerala and other parts of south India. These are important for the study of social and economic history. They throw light on the cohesion and strength of the property-owning upper caste corporations and the ruthless measures which they had adopted towards erring members of their own community in order to preserve intact their material privileges and social dominance.

The social implications of this type of sin, with the original and extended connotations, are described in straight forward manner in some other Cera inscriptions of Kerala. A passage in Tiruvalla copper plates asserts that the offending *Uralan* (member of the Brahmin village council) and his associates will be regarded as those who murdered the father and married the mother, and elaborates it further by stating that their lands and homesteads will be cofiscated by the village council, the proceeds being utilised for the expenses of the temple.[11]

An undated record from Iranikulam, late in the ninth century, has improved upon this theme by clarifying that he who abuses the rights in regard to a particular village under the protection of the council shall be guilty of murdering his own father and the teacher who initiated him into the Vedas and his mother. As a result he will be disqualified from having *Tanam* and *Paratai* (*Sthānam* and *Pariṣad,* i.e. membership or seat of the village council called Ur and *Sabhā* and its executive committee). Not only that, a cryptic expression at the end says that he will be 'Urkkupuram' i.e. outside the village. The disqualification regarding *Sabhā* and *Pariṣad* naturally signified loss of the share of both Devasvam and Brahmasvam property, which a Brahmin possessed by virtue of his membership in the corporate body of the village. When he is removed from this body as a result of his triple crime, he loses his landed property and all the social and political privileges attached to it. He is no longer a member of the privileged classes.

It is from the Ur or *Sabhā* that members were recruited to the *gaṇas* or boards of trustees for particular endowments. The patronage of temple servants, the right to appoint and change tenants for the temple property and the authority to fix their conditions of tenure and service—all these went with a seat in the village council. This meant enormous power and prestige in the neighbourhood of the Brahmin centre. Dismissal from the council implied the termination of all such benefits in addition to the loss of reputation and the usual caste privileges. A Brahmin without membership in his own village council, without referees or the identity of Brahmin parentage, cut off from the *gotra* and the *sâkhā,* was no Brahmin at all. He was doubly accursed since the definition of the great sins included his associates also among the sinners deserving the same punishment. Punishment also was hereditary like the offices; it also took the family and not the individual as the unit as in the case of inheritance. People shunned the outcaste like a leper and he was beyond redemption. He was thrown back to the level of the low-caste people. It was not only a matter of shame but also a matter of complete loss of identity, virtually going out of the pale of civilised society. In a situation where all property rights, powers and privileges were dependent on one's birth and family status, within the framework of community and country, such loss of identity was equal to extinction in a social sense.

The short sentence at the end of the passage in an undated Iranikkulam record—*urkkupuram*—suggests all this at one stroke. The person who is punished is not merely physically banished but also politically and socially ostracised. His misery in ex-communication must have been great and almost in direct proportion to the prestige he enjoyed in the normal course. This is where equation with the five great sins counts by lending scriptural support to political action. Once it is decreed that a socio-economic offence corresponds to moral turpitude, the whole paraphernalia of consequences follow from such action.

To the extent to which *Manusmṛti* and other Śāstraic texts fulfilled the function of basic laws or constitution whithin the socio-political set-up of ancient India, these additions to the Śāstraic lists of *Mahāpātaka* certainly had the effect of amending that constitution, updating it and bringing it closer to the model of the property ownership in a fedual age. Written laws were amended by specific written clauses applicable only to given situations in a given place. Incidentally this exhibits a relatively unnoticed phase of Śāstraic law in traditional India: the amendment of laws by precedent and judicial review. This proves the flexibility and adaptability of Indian tradition and disproves the common assumption of many Indologists that Indian social organisation has remained unchanging for ages. The written codes in the ancient texts did remain unchanged, though some clauses gained popularity while others fell into disuse. By the process of equation, some new general prohibitons like those against, sea travel, trade and profession of the arts came into existence. By the same process, a few specific prohibitions in the historical context of time and place also entered into the epigraphic records which must be read along with the Śāstra literature. Indologists who studied these texts without looking into the applied context and concluded that basic laws in Hindu society remained unchanged were committing a serious blunder. They may be stated to have missed the whole range of historical change because of the restricted nature of literary evidence.

When we recognise that the seemingly spiritual threat was a real warning about political action against socio-economic offences, it leads to the next step in understanding that the same threat is expressed in various other forms also. For instance there are inscriptions in different parts of Kerala which refer to the precedent in Muzhikkalam temple.[12] Prof. Elamkulam, who brought out their significance for the first time thought that the Muzhikkalam *Kaccam* or agreement of Muzhikkalam must have been formulated at a grand assembly of all the temples in the country under the presidentship of the sovereign.[13] However, there is no evidence to warrant such an assumption. It could as well be that at Muzhikkalam, one of the four Brahmin settlements around the capital with representative in the Perumal's Council of Nalu Tali, they prepared in detail the regulations governing temple administration which received the Perumal's stamp of recognition and came to be generally followed as a code of conduct in Kerala Hindu temples. There were other *Kaccams* (Argreements) like Katankattu *Kaccam*, Tavaranur *Kaccam* Śaṅkaramaṅgalattu *Kaccam*, Kaitavarattu *Kaccam*, etc., in the records of the age dealing with different aspects or types of administrative problems.[14] In Muzhikkalam *Kaccam*, as well as other *Kaccams* we find that some clauses refer to excommunication of the offenders after the confiscation of their property and cancellation of all privileges.[15] The traditional chronicle of Tulu country to the north of Kerala known as *Grāmapaddhati*, speeks of ostracism, confiscation of property, etc. The sinners are said to become *Sthānahīnāh* (deprived of *sthāṇa* or seat in the council) *Parityaktāh* (abandoned) and *Sarvakarma bahiṣkṛta* (outcastes from all rituals)[16] In the *Kaccams* of Kerala there are several items of minor offences for which higher punishment is prescribed in the form of fines. However, the supreme punishment meted to the Brahmin *Uralan* (member of the proprietory council of the village) who was guilty of any of the socio-economic offences, appears to have been excommunication as mentioned above.

As per the available records to the procedure laid down for excommunication was followed at least once in the case of a person called Tenceri Cennan Tayan of the Brahmin village of Trikkadittanam who was excommunicated, after the confiscation of all his property, for having stolen from the Bhāṇḍara or treasury of the temple Manalmanrattu Yakkan Cirikantan, the Nayar governor of the district confiscated all the lands and shares in land belonging to this Brahmin, as member of the village council and member of the *gaṇa* (board of trustees)—the details are outlined in the document,—Paratai (Executive Committee) and *Sabhā* (Council of the *Uralar*, the learned Brahmin proprietors of the village) and used all the proceeds for instituting *Pañcamaśabda* (the worship With five musical instruments) in Trikkadittanam temple.[17]

In discussing the Muzhikkalam *Kaccam*, Professor Elamkulam has argued that such strict measures were designed chiefly to protect the interests of the tenants cultivating the lands of the temple.[18] This appears to be the result of a misunderstanding about the real objective. It is true that the punishments are prescribed for Brahmin proprietors who cause obstruction to cultivation or misappropriate the profits from lands given to the tenants. Incidentally the tenants also benefited, but the chief aim was to guarantee the uninterrupted flow of tenants/dues from their hands to the coffers of the temple so that rituals may be carried on without break or decrease. Thus, in the joint proprietorship of Devasvam or temple property, the individual member proprietor should not be permitted to commit any excess, inconsistent with the common interest of the group or corporation. Therefore, the threatening clauses were devised to restrain individual impulses and protect the Common interest of the Brahmin elite. The prosperity of the temple was closely interwoven with the unity and cohesion of the ruling Brahmin group of the village which was the power behind the temple and the success of the whole movement of Aryanization depended on the strength of this institutional base. In this context, the proviso for cancellation of membership rights, confiscation of property and excommunication of erring Brahmin proprietors guilty of economic offences play a key part in ensuring the cohesion, unity of the *Sabhā*, or council of Uralar, the basic unit of the Brahmin oligarchy in the scattered Aryan settlements in Kerala and other parts of south India. This rigidity of the constitution of the village council with the ruthless elimination of unhealthy elements constituted the price that Brahmins had to pay for the social dominance.

Notes

1. The outlines of the political and social history of this period were brought out for the first time by Prof. Elamkulam P.N. Kunhan Pillai, *Studies in Kerala History*. Further study in this field with substantial alterations in chronology, political history, social and economic history and history of art and culture has been attempted by the present author. See M.G.S. Narayanan, 'Poltical and Social Conditions of Kerala under the Kulasekhara Empire' (unpublished Ph.D. thesis). The findings regarding Aryan Brahman settlements mentioned in the dissertation are developed further in this paper.
2. For the purpose of the present study only the punishments prescribed for the Uralar are taken up for discussion. There are several other exhortations and admonitions against outsiders, rulers, officials and others—who might offend against Devasvam and Brahniasvam, both in Kerala and in other parts of India. For a general account of these, refer D.C. Sircar, pp. 141–3 and 169–201. While the exhortations are generally designed to protect Brahmin property from harm done by others, those under discussion at present were intended to protect Brahman property from harm by fellow-Brahmans within the village council.
3. *Travancore Archaeological Series*, vol. II, pp. 8–14, lines 1–4. Some landed property is assigned for the conduct of the Muttappaii or daily sacrifice in the temple. Violation of the property by a Council member for promoting self-interest would mean obstruction of the sacrifice.
4. *Bulletin of Sri Rama Varma Research Institute*, vol. IX, pt. I, p. 43, lines 10–13.
5. *Epigraphia Carnatica*, vol. VI, Kp. 37, p. 82. There are other instances where the violation of agreement is equated to one of the five great sins, i.e. the Stealing of

silver and gold ornaments, or to the five great sins and the great sin of having destroyed Brahmapura of Sivalli in Tuluva or Vasanasi Rameswaram and Kurukshera, See ibid, Kp. 38 p. 82. See also 98, 100, 102, 171 of 1961; *EI*, IX, pp. 20–1.

6. B.A, Saletore, *Ancient Karnataka*, I, p. 188.
7. K.A. Nilakanta Sastri, *Pandyam Kingdom*, pp. 228–30.
8. *Manusmṛti*, XT, 54 and 55, See also *Yājñavalkya*., III, 227ff.
9. D.C. Sircar, op. cit., p. 142.
10. *Baudh"ayana Dharmasūtra*, 7–19. There is some disparity between these two works in the enumeration and classification of sins. They also provide material of historical interest since greed for land, voyages, trade arts, etc., are grouped among sins. For a discussion, See W. Campert, 'Old Classification of Sins in South India', *Bulletin of Sree Rama Varma Research Institute*, I, pp. 9, 11.
11. *Travāncore Archaeological Series*, vol. II, pt. III, pp. 131–207, lines 28–30.
12. *Bulletin of Sree Rama Varma Research Institute*, vol. IX, pt. II, p. 134.
13. Elamkulam P.N. Kunjan Pillai, *Janmi Sampradayam Keralatti*, pp. 28–35.
14. Ibid., pp. 35–36, M.G.S. Narayanan, *Kulasekhara Empire*, op. cit. p. 332.
15. M.G.S. Narayanan, op. cit., pp. 335–48.
16. See B.A. Saletore, *Ancient Karnataka*, I, pp. 310–20.
17. M.G.S. Narayanan, *Index to Cera Inscriptions*, A-64, lines 1–2.
18. Elamkulam, op. cit., pp. 32–5.

Index